BEER
NewEngland

Art's Sportsmen's Tavern
Colchester, Connecticut
November, 1940

An Affectionate Look at Our Six States' Past and Present Brews and Breweries

BEER
NewEngland

by Will Anderson

Studio Photography by Paul J. Luise, Limington, Maine
The Hug Collection Photography by Bill Higgins, Lorain, Ohio
Field Photography by the author

Will Anderson
Portland, Maine

Other Books by the Author

Andersons' Turn-of-the-Century Brewery Directory (1968)
Beers, Breweries and Breweriana (1969)
The Beer Book (1973)
The Breweries of Brooklyn (1976)
The Beer Poster Book (1977)
Beer, USA (1986)
From Beer to Eternity (1987)

Library of Congress Catalogue Card Number 88-91324

Anderson, Will, 1940-
1. Beer   2. New England

ISBN 0-9601056-2-X

Designed and typeset by PrintMedia, Portland, Maine
Printed by Spectrum Printing and Graphics, Saco, Maine

Cover design: David Adams, PrintMedia

Cover Photo: Model Package Store
White Street, Haverhill, Mass., circa 1938
Courtesy Haverhill Public Library

Contents

Acknowledgments

**In researching and writing BEER, NEW ENGLAND I was fortunate to have been helped
by a whole host of wonderful folks. Cheers and thanks to . . .**

Sally Anderson, Editor, Town Crier, Bellows Falls, Vt.;
Gloria Bishop, Portland, Me.;
Bob Blezard, Worcester Telegram & Gazette, Worcester, Mass.;
Peter Blum, Stroh Brewery Co., Detroit, Mich.;
Pauline Bolduc, New Bedford Public Library, New Bedford, Mass;
Pat Buckley, Portland, Me.;
Christine Burchstead, Rockingham Free Public Library, Bellows Falls, Vt.;
Don Bull, Stamford, Conn.;
Robert Callahan, Captain, New Haven Fire Department, New Haven, Conn.;
Lynda Conner, Yarmouth, Me.;
John Corrado, Purdys, N.Y.;
Carol Coverly, Morse Institute, Natick, Mass.;
Paul Cyr, New Bedford Public Library, New Bedford, Mass.;
Michael Diamantopoulos, Sr. and his son, Michael, Jr., and daughter, Millisa, Lawrence, Mass.;
Frances Dowd, Haverhill Public Library, Haverhill, Mass.;
Anna Mary Dunton, Canaan Historical Society, Canaan, N.Y.;
Nancy Florence, Derby Public Library, Derby, Conn.;
Richard L. Fox, Hartford Provision Co., New Britain, Conn.;
Jim Fraser, Queen City Tavern, Burlington, Vt.;
Cynthia Gabrielli, Manchester Historic Assn., Manchester, N.H.;
Ellen Gambini, Silas Bronson Library, Waterbury, Conn.;
Dave Graci, Dave's Y Package Store, Chicopee, Mass.;
Augie Helms, Union, N.J.;
Thomas J. Kabelka, Waterbury Republican, Waterbury, Conn.;
Catherine Largary, Middlebury, Conn.;
Elizabeth Lessard, Manchester Historic Assn., Manchester, N.H.;
Maragaret Humberston, Springfield City Library, Springfield, Mass.;
Patricia Mark, Rockingham Free Public Library, Bellows Falls, Vt.;
Mary Maynard, Chatham Public Library, Chatham, N.Y.;
Edith McCauley, Portland Room, Portland Public Library, Portland, Me.;
Jack McDougall, Cranford, N.J.;
Valerie McQuillan, Springfield City Library, Springfield, Mass.;
Rose Mesite, Mesite's Florist, Meriden, Conn.;
Wanda Moskwa, Pawtucket Public Library, Pawtucket, R.I.;
Barbara Nelson, Pelham Manor, N.Y.;
Ed Nichols, Valley Stream, N.Y.;
George W. Nowacki, New Haven Public Library, New Haven, Conn.;
Mary Frances O'Brien, Boston Public Library, Boston, Mass.;
Ernie Oest, Port Jefferson Station, N.Y.;
Ken Ostrow, Newton, Mass.;
Arlene C. Palmer, New Britain Public Library, New Britain, Conn.;
Frank Pearce, New Haven Fire Department, New Haven, Conn.;
Dale Rand, Portland, Me.;
Mike Rissetto, Floral Park, N.Y.;
Mary Jane Ryan, Boston Red Sox, Boston, Mass.;
Carolyn M. Schinzel, Silas Bronson Library, Waterbury, Conn.;
George Sigel, Boston Beef Co., Worcester, Mass.;
Ken Skulski, Lawrence Public Library, Lawrence, Mass.;
Jim Starkman, Fairport, N.Y.;
Mary Ellen Squeglia, Brewery Square, New Haven, Conn.;
Irva M. Torres, New Bedford Public Library, New Bedford, Mass.;
Austin Ward, Lyme, Conn.
Martin Waters, Boston Public Library, Boston, Mass.;
Russ Waters, Lowell, Mass.;
Carolyn Wakefield,Lynn Public Library, Lynn, Mass.
Greg Whelan, Weeks, Whelan & Gamester, Portsmouth, N.H.;
Keith Whitmore, Waltham, Mass.;
Richard E. Winslow, II, Portsmouth Public Library, Portsmouth, N.H.

Special Thanks To
Jennifer Bugbee and Jayne Sawtelle and the whole gang at PrintMedia for their care and wonderful job.

And Special, Special Thanks To
Tom, Vic, and Bob Hug of Lorain, Ohio for most generous access to their marvelous breweriana collection.

Preface

There once was a time not so very long ago when towns and cities throughout New England were proud of their uniqueness; proud of their own local hotels, soda fountains, soda bottling works, restaurants.

McDonald was the last name of a kid you knew in the third grade. Holiday Inn was a Bing Crosby movie you'd seen from the balcony of the Bijou. Burgers were hamburgers... and the Hamburger King was Sal down at the corner luncheonette. Ramada sounded vaguely like a good field/no hit thirdbaseman - was it Joe Ramada? - who had a cup of coffee with the Sox just after the war.

But maybe - just maybe - New England was proudest of its own beers. And ales. Ales ruled supreme.

Sure there was Bud and Schlitz and Miller... but they were pretty much beers you got if you went "out west"; Coors if you went further out west. Stroh's and Rolling Rock you'd never heard of.

Who needed 'em? We had Dawson's ("Time Out For Dawson's") and Star and Frank Jones and Narragansett ("Hi Neighbor") and Cremo and Holihan's, Hampden, Harvard, Hanley's and Hull (we were big on H's!) and Pickwick ("The Poor Man's Whiskey") and oh so many more. All local, all our own... all good. Real good.

Yep, BEER, NEW ENGLAND is a tribute to those days of yesteryear. But it's also - very definitely - a tribute to the present...to (a) the micro brewery movement that's brought excitement and some magnificent brews back to Boston, Portland, Northampton, White River Junction and a lot of beer drinkers in between, and to (b) some of the neatest and most charismatic bars/taverns/tap rooms to be found on either side of the Androscoggin.

One last note: BEER, NEW ENGLAND is written in an A to Z fashion... somewhat for the sake of structure, and somewhat - actually mostly - because it seemed that it would be more fun to write that way. And that's the key: fun. I know I've had a lot of fun researching and writing BEER, NEW ENGLAND. I hope you have a lot of fun reading it!

Will Anderson

Portland, Maine
August 16, 1988

To Penny Ward of Avon and Lyme, Connecticut…
without whose assistance and encouragement BEER, NEW ENGLAND
would be but a flat and pale shadow of its present being.

Ale, Ale

NEW ENGLAND'S - AND AMERICA'S - ORIGINAL BEER

"So, I guess the Germans brought beer over here with them when they came," commented an acquaintance recently. A high school history teacher at a rather prestigious Connecticut prep school, at that. And he didn't mean that our first German-Americans brought a six-pack or a case or two over on the boat with them. No, he meant that we didn't have malt beverages

---

There Is a Difference

Ale differs from lager in several ways. It has a greater hop content, a more bitter taste, is generally more full-bodied, usually has a higher alcoholic content, and is apt to be less carbonated. True ales are top fermented — as opposed to lagers, which are bottom fermented — but there are quite a number of very satisfying ales that are bottom fermented. Ale tends to be of English/Irish heritage; lager of German/Czech. Both porter and stout are types of ale.

One last major difference: lagers are generally brewed to be served on the cold — although not frozen! — side, while the full flavor and character of ale benefits by its being served warmer. Try some at room temperature. I think you'll be most pleasantly surprised.

---

until the Germans arrived in the 1840s. That we were a deprived nation.

How misinformed he be!

There was beer before the Germans arrived. It was called ale. It was brewed by the likes of the Pilgrims, Samuel Adams, Israel Putnam, George Washington . . . and just about every household in New England and the rest of the colonies. It was as much a staple as bread. And much tastier.

English rule departed in 1783. Lager beer — that which we know as "beer" today — made its American debut in 1840 (see page 76). But ale continued as the choice of many. And nowhere was this more true than east of the Hudson.

Edgar Allan Poe, pausing to refresh at a Lowell, Massachusetts' pub in 1848, paid tribute to the hoppy nectar, not only by enjoying a fair amount of it, but by composing a poem in its honor:

> Fill with mingled cream and amber
> I will dram that glass again.
> Such hilarious visions clamber
> Through the chamber of my brain —
> Quaintest thoughts — queerest fancies
> Come to life and fade away:
> Who cares how time advances?
> I am drinking ale today.

1906 advertising lithograph, Frank Jones Brewing Company,
Portsmouth, New Hampshire. Courtesy the Hug collection.

Brewer of Fine Ales

Frank Jones: New Hampshire state senator, railroad magnate,
proprietor of hotels of distinction, all around bon vivant . . .
and brewer of fine ales. For more on Frank, his life and his
ales, please see pages 68-74.

Vassar College was founded by Poughkeepsie, New York ale brewer Matthew
Vassar in 1861. And "ale brewer" is certainly the correct term: even as lager was
ever gaining in popularity in the second
half of the nineteenth century, Vassar
refused to brew other than ale. No weak-
bodied lager for him. Alas, no profits,
either. And his refusal to go with the flow
eventually lead to the brewery's failure in
1896. All is not lost, however: the college's
founding father is yet remembered in a
little ditty heard to this day on Vassar's
storied campus:

> And so you see, for old V.C.
> Our love shall never fail.
> Full well we know
> That all we owe
> To Matthew Vassar's ale!

And in 1866, John Taylor's Sons' brewery,
of Albany, New York, published a book
—a 100-page book — entitled ALE: IN
PROSE AND VERSE. Lager is excluded.

Then there's Shakespeare, who wrote, "A
quart of ale is a dish fit for a king" in
WINTER'S TALE; the word "bridal,"
which comes from bride ale . . . a special
brew to honor the bride in days of yore;
etc; etc.

So Ale Got a Lot of Good Press in the Old Days ... What about Lately?

More recently, ale kept nicely afloat in New
England — as well as upstate New York
—long after the rest of the nation had
drifted off to lager and only lager. In
seems-like-just-yesterday 1945, for in-
stance, every one of New England's brewers,

Cont'd. on page 5

2

LONG TIME USERS OF CCS CROWNS

I'M TELLIN' YOU!

The newspaper advertising used in the promotion of Hanley's Extra Pale Ale is characterized by attention-compelling illustration and generous space. It appears in 64 papers throughout the 6 New England States.

...IT'S THE
Silver Spring WATER
THAT MAKES
HANLEY'S **EXTRA PALE**
SO **EXTRA GOOD**

Yes, it's the Silver Spring Water — one of the few naturally perfect brewing waters known to the world — that helps to make Hanley's Extra Pale so light, so dry, so clean in flavor, that it never tires the taste.

Silver Spring Water is so important in making a really fine brew, that James Hanley literally built his brewery around the Silver Spring back in 1876.

And the celebrated Silver Spring flows as crystal pure, as generously today, as it has since Colonial times — to help brew Hanley's — NEW ENGLAND'S LEADING ALE.

HELP! Help us beat the bottle shortage. Help us keep you supplied with Hanley's by returning your empties NOW! (They're worth money to you, too.)

HANLEY'S *Extra Pale*
THE JAMES HANLEY COMPANY · PROVIDENCE, RHODE ISLAND

Sketch of the plant of the James Hanley Company of Providence, R. I., built around Hanley's celebrated Silver Spring, from which flows one of the few naturally perfect brewing waters known.

CROWN CORK & SEAL COMPANY
Originators and World's Largest Makers of Crowns
ST. LOUIS · LOS ANGELES · SAN FRANCISCO
Plants at: BALTIMORE

Say you saw it in Modern Brewery Age

Hanley's: Long Before there Was Spuds there Was "Watchdog"!

Here's a thirst-provoking array of 1935-1955 items from Providence's James Hanley Company, one of THE famous names in New England ale history. James Hanley, the man, was born in Ireland in 1842, and came to America — and Providence — at the tender age of four. James Hanley, the brewery, was fiercely proud of both its Silver Spring water ("one of the few naturally perfect brewing waters known to the world") and its "Watchdog of Quality" bulldog. "Watchdog" originated in 1913, when the brewery first bottled its ale. One of the Hanleys, a bulldog fancier, thought the dog would make a good trademark. The rest of the family agreed, and portrait artist Frederick Stanley was commissioned to capture the faithful pooch on canvas. Used extensively on Hanley's packages and in its advertising, "Watchdog" — or his portrait, anyway — was insured with Lloyds of London in 1946. Eleven years later, in 1957, Hanley succombed to the relentless pressure from the nationals/large regionals and sold out to long time rival Narragansett. "Watchdog's" watching days were over.

HANLEY'S Ale PEERLESS
Brewed in Rhode Island's Largest Ale Brewery
PROVIDENCE, R.I.

HANLEY'S Ale
THE JAMES HANLEY COMPANY
Ale Brewers SINCE 1876
PROVIDENCE, R.I.
CLOSE COVER BEFORE STRIKING MATCH

TRIPLE TESTED
Hanley ALE

HANLEY'S **for** ALE

HANLEY'S
PURPLE LABEL
IN BOTTLES ONLY
LIGHT AS LAGER
EXTRA PALE
THE JAMES HANLEY COMPANY - PROVIDENCE, R.I.

QUALITY GUARDED
SINCE 1876
HANLEY'S *Extra Pale* ALE
TWELVE FLUID OUNCES · INTERNAL REVENUE

The Story of the "New Super-Duper Coating"

That it sometimes doesn't pay to mess with a good thing is a lesson Boston's Croft Brewing Company learned. The hard way. Recalls 72-year old Milton Allen, in the beer business most all his life and a man who knows a story or two about the industry (please see pages 169-171): "Ballantine was the big seller in the mid and late 1930s. Ballantine Ale in the tall green bottles. Croft came out in the same type of bottle. They had a beautiful product. Very nice. It was so successful that everything was on quota: you could get so many cases a week and so many halves, and that's it until an increase in production. The quota was sold out every week. Things are going along fine. The brewmaster's name was Walter Croft. And he was going on a trip to Europe. He was going to visit the breweries in Europe and get awards and so on and so forth. He was supposed to be a very famous brewmaster.

Well, somebody came in to see him just before he left, and they had something new to sell. Instead of putting the coating (that lined the inside of the aging tanks) on the tanks, which could be knocked off by hitting it or something like that, they've got something which is impervious to blows. They had small tanks to demonstrate. This was a new super-duper coating. They took a hammer and hit it and banged it: wouldn't come off. Mr. Croft thought it was wonderful, and he gave them the contract to re-coat all the tanks with the new coating.

But nobody tested it when it was wet. When they put the beer in there, all the coating just slid down to the bottom of the tank and the ale was exposed to the iron in the tank. You know, if you threw one iron bolt in the tank of beer that would spoil the taste of it. So, he's in Europe and the beer's no good. My dad used to open a quarter keg of beer once in a while down there in the south end (of Springfield) for the fellows. And Hugh Lennon, who was the salesman for Croft, came in and my dad said to Hugh, 'Something's wrong with your ale.' 'What's the matter with it?' Lennon said. 'There's something wrong with it.' Lennon tried it —he (Lennon) told me this afterwards when he was working for us (Springfield's Commonwealth Brewing Company) — and he said to my dad, 'There's nothing wrong with it. It's perfect.' Then he said (recounting later): 'I walked out of there and ran like hell to the nearest pay station. I called Boston and I said, 'There's something wrong with the ale.'

He (Hugh Lennon still) said it was terrible: from being a top quality product, Croft went down to nothing. Then they came out with cream ale and so on and so forth, but they folded. And that was the incident that did it. One incident."

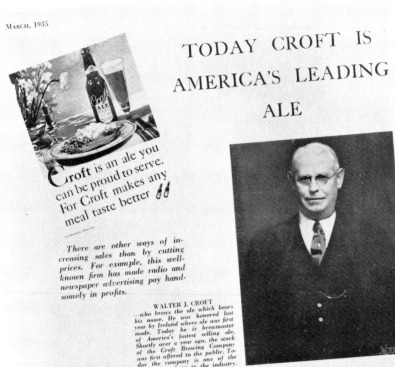

MARCH, 1935

TODAY CROFT IS AMERICA'S LEADING ALE

Croft is an ale you can be proud to serve. For Croft makes any meal taste better

There are other ways of increasing sales than by cutting prices. For example, this well-known firm has made radio and newspaper advertising pay handsomely in profits.

WALTER J. CROFT
—*who brews the ale which bears his name. He was honored last year by Ireland where ale was first made. Today he is brewmaster of America's fastest selling ale. Shortly over a year ago, the stock of the Croft Brewing Company was first offered to the public. Today the company is one of the outstanding firms in the industry.*

JOHN J. McCARTHY
—*Account Executive for the agency handling the Croft advertising.*

IN the February 26th, 1935, issue of the New York Times, there appeared the following on the financial page—
*Croft Brewing Company — For 1934:
Net profit after depreciation, Federal taxes and other charges, $474,054, equal to 27 cents a share on 1,732,441 $1 par capital shares, excluding 61,777 shares in treasury; net sales, $4,163,698.*
Behind this brief financial paragraph is the story of one of the most outstanding successes not only in the brewing industry but in the whole gamut of American business. The Croft Brewing Company has been in business a little over a year. It literally started from scratch with a remodeled plant and a new

product in one of the most highly competitive ale and beer markets in America, namely, Boston.

Now the Leading Ale

In the short span since December 6th, 1933, when the first shipment left the Brewery, Croft Ale jumped into the leadership in ales and beers, not only in Boston but throughout New England. It has held this leadership in sales ever since. No mean feat! According to a recent survey made by the Boston American, there are fifty-four ales and beers being marketed in Metropolitan Boston. Besides the competition of the big Western brewers and the New York brewers, Croft has had to compete for supremacy with a host of local brewers, all of them marketing ales.

The first page of a *Modern Brewery* magazine article from March of 1935, when Croft Ale was riding high. The Croft Brewing Company survived until July of 1952, when it was purchased by Narragansett.

numbering twenty, boasted one or more ales in their lineup, including very often the star of that lineup. Twenty out of twenty is, of course, 100% . . . far, far more than the other forty-two states' reading of closer to 50%. As recently as 1962, when the number of New England brewers had sadly declined to nine, the number of them that brewed ale still hung in there at 100%.

More Recently Yet

Today, all three of New England's locally-owned breweries — D.L. Geary in Portland, Maine; Catamount in White River Junction, Vermont; Mass. Bay in Boston — produce

> "We (New England's brewers) were all ale. We turned to beer after World War II ... slowly and reluctantly. When the boys came back all they wanted was beer, beer. Ale was an oldtimer's drink. And everytime an oldtimer died, we lost a customer."
>
> M. Joseph "Matt" Stacey
> President, Brockert/Worcester
> Brewing Company, 1942-62
> Worcester, Massachusetts
> February 19, 1988

ale ... and only ale. And we're talking real ales here. The kind grandma used to sprinkle on grandpa's Indian pudding when she wanted to get him in a good mood. Plus the region's two brew pubs bat .500. Boston's Commonwealth Brewing Company lives up to its "Let No Man Thirst for Lack of Real Ale" slogan. Very nicely. And while the Northampton Brewery/Brewster Court Bar & Grill in Northampton, Massachusetts' regular brews are lagers, their third tap — the special tap —is very often an ale. (Note: for more, lots more, on New England's contributions to the exciting micro-brewery renaissance, please see page 59-67.)

Could the Pilgrims, Samuel Adams, George Washington, Matthew Vassar, Edgar Allan Poe, Shakespeare — and generations of New England ale drinkers — be wrong?!

Today

The ales of New England today: a hearty — and mighty tasty —lineup. As some spaghetti company, the name of which escapes me, used to like to say: "Get to know what good is."

Beantown Brews And Breweries

BOSTON'S BREWING PAST AND PRESENT

Of course Boston was a major brewing center. How could the Hub have been anything else but!? During the heyday of American brewing — when there were over 2,000 breweries in operation nationwide and every city and town of any consequence had its own brew or brews — Boston was undisputedly up there among the kingpins. In the late 1870s, the rare pre-prohibition period for which complete statistics are available, Boston was home to twenty-two breweries.

a year at the time, six (or almost 10%) of them were Beantown operations. Boston Beer and Rueter & Alley, two of the city's giants of the day, were both in the top twenty (the top sixteen, in fact!).

At the start of this very century — when your grandparents were grumbling that McKinley's promises of a full dinner pail were just so much malarkey and that egg and meat prices were too high — Boston ruled - sort of - the brewing world: its number of oper-

Habich & Co., Norfolk Brewery (earlier known as A. Richardson, Norfolk Brewery from 1864 to 1874; and Edward Habich, Norfolk Brewery from 1874 to 1888)
171 Cedar Street
1864-1902
Nothing of the brewery survives. Its former site is now part of the campus of Roxbury Community College.

Circa 1910 lithograph, courtesy the Hug collection

Augustus Richardson's brews, at the time of this view, were Richardson's Norfolk Ale and Parker House Ale (as in the Parker House, Boston's venerable hotel of Parker House roll fame). A porter was brewed as well.

It's certainly difficult to believe that the Roxbury Crossing area ever looked as countryfied as this. But it did... when Augustus Richardson ran the Norfolk Brewery, situated just above Columbus Avenue. Richardson, who began operations in 1864, was proprieter until 1874, when he sold out to one Edward Habich (although he, Richardson, stayed on at the brewery in the capacity of maltster). Ales and porter were brewed. In that magic year of 1900 Habich, too, joined the ranks of the Massachusetts Breweries. The Habich branch was soon deemed inefficient — most likely because of its age — and was closed in 1902.

And these were not drop-in-the-bucket breweries: of the sixty-five American brewers with output of over 30,000 barrels

ating breweries had increased to twenty-nine, ranking it at the very top with respect to most breweries per capita among the nation's super — in size — cities.

City	Turn-of-the Century Population	Population Rank	# of Breweries	Breweries per Capita	Breweries per Capita Rank
Boston	560,892	5	28	.0000499	1
Baltimore	508,896	6	25	.0000491	2
Philadelphia	1,293,697	3	59	.0000456	3
St. Louis	575,238	4	26	.0000451	4
Chicago	1,698,575	2	59	.0000347	5
New York	3,437,202	1	111	.0000322	6

Call it the LCBPCR (Largest Cities' Breweries Per Capita Ratio!) if you will. Or call it whatever you want: it meant that the good

citizens of Boston were enjoying a lot of local suds.

It would be nice to be able to say that every Hub neighborhood had its own brewhouse in those golden, olden days but, in truth, most of the twenty-nine were in a tight little band in Roxbury and Jamaica Plain. Oh, sure, there were two in Charlestown, three in Southie, and a scattering elsewhere around town, but the bulk was in an area bounded

Note: An entire book could — and should — be written on the breweries of Boston. Such, however, is not the purpose of BEER, NEW ENGLAND. Over this and the next fourteen pages is included an overview of the Hub's brewing history and capsule accounts for twenty-three of the city's more important breweries through the years.

Roessle Brewery (became part of the New England Breweries Company in 1890; was a branch of Haffenreffer & Company from 1933 to 1951)
1250 Columbus Avenue
1846-1951
Nothing of the brewery remains. On its site is now Roxbury Community College.

Two early (circa 1890) Roessle labels that serve as fine examples of the labelmaker's art. Although on use on drug vials and early patent medicines as early as the 17th century, labels did not appear on beer bottles to any appreciable extent until the second half of the 19th century. For more on John Roessle, a pioneer New England lager brewer, please see page 77.

1890's McCormick Red Label Ale bottle.

McCormick Brewery Company (also known as James McCormick in 1885-86; James W. McCormick & Co. from 1886 to 1888; and the McCormick Brewing Company from 1888 to 1895)
95 Central Street/89 Conant Street
1885-1918
Nothing of the former brewery remains. In fact, even Conant Street no longer exists.

Looking as if it should've held wine instead of beer is this late 1890's McCormick Red Label Ale bottle discovered not long ago in a back road antique shop in Ossipee, New Hampshire. Note the bold reference to "brewery bottling." Many pre-prohibition brewers farmed their bottling out; i.e., they preferred to have someone else handle the task for them. Those brewers that did do their own bottling, consequently, tended to be boastful of it.

McCormick was founded by James McCormick in 1885 (though he claimed the brewery was the successor to Isaac Cook & Company, established in 1870, and also located on Central Street, but at a substantially different number). Stock and India pale ales were the brewery's proudest products, although lager was also produced at least from the late 1890s on. In what was undoubtedly a rare endorsement from a public official, McCormick IPA ads in the late 1880s were known to include a statement from the State Assayer, Dr. James F. Babcock, attesting to the purity of the brew and that it was "well calculated to compete with the best foreign ales." For the last three years of its existence the brewery operated under the name of Fenway Breweries.

=ALE AND=
Lager Beer Brewery
...For Sale...

THE HUB BREWERY, Roxbury District, BOSTON, MASS.,
of 100,000 barrels capacity, will be sold

At a Low Figure, on Easy Terms!

Handsome, substantial buildings of brick with granite trim, concrete, steel
and iron, with **complete modern equipment,** capacity 100,000 barrels; 275-
barrel kettle, 75-ton De La Vergne refrigerating machine; 10 ale fermenting
tubs, each 150 barrels; 12 ale storage tubs, each 225 barrels; 9 lager beer fermenting tubs, each 155 barrels; 6 chip casks, 150 barrels; 11 chip casks, 100
barrels. The brewery has four malt storage bins, each of 1,100 bushels capacity.

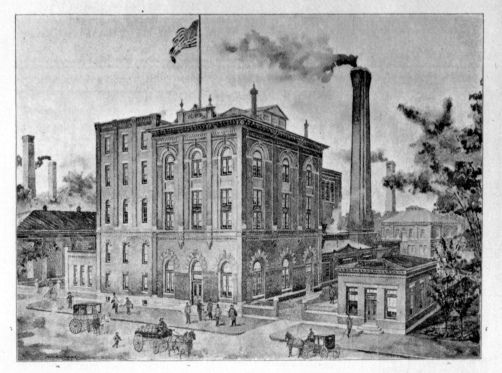

PLANT IS ALL READY TO BEGIN OPERATION

with large amount of **small cooperage wagons, teams and harness,** all in perfect order. Brick stable, with
granite trim, for thirty horses. Boston and suburbs, with a population of 1,500,000, consumes annually 600,000
barrels of beer and ale from outside breweries. **An excellent chance to establish a paying and growing business.**

——— ADDRESS ———

WILLIAM DWYER,   TREMONT BUILDING, ROOM 1024,   BOSTON, MASS.

Hub Brewing Company
193-197 Norfolk and Shirley Streets
1898-1903
The lower part of the shortlived brewery remains extant, although unimpressive, the home of the Blue Sea Fish Company and Char Fish Processing Company. That's right, the lower part: the top thre floors of the lefthand part of the brewery and the top two of the righthand have been lopped off. A disgrace... but I suppose better having all the floors lopped off and the site turned into yet anothe parking lot.

What a deal: a fully equipped brewery, all set up and ready to go, "at a low figure, on easy terms." The *Western Brewer*, the trade magazine in which this 1903 ad ran, agreed. Waxed they: This offering "presents an excellent opening for anyone who is desirous of entering upon the brewing business. The Hub Brewery plant is up to date in every respect, and in first-class condition, and when it is considered that the consumption of ale and beer is not only large but steadily increasing in Boston and the immediate suburbs of that city, it will be understood that the purchase of this property upon favorable terms is bound to prove a profitable investment."

Good deal or not, there were no takers: by the end of 1903 brewing operations appear to have come to a halt (although the Hub name did appear in the BOSTON CITY DIRECTORY's list of brewers for another two years, through 1905).

by Huntington and South Huntington Avenues, and Ruggles, New Dudley, Washington, Lamartine, and Centre Streets.

The reasons why were basic. Greater Boston didn't become home to large numbers of Germans — Oscar Handlin, in his 1979 book BOSTON'S IMMIGRANTS, states that no more than 6,500 Germans in total dwelt in the entire metropolitan area at any one time — but those that it did attract settled primarily in West Roxbury and Jamaica Plain. To this day there's a section in West Roxbury that's called Germantown by the people who live there. Martin Waters, the seventy-year old curator of maps for the Boston Public Library, recalls visiting German clubs as a youth: "There was one out on the corner of Lamartine and Boylston Streets —in Jamaica Plain, on the Roxbury boundary line — and on Sunday afternoons they would have people sitting around eating and drinking beer."

Cont'd. on page 12

1889 billhead, courtesy the Hug collection

BURKHARDT'S BREWERY, CITY OFFICE, 115 WATER ST.

Burkhardt Brewing Company (known as just G.F. Burkhardt from 1850-1891) Parker and Station Streets
1850-1918 (and then until 1927 as a manufacturer of cereal beverages)
Appears to be largely extant; now occupied by Great Eastern Packing and Paper Stock Corp. and by Northeastern University (as its central receiving facility).

BURKHARDT BREWING CO.
ROXBURY, MASS.

1895 advertisement

1895.

Bottling Dept.
125 Halleck Street.

Brewery,
Cor. Parker and Station Sts.

Long Distance Telephone, Roxbury 265.

Circa 1900 bottle opener

George F. Burkhardt is generally credited with being among those who introduced lager to Boston's beer drinkers. He passed away in 1884, but the brewery he'd founded did its thing right up until prohibition. Lager, bock, ale, and stout were all brewed (sometimes with imaginative names: in October of 1912, in celebration of the Red Sox' championship season, Burkhardt came out with both Pennant Ale and Red Sox Beer). As the Burkhardt Corporation, the company labored on, manufacturing cereal beverages — non-alcoholic beer — through most of the 1920s. The plant did not reopen after prohibition was repealed.

George F. Burkhardt, circa 1880

9

April 1988

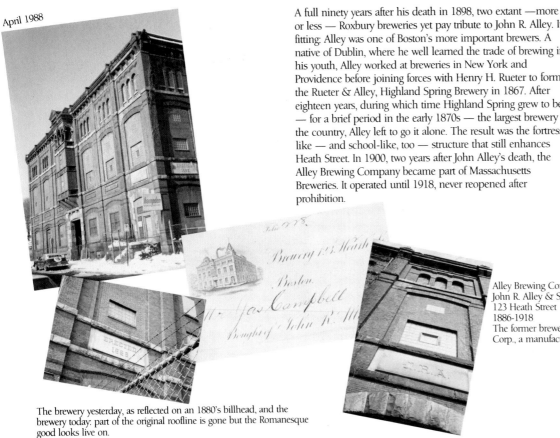

A full ninety years after his death in 1898, two extant —more or less — Roxbury breweries yet pay tribute to John R. Alley. It's fitting: Alley was one of Boston's more important brewers. A native of Dublin, where he well learned the trade of brewing in his youth, Alley worked at breweries in New York and Providence before joining forces with Henry H. Rueter to form the Rueter & Alley, Highland Spring Brewery in 1867. After eighteen years, during which time Highland Spring grew to be — for a brief period in the early 1870s — the largest brewery in the country, Alley left to go it alone. The result was the fortress-like — and school-like, too — structure that still enhances Heath Street. In 1900, two years after John Alley's death, the Alley Brewing Company became part of Massachusetts Breweries. It operated until 1918, never reopened after prohibition.

John R. Alley, circa 1895

The brewery yesterday, as reflected on an 1880's billhead, and the brewery today: part of the original roofline is gone but the Romanesque good looks live on.

Alley Brewing Company (known as John R. Alley from 1886 to 1893; John R. Alley & Sons from 1893 to 1895)
123 Heath Street
1886-1918
The former brewery is now occupied by Hampden Automotive Sales Corp., a manufacturer of auto parts.

circa 1895 advertising mirror, courtesy the Hug collection

Rueter & Co., Highland Spring Brewery (earlier known as Rueter & Alley, Highland Spring Brewery)
Heath and Terrace Streets
1867-1953
Much of the once-mammoth brewing complex has been torn down in the past few years and is now an expanse of rubble and piles of dirt. A huge section, however, remains, sandblasted to look a lot newer than it really is. It reads "Oliver Ditson Company," but underneath can be seen "Rueter" and "Brewing." Neither Rueter, of course, nor Oliver Ditson are using it today. It's occupied by Aura Design Posters and Graphique de France. P.S. Look for the words "Highland Spring Sterling Ale Store," still clearly visable from Columbus Avenue.

After John Alley's departure, Henry H. Rueter carried on at Highland Spring (renamed Rueter & Co., Highland Spring). A native of Westphalia, Prussia, Rueter had gained a wealth of experience at various Boston breweries for a solid sixteen years before having co-founded Rueter & Alley, Highland Spring in 1867. (The "Highland Spring" name was not just puff: it was the name given to the brewery's water source, located at the base of the slope upon which the brewhouse was built). In 1875 Rueter was elected president of the U.S. Brewers' Association, a post he held with distinction for five years.

Although active in legislative and governmental affairs on behalf of the country's brewers, Rueter did not ignore the home front: Rueter & Co. was one of the nation's first breweries to make use of artifical refrigeration and, with its huge storage capacity, was for many years the largest exclusively ale and porter brewery in the Hub. Its major product, Sterling Ale, was especially well respected.

Circa 1890 Rueter & Co. Sterling Ale label. "Semper Idem," the company's motto, means "Always the Same" in Latin.

Henry H. Rueter passed away in 1899 but his brewery, under the direction of his three sons, Henry A., Frederick T., and Ernest L, prospered until prohibition reared its head.

Henry H. Rueter, circa 1895

Cont'd.

Croft Brewing Company
Heath and Terrace Streets
1933-1953
See Rueter & Co., Highland Spring

Croft's snappy-looking 1930's label.
The brewery's slogan: "Friends Linger Longer."

Utilized by a metal and rubber company during prohibition, the former Highland Spring plant bounced back in 1933. But it bounced back not as Highland Spring or Rueter, but as the Croft Brewing Company. It was appropriate: Walter J. Croft, the brewery's namesake and brewmaster, had been brewmaster at Highland Spring for over two decades prior to prohibition. Under the direction of Croft and Rudolph P. Bischoff, the brewery's president, the plant was thoroughly modernized, beginning with the steam heat sterilization of every room of every building, and ending with the installation of over $500,000 worth of the best equipment money could buy. A branch brewery — the former Bismark Brewing Company — was even set up in Baltimore (although not for long: it lasted but a year). Things looked rosy. And, the Maryland failure aside, they were rosy. By early 1935 the brewery was advertising Croft as "America's most popular ale." The industry's leading trade mag, *Modern Brewery*, agreed (see page 4). What finally did Croft in, more than brutal competition or the switch in taste from ale to lager, was a bad batch that got out (again, page 4). In the beer business sometimes all it takes is one goof, and Croft's one goof was one from which it never fully recovered. Purchased by Narragansett in 1952, Croft was closed a year later (although Narragansett continued to brew Croft Ale for almost a quarter of a century thereafter, up until 1976).

Circa 1905 King's Bohemian Food Beer label.

Continental Brewing Company (earlier known as Frey, King & Co. in 1877-78; Lang & King from 1878 to 1883; Charles A. King from 1883 to 1896
86-90 Longwood Avenue
1877-1902?
Nothing of the brewery, now the site of public housing, remains.

The first brewery in New England to be lighted by electricity, and one of the first to make use of a refrigerating machine: such were two of the Continental Brewing Company's claims to fame. Another was their beer. The brewery touted its King's Bohemian as a food beer, "specially brewed to contain a large amount of malt extract, with only a small percentage of alcohol." A second product was King's Culmbacher which, the reverse of Bohemian, was billed as strong. And very old: "Sent out only after it is at least One Year Old." Continental, founded by Gustav Frey, Charles A. King, and John P. Lang in 1877, became a branch of the Massachusetts Breweries' combine in 1900. How long it remained in operation as a branch is a matter of conjecture, however. The usually reliable AMERICAN BREWERIES lists 1902 as Continental's last year, while the BOSTON CITY DIRECTORY lists it right through to 1919. Both agree that it never opened after prohibition.

The brewery also maintained a separate Puremalt Department, for a time at 60 Conant Street, later at 36-38 Hawley Street (Mass. Breweries' headquarters). Puremalt was a non-alcoholic malt extract, touted as a body builder "especially valuable for convalescents, nursing mothers and for all who are troubled with insomnia or nervousness." It was manufactured at least as early as the 1890s and was still showing up in ads in the early 1930s.

Circa 1918 King's Puremalt tip tray

Beautifully-lettered 1909 ad for
Massachusetts Breweries Company

Martin also stresses the relative availability of cheap land in Roxbury and Jamaica Plain, as opposed to Boston proper, during the Boston brewing industry's formative years in the mid and late 19th century. "Breweries use up a lot of territory," as he so graphically phrases it. Daniel Dunn, a knowledgeable local history buff whose family owned the former Franklin Brewing Company in Jamaica Plain from 1926 on, advances another theory. "The Germans came over and they settled there (in Roxbury and Jamaica Plain) because of the purity of the water, the kind they wanted," says he. That the water was indeed excellent can be attested to by the fact that, at the Centennial Exposition in Philadelphia in 1876 — in competition with the nation's very best — Roxbury Crossing's Highland Spring Brewing Company brought the first prize for ale back to Boston. "Perfection in every requisite of good ale, namely: in color, brightness, taste and aroma" are the words used to characterize Highland Spring's standard bearer.

Whether it was a German population, availability of land, or good water — or, as is most likely, a combination of the three — after impressive beginnings in South Boston and Charlestown, Boston's brewing industry rose to its degree of prominence primarily on the doings in Roxbury/Jamaica Plain. It was there that both John Roessle and George

Cont'd. on page 18

Andrew J. Houghton was a fairly ripe forty before he broke into the brewing business. A native of Vermont, he'd followed in his father's steps as a merchant until 1870, when he, in partnership with John A. Kohl, founded the brewery that bore his name. Houghton died in 1892, Kohl in 1901; but the brewery continued on until prohibition.

1909 ad for Vienna. Houghton's other brand was Pavonia, also a lager.

AN HONEST BREW

Old-Fashioned Ways Mark Every Step in Brewing

**HOUGHTON'S VIENNA
OLD-TIME LAGER BEER**

No stinting of Hops or Malt—no short cuts
—nothing, either in material or method, but
the best. And the beer shows it. . . . . .

T. J. Dempsey, Agent

A. J. Houghton Co., Boston

A. J. Houghton Co.
Station and Halleck Streets
1870-1918
Absolutely nothing remains
of the brewery; the site is now a
large, level
"Authorized Permit Parking Only"
Masco lot

1905 lithograph, courtesy the Hug collection

Circa 1910 litograph, courtesy the Hug collection

Robinson Brewing Company/Rockland Brewery (known as A. Robinson
& Co. from 1884 to 1893)
25 Amory Street
1884-1902
Nothing of the brewery remains. Its site is now an open field.

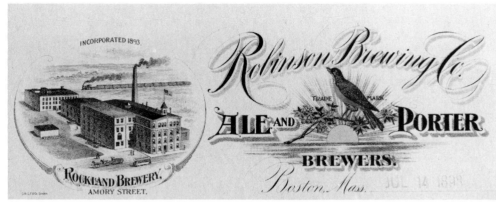

1890's letterhead, courtesy the Hug collection

If you had a son, would you name him Elmo?
If you had a brewery, would you name your beer Elmo?!
Well, that's exactly what Alexander Robinson named his ale:
Elmo ("Always Sparkling! Excellent Flavor!") Ale.

Robinson, a Scot who came to America at age eleven, served as
brewmaster at True W. Jones' brewery in Manchester, New
Hampshire for a number of years, then started his own brewery
in 1884. Known as the Rockland Brewery, it operated as an
independent entity until 1900. Elmo Ale really was the firm's
featured brew, at least in the late 1890s. Porter and India pale
ales - including East India Pale Ale - were also brewed. In
1900, three years after Alexander Robinson passed away, the
brewery became a branch of the Massachusetts Breweries
Company. Its days in that capacity were few, however: the
powers to be at Mass. Breweries shut it down in 1902.

1902 lithograph, courtesy the Hug collection.

J.W. Kenney, Park Brewery
79 Terrace Street
1881-1918
Nothing of the brewery remains; site is now basically a field of rubble.

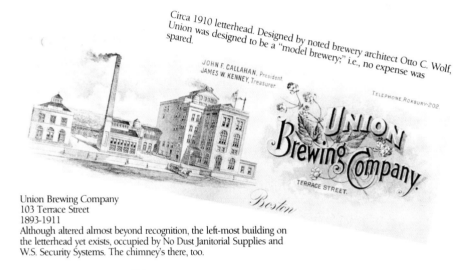

Circa 1910 letterhead. Designed by noted brewery architect Otto C. Wolf,
Union was designed to be a "model brewery;" i.e., no expense was
spared.

Union Brewing Company
103 Terrace Street
1893-1911
Although altered almost beyond recognition, the left-most building on
the letterhead yet exists, occupied by No Dust Janitorial Supplies and
W.S. Security Systems. The chimney's there, too.

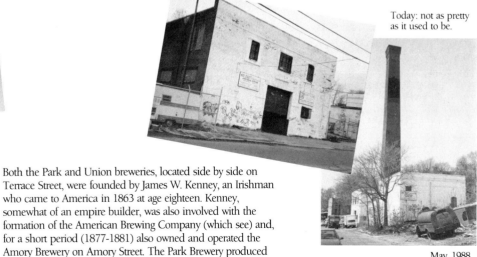

Today: not as pretty
as it used to be.

Both the Park and Union breweries, located side by side on
Terrace Street, were founded by James W. Kenney, an Irishman
who came to America in 1863 at age eighteen. Kenney,
somewhat of an empire builder, was also involved with the
formation of the American Brewing Company (which see) and,
for a short period (1877-1881) also owned and operated the
Amory Brewery on Amory Street. The Park Brewery produced
strictly ales; Union strictly lager (a 1904 ad proclaimed Union's
Extra Lager to be "Equal to any brewed in the United States").
Neither reopened after prohibition.

May, 1988

13

Circa 1935 Old Homestead bottle. Note that the body label reads "12 oz." while the neck label reads "One Pint."

1873 lithograph, courtesy the Hug collection

Circa 1915 Old India tip tray

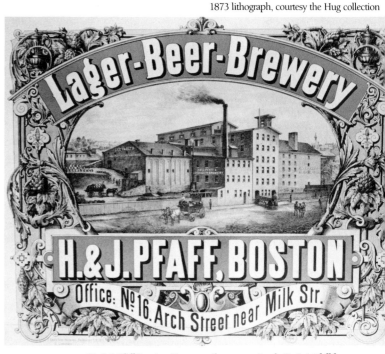

Commercial Brewing Company (known as Puritan Brewing Company from 1897 to 1906; Commericial thereafter)
40-46 Roland Street, Charlestown
1897-1940
A large portion of the former brewery remains, today a part of the Boston Paper Board Corp.

H. & J. Pfaff Brewing Company (known as simply H. & J. Pfaff from 1857 until 1893)
1276 Columbus Avenue
1857-1918
Nothing remains of the brewery; the site is now utilized as part of the new home of Roxbury Community College.

Commercial, organized in 1897 as the Puritan Brewing Company, was a longtime fixture in Charlestown. Best known for its ales, the brewery also produced 8 Bells Lager for a time in its last few years of operation. Brewing ceased in 1940.

Bavarians Henry and Jacob Pfaff founded what became the H. & J. Pfaff Brewing Company in 1857. Lager, of course, was their product . . . and they were proud that it was a Boston product. "A BOSTON PRODUCTION. No claim is made that this beer is made in Vienna, or Pilsen, or Cincinnati, or Milwaukee, or in any other place except in Pfaff's Brewery, in Boston Highlands," read an 1880's ad which continued on: "But it is claimed that no beer richer in flavor, purer in composition, more brilliant in sparkle, more healthful in character, is made in this country or Europe." Ok!

Pfaff was one of the ten breweries that banded together to form the Massachusetts Breweries Company, headed by Charles Pfaff, Jacob's son. The brewery closed with prohibition and never reopened.

1937 ad introducing 8 Bells Lager

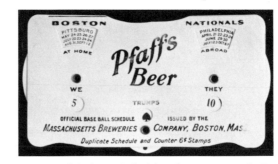

Circa 1915 celluloid Braves' schedule and scorer, courtesy the Hug collection (this nifty little piece of advertising is especially apropos: Charles Pfaff was a member of the Braves' Board of Directors in the late teens.)

Bottle opener, trademarked 1901

Circa 1910 Suffolk advertising poster

Suffolk Brewing Company
423-444 East 8th and G Streets, South Boston
1861-1918
Suffolk is the only one of South Boston's three former breweries that isn't still gracing the neighborhood. On its site is Bay Towers, a fourteen-story apartment building.

Although it was certainly a substantial operation, little of any consequence is known about the Suffolk Brewing Company, which opened in 1861 and closed in 1918. Both ale and lager were brewed. Suffolk was also involved very early in the game with a non-alcoholic brew. Called Uno, it was introduced in 1895. For the last twenty-eight years of its life the brewery was a part of the New England Breweries Company (see page 21). It did not open after repeal.

American Brewing Company
235-251 Heath Street
1891-1934
Appears to be fully extant; now utilized by F.A.E. Worldwide, a moving and storage outfit.

One almost expects to find a moat hidden somewhere on the premises of the American Brewing Company, a multi-faceted jewel of an example of pre-prohibition brewery architecture. It's all there in the castle-like structure: a magnificent turreted corner (look for the stained glass —albeit dirty stained glass — windows), massive arch courtyard entranceways, a plentitude of terra cotta, block "AMERICAN BREWING Co." lettering, and a most impressive — and large — A.B.C. metal sign that serves to crown the former brewery almost as much as does the turret.

The American Brewing Company began life in 1891. Frank E. Magullion was president, Gottlieb Rothfuss treasurer and general manager. Within the space of a few years Magullion was out as president, replaced by H.W. Huguley, but Rothfuss remained as treasurer and GM. Only lager, A.B.C. Lager, appears to have been brewed. After less than a decade as an independent, American, in 1900, became part of Massachusetts Breweries, operating as a branch until prohibition. In mid-May of 1933, Theodore C. Haffenreffer, head of Haffenreffer & Company, announced that big plans were in the offing for the brewery: capacity was to be increased from 300,000 barrels to 500,000, and the plant — which had been utilized as a laundry during prohibition — was to be operated as a unit of Haffenreffer. Such plans were of short duration, however: within a year Haffenreffer ceased operations as its newly-acquired facility, and A.B.C.'s days as a brewery were over.

All photos: April and May 1988

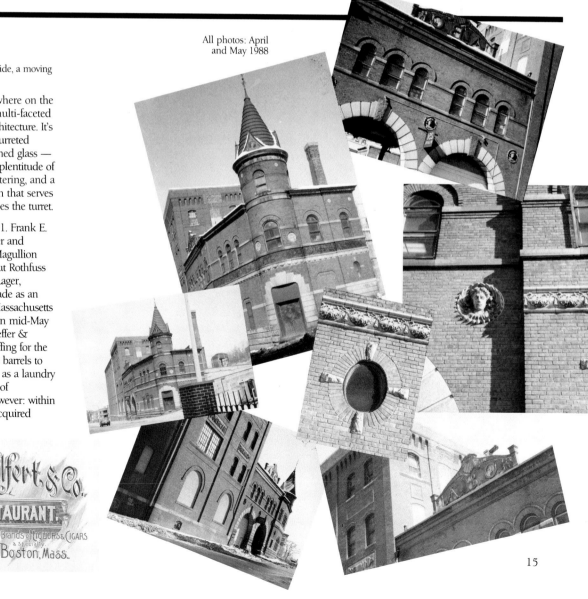

1895 ad for John N. Wilfert's Restaurant, proud purveyors of ABC's Lager

15

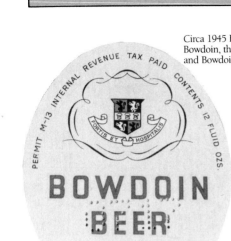

Circa 1945 Bowdoin Beer label (Roxbury was the birthplace of James Bowdoin, the Massachusetts governor for whom Bowdoin College - and Bowdoin Beer! - was named.

Circa 1935 electric light-up sign

Circa 1935 Star Banner Ale label

Star Brewing Company
69 Shirley Street/197 Norfolk Avenue
1896-1952
One smallish and not very impressive building yet stands, utilized by Balance One, Inc. The remainder of the brewery's former site is now, the ultimate ignominy, a parking lot.

Star was long known as "The Irish Brewery" of Boston, founded by John Joyce, Daniel Shea, Thomas F. Croak, John J. Murphy, and M.P. Murphy . . . and seemingly run by Murphys ever after.

The brewery was a pioneer in the development of sparkling ale. It may well also have been, as the century turned, the only brewery in the world with a garden in its brewhouse. Arthur P. Fegert, Star's brewmaster, felt plants would contribute to a feeling of cleanliness and pure air; that working would be more pleasurable; and that better beer would be the end result.

Star remained in operation until 1962, brewing Murphy's ("The Flavor That's In Favor") Ale, Star Banner Ale, and Bowdoin Beer.

Circa 1950 Murphy's plastic coaster

Circa 1938 serving tray

Hanley and Casey Brewing Company (known as Cook's Brewery/Phoenix Brewing Company from 1884 to 1890)
104 Ward Street
1884-1916
Most of the brewery has been demolished. One smallish but solid building remains, however, utilized today as the physical plant (maintenance) facility for Wentworth Institute of Technology.

What became Hanley and Casey was founded in 1884 by Charles H. Nichols and Thomas Carberry as Cook's Brewery (also known as the Phoenix Brewing Company). In 1890, ownership changed to Patrick T. Hanley and James D. Casey who, naturally enough, changed the firm's name to Hanley and Casey. Fine ales — stock, old stock, India pale and porter — were H & C's speciality. The brewery became part of the Massachusetts Breweries Company in 1900, operating as the Hanley and Casey branch until 1916. Descendant Edmund J. Casey incorporated the Casey Brewing Company in 1933, intending to brew in Boston, but nothing ever came of it.

April, 1988

What remains today: the maintenance building for Wentworth Institute.

April, 1988

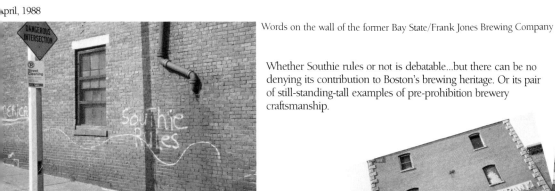

Words on the wall of the former Bay State/Frank Jones Brewing Company

Whether Southie rules or not is debatable...but there can be no denying its contribution to Boston's brewing heritage. Or its pair of still-standing-tall examples of pre-prohibition brewery craftsmanship.

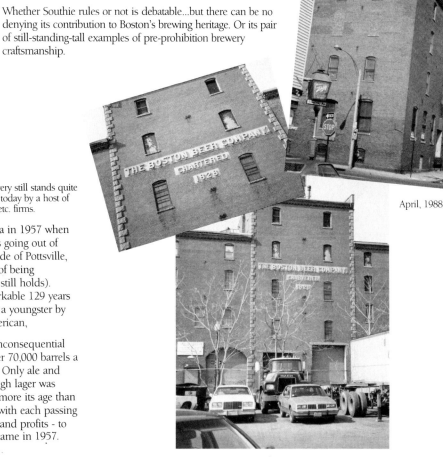

April, 1988

Boston Beer Company
225-249 West Second and D Streets, South Boston
1828-1958
What was, for so many years, America's oldest brewery still stands quite majestically in the heart of South Boston, occupied today by a host of small marine supply, textile by-product, millwork, etc. firms.

It was a joyous day in Pottsville, Pennsylvania in 1957 when the Boston Beer Company announced it was going out of business. With Boston Beer's demise, the pride of Pottsville, D.G. Yuengling & Son, inherited the honor of being America's oldest operating brewery (a title it still holds). Boston Beer had been around a rather remarkable 129 years (one more than Yuengling), since 1828. Just a youngster by European measurement, but ancient by American,

Prior to prohibition, Boston Beer was a not inconsequential force in eastern brewing. It regularly sold over 70,000 barrels a year, substantial by the standards of the day. Only ale and porter were brewed. After prohibition, although lager was added, the brewery's claim to reknown was more its age than its output. And this became increasingly so with each passing year: another year older but with less sales - and profits - to show for it. The end came in 1957.

A lithographed calendar from 1889, the year Frank Jones became sole proprietor of his Boston brewery.

Frank Jones Brewing Company (earlier known as Henry Souther, Bay State Brewery; Jones, Johnson & Co., Bay State Brewery; and Jones, Cook & Co.)
524 East Second Street, South Boston
Early 1850s — 1903
Still standing. And huge. Occupied today by a variety of firms, including Able Steel Rule Die Company, B & G Custom Woodworking, City Point Marine, Art Press, and South Boston Wood Works.

Boston's Beer's neighbor — just about six blocks over on Second Street — is another brewery with a lot of years under its brick. What was first known as the Bay State Brewery was founded in the early 1850s by Henry Souther, who operated it into the 1870s, when Frank Jones ("The King of Ales": see pages 68-75), in conjunction with others, took over. In 1889 Jones became sole proprietor, a distinction he held until 1903 when the brewery closed.

Ringing much of the top of the brewery of long ago is lettering that's hung in there a century or so. It's a joy to behold.

Courtesy of the Hug collection

All photos April and May, 1988

I couldn't resist snapping this reserved parking spot sign in the former brewery's courtyard.

F. Burkhardt, the Hub's earliest lager brewers, set up shop. Roessle's exploits are detailed on page 77, but Burkhardt's achievements are worthy of note as well.

In 1849 Burkhardt, a German immigrant who'd brought the necessary lager yeast up from Philadelphia, brewed his first lager while in the employ of Matthias Kramer and Charles Roessle (father of John), who operated a tiny brewhouse on Pynchon Street in Roxbury Crossing. By the time 1850 had arrived, however, Burkhardt —whose wages were considered too high by Roessle — was out on his own. As narrated in BACON'S DICTIONARY OF BOSTON (Houghton, Mifflin & Co., 1886): "Burkhardt thereupon formed a partnership with a man who'd

been a cooper in Kramer's employ; Burkhardt putting in as capital $250 which he'd saved, and the other man agreeing to put in some 500 florins which he expected to get from Germany, but which never came. An old, low brick building, No. 62 Northampton Street, near Harrison Avenue, was hired by the new firm, and a copper kettle ordered and delivered. When the remittance from Germany failed to arrive, the kettle could not be paid for and the coppersmith had to take his choice of removing his property or trusting Burkhardt, who had terminated the partnership and was pushing the business alone. The coppersmith took the latter course, and never had reason to regret his choice."

Haffenreffer & Co., Boylston Brewery
Bismark and Germania Streets, Jamaica Plain
1870-1964
The former brewery consists of a hodge-podge of buildings, half of which are slated to be restored and again used for brewing by Jim (Samuel Adams) Koch and his Boston Beer Company; others of which are occupied by 21st Century Foods, the Metropolitan Cleaning Corp., the M. Abelman Co. and the set shop of the American Repertory Theatre.

April, 1988

Today the former brewery is abuzz with the promise of a new life . . . as a brewery! (See page 66). Great!!

Strange how you never know. On the exact same day I telephone-interviewed two septuagenarians (the fancy word for seventy-year olds.) One, Martin Waters of the Social Sciences Department of the Boston Public Library, was most cordial and helpful. The other, T.C. (Ted) Haffenreffer, Jr., the last president of the Haffenreffer brewery, was most uncordial and unhelpful. Almost every question I asked was greeted with a "that was before my time" response. (And I don't think it would've made any difference what the question was; the response would've been the same. As in: "Mr. Haffenreffer, who won the Spanish-American War?" Answer: "That was before my time."). "Frankly," he summed up the topic of beer and brewing yesterdays, "I think it's kind of a boring subject."

What a shame: the patriarch of the most important name in New England brewing history (at one time or another the Haffenreffer family owned or controlled breweries in Providence, Fall River and New London as well as, of course, Boston) finds the subject boring. It may just be, though, that that's why Haffenreffer isn't in the brewing business anymore: a generation came along that had little interest in it.

The Bolyston Lager Beer Brewery, Haffenreffer & Co., was founded in 1870. As the name made clear, lager — advertised as being "for export and home trade" — was the product. Malt wine, so named because of its high alcohol content (usually around 10 or 11%), was added in the mid 1880s. In 1890 Haffenreffer and Co., along with Roessle, Suffolk, and Lawrence's Stanley & Co., were bought up by British interests and combined to form the New England Breweries Co., Ltd. There appears, however, to have been minimal interlocking between them, with Haffenreffer pretty much just continuing to roll along on its own. The year 1901 saw the addition of ale and porter. The company's product line, then, consisted of lager, export, Bayrisch (a lager that was the firm's featured brand), sparkling ale, stock ale, and porter. No malt wine.

Prohibition, needless to say, meant an end to the whole line-up. Haffenreffer put several non-alcoholic brews on the market, but with less than overwhelming success. The company's most notable achievement during the 1920s would have to be the acquisition of the rights to the name "Pickwick." The name was

A circa 1910 etched Boylston Brewery ceramic mug

And the evolution of Pickwick...

...a 1916 Harvard Brewing Company Pickwick Ale ad

. . . a trio of 1920's Haffenreffer & Co. Pickwick Pale ads

Growth at Burkhardt's and an increasing number of contemporaries was quite phenomenal. BACON'S described the industry, especially the lager industry, as having "shown a growth that is marvellous (sic) for a new industry." Continuing on, the DICTIONARY's section on beer and brewing reflected that the number of breweries had "increased until now a large area of country in the Roxbury District is covered with their solid brick buildings, yards, and vaults."

George W. Engelhardt, writing in his BOSTON, MASSACHUSETTS, published in 1897, quantified the growth: in 1886 ten Boston breweries sold 220,000 barrels of beer and ale; in 1895, twenty-three sold 1,092,340. Engelhardt also reported that about 1,500 persons — a considerable number — were employed in the brewing industry in 1895, with an annual payroll of approximately $1,225.000. "Only two industries pay higher wages than this one," he noted.

Such progress did not go unnoticed by the investment community, especially foreign investors. During the late 1880s a depression in Great Britain caused many English financiers to look elsewhere to invest their capital. American brewing stock particularly caught their fancy and, beginning in 1888 in Philadelphia and New York City, British

not new: it had been trademark registerd by Lowell's Harvard Brewing Company, as a name for its ale and porter, in March of 1913, and used extensively by them in the 1913 to 1918 period. But by the 1920s the name — for Pickwick Pale, a non-alcoholic beverage — had become the property of Haffenreffer. What a splendid name it was: the name of one of Charles Dicken's most popular characters and one who, it just so happens, was an ardent devotee of good ale.

After prohibition the brewery, dropping Bayrisch and other pre-pro favorites, pinned its sales efforts on Pickwick Ale. It succeeded. To this day ask most any oldtimer in eastern Massachusetts about Pickwick Ale and chances are they'll beam. "The poor man's whiskey" and "ten-cent whiskey" (in deference to the brew's high alcohol content at a low price), I heard it referred to over and over.

Haffenreffer operated three plants, the former American and Roessle breweries as well as its own flagship operation, for a brief period after repeal. Very brief: American was closed down within a year. But the old Roessle plant remained operative until 1951. Steadily, however, as with all but a relative handful of giant brewers, the company's fortunes began to wane. There was no competing against Anheuser-Busch, Schlitz, Pabst, Miller et al. "We could see the handwriting on the wall" is how T.C. Haffenreffer, Jr. phrased it in one of his few non "before my time" responses. In 1964, Haffenreffer and Co. closed down its 94-year old Jamaica Plain landmark.

. . . and an after repeal Pickwick Ale — "Ale that is Ale" — coaster.

investment syndicates sought to gain control of numerous breweries. In Boston this resulted in the establishment, in 1890, of the New England Breweries Company, Ltd., a loosely-structured consolidation of the Haffenreffer & Co., Roessle, and Suffolk breweries in Boston plus Stanley & Co. in Lawrence.

A decade later, at least somewhat in response to the "British invasion," ten breweries — all in the Hub — combined forces as the Massachusetts Breweries Company. The ten, in alphabetical order, were: Alley Brewing Co., American Brewing Co., Continental Brewing Co., Franklin Brewing Co., Habich & Co., Hanley & Casey Brewery Co., H. & J. Pfaff Brewing Co., Robinson Brewing Co., and the East Boston and Elmwood plants of the William Smith & Sons Brewing Co. The Elmwood, Habich and Robinson operations were shut down soon after consolidation but the rest, with varying degrees of activity or inactivity, appear to have remained in

Franklin Brewing Company
3175 Washington Street
1898-1902?
Still very much standing, the home of Dunn Moving and Storage

Lots of ornamentation.
Lots of grandeur.
A Beaux-Arts gem.

The envelope, please.
In what would come down to American Brewing (with Alley getting some support, too) vs. Franklin Brewing, my vote for Boston's Most Beautiful Brewery (that's still standing, of course) would go to Franklin. Maybe it's because Franklin is an underdog, having always lived in the shadow of its immediate neighbor, the Haffenreffer & Co.'s Bolyston Brewery. Or maybe it's because, being a rather shortlived operation, one expects to find nothing remaining. Yet, what one does find is a soaring, fortress-like structure that beautifies the neighborhood skyline from many a block.

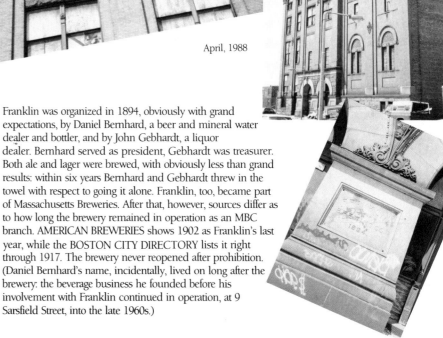

April, 1988

Franklin was organized in 1894, obviously with grand expectations, by Daniel Bernhard, a beer and mineral water dealer and bottler, and by John Gebhardt, a liquor dealer. Bernhard served as president, Gebhardt was treasurer. Both ale and lager were brewed, with obviously less than grand results: within six years Bernhard and Gebhardt threw in the towel with respect to going it alone. Franklin, too, became part of Massachusetts Breweries. After that, however, sources differ as to how long the brewery remained in operation as an MBC branch. AMERICAN BREWERIES shows 1902 as Franklin's last year, while the BOSTON CITY DIRECTORY lists it right through 1917. The brewery never reopened after prohibition. (Daniel Bernhard's name, incidentally, lived on long after the brewery: the beverage business he founded before his involvement with Franklin continued in operation, at 9 Sarsfield Street, into the late 1960s.)

existence until prohibition arrived on the scene in the Bay State in 1918. They, along with almost a dozen independents, constituted an impressive brewing bloc for the first two decades of the century.

Prohibition witnessed many, many adjustments. Some brewers, among them Haffenreffer, Burkhardt, and Star, tried to make a go of non-alcoholic beverages. Products with names like Dry Town, Uno, and Pickwick Pale were offered up . . . to a generally less than fully appreciative audience. The American Brewing Company, turret and all, was turned into a laundry. H & J Pfaff was converted to storage under the name of the Columbus Avenue Storage Company, with a part of it, known as Eliot Square Storage, set aside solely for automobile storage. Fenway (nee McCormick) became an auto repair shop. Most former brewing facilities just stood idle, slowly rotting. The moral of it all: legislate a proud industry out of business and you may well get some pretty un-proud results.

When FDR, as part of his let's-get-the-country-out-of-its-doldrums plan, re-legalized beer in 1933 it was a grand day for but a few of Boston's old line brewers. While happy days were here again for Boston Beer, Commercial, Haffenreffer, and Star, it was too late for all the rest. But, if so many of the old names didn't make it back, at least there was one new one. Croft. And it was most fitting that it was an ale brewery, for, while the Hub's brewing industry was certainly very much influenced by its Roxbury/Jamaica Plain Germanic heritage, it was never overwhelmed by it. Ale remained the core — heart might be a better word — of Boston brewing. As Rudy Bischoff, Croft prexy, said in discussing his new ale: "You must remember that Boston and New England have always been particularly partial to a fine ale as compared to beer."

This allegiance to ale was eventually, of course, to prove a negative . . . to Croft as well as to the rest of Boston's brewing fraternity,

Dry Town: not a big hit.

all of whom continued to peg most of their hopes on ale a long time after they should have. Returning World War II servicemen, exposed to little but Schlitz, Bud and other light lagers during their stay in uniform, found the once friendly ales too heavy. Women, an ever-increasing force in the marketplace, agreed. Add this loss of taste for ale to the legion of other problems faced by small/medium brewers in the past forty to fifty years (well documented in several chapters of BEER, NEW ENGLAND) and it becomes clear that Boston's five after-repeal breweries had little real chance to survive.

And survive they did not. Commercial was the first to go, folding in 1940. Star was next, closing its doors in 1952. Croft followed the same year, selling out to Narragansett. Boston Beer, which had been in existence in one form or another since 1828, gave up the ghost in 1957. That left Haffenreffer to carry on alone, which it did for another seven years, shutting down in 1964.

At the time of Haffenreffer's closing, I think it can safely be stated that most industry analysts would have said the chances of Boston ever seeing another operating brewery were about as good as the Orioles' chances of winning the 1988 pennant after their 0-21 start. But the exciting advent of micro brewing (see "Just Like the Good Old Days," pages 59-67) changed all that. Result: the Hub is once again in the thick of brewing . . . the only eastern city — as of this writing — with a micro brewery (Mass. Bay, brewers of Harpoon Ale), a brew pub (Commonwealth Brewing), and a contract brewer (Boston Beer Company/Samuel Adams).

The Beantown's back as a Brewtown!

Can You Tap This?

◆

THE STORY OF THE BEER CAN

The beer can is not a spring chicken anymore. As a matter of fact, it's going on fifty-four years since the G. (for Gottfried) Krueger Brewing Company, of Newark, New Jersey, introduced canned beer to the world in January of 1935. Actually, they didn't introduce it to the world... just to the prospective beer-buying folks of Richmond, Virginia. The reason for Richmond was simple: Krueger management was fearful the can might flop, so they picked a test market on the fringe of their sales area, far, far away from the bulk of their customers in the Newark/New York City area.

But the can did not flop. Quite to the contrary, it proved to be a smash success. While many customers obviously gave it a try for novelty's sake, they quickly came to appreciate that the can was lighter in weight than the bottle, and was more compact, too. They became repeat Krueger-in-the-can customers.

This success, naturally, did not remain a secret. Pabst and other brewers far larger than Krueger soon jumped aboard the can bandwagon, too. Today, billions and billions of cans later, the beer can is as much a part of American life as baseball, and hot dogs, and apple pie...and beer.

Grocery store, Richmond, Virginia, early 1935

Richmond: The Birth of the Beer Can

When launched in its Richmond test market, Krueger in cans was backed by heavy support on the part of American Can. They had a lot at stake. Krueger had done its homework, too. In the spring of 1934 they'd sent four sample tin can containers into the homes of a thousand families, along with a questionnaire allowing each family to voice their views on canned beer in general and the four sample cans specifically. The result, come the winter/spring of 1935, was a hard-hitting campaign -featuring the brewery's "K-Man" - for Krueger in cans.

Letting the Can Out of the Bag

The real credit for the beer can goes not to Krueger, but to the American Can Company. It was their determination and dogged persistance, starting even before prohibition, that overcame all the obstacles to successfully sealing beer - a very sensitive and highly carbonated beverage - in cans.

While much of the developmental work and progress with respect to the can was guarded, lest someone else beat them to the punch, American Can decided to let the can out of the bag in late 1933. This announcement, in the October issue of *Brewery Age*, was the result.

North to New England

New England's brewers were no dummies: they knew that if beer could be sold in cans in Richmond, it could be sold in cans in Boston, Burlington, Bangor et al, too. Here's a trade ad in the July, 1936 issue of *Modern Brewer* - from one of American Can's rivals, the National Can Company -heralding the arrival of Bay State Ale and Beer (Commonwealth Brewing Company, Springfield) in cans . . . their cans, of course.

Not All Cans Were Created Equal

In their early years not all beer cans were created equal. There were cans with the flat top we've all come to know well. But then there were cans that looked almost like a bottle. Many brewers, especially smaller ones, opted for the "bottle can" (also known as the spout top or cone top can) as it could be filled via their already-in-place bottling line. Then, too, the fact that the bottle can did indeed resemble a bottle was considered a plus: customers accustomed to drinking from a bottle would feel right at home. And they wouldn't have to wrestle with that newfangled invention - the can opener - that was neccesary to tap open a flat top. Eventually, of course, the advantages of the flat top - that they could be filled faster at the brewery because of their wider mouth, and that they could be stacked and stored more easily with less space taken - won out…and the bottle can went the way of the growler.

THE GREAT NEW ENGLAND BEER CAN BEAUTY CONTEST

There are beauty contests…

New York N

Finalists in the 1961 Miss Rheingold Contest: during its heyday the annual Miss R. competition was the second most heavily voted election in America.

…and there are beauty contests…

Jack Dempsey and Mr. Bock Beer of 1934-35 line up outside Jack's popular New York City restaurant in March, 1935. The Big Apple's brewers conducted a who's-the-handsomest-goat in New York City contest for several years after repeal as part of their drive to promote bock beer.

…and then there are really beauty contests!

Six beauties!
From left to right: Harvard Ale, Harvard Brewing Co., Lowell, Mass.; Dawson's Pale Ale, Dawson's Brewery, New Bedford, Mass.; Old Tap Ale, Enterprise Brewing Co., Fall River, Mass.; Red Fox Ale, Largay Brewing Co., Waterbury, Conn.; Clyde Premium Beer, Enterprise Brewing Co., Fall River, Mass.; Old England Cream Ale Old England Brewing Co., Derby, Conn.

Of all the cans and can designs put on the market by New England's brewers in the fifty-three years since Krueger started it all, BEER, NEW ENGLAND's esteemed panel of judges (in other words, me) has selected the six that it feels most fully typify the beauty of the beer can. All six are relatively early cans, from the period when:

● Designs were simpler…yet more dramatic, too.
● Cans were solid: it really did take a man (or one heck of a strong woman!) to crush one.

And last, but far from least,

● There were breweries in operation large enough to have a canning line (since 1983 there's been but one brewery in all of New England that cans beer…Anheuser-Busch's monster facility in Merrimack, New Hampshire).

Finalists were chosen on the basis of design, color contrast, and of course, shapeliness.

But enough with the words…let the spotlights shine. And let them shine brightly. It's time to announce the winners of THE GREAT NEW ENGLAND BEER CAN BEAUTY CONTEST!

The biggest and brighest spotlight beams on a can I feel is not only the prettiest in New England's can history, but also one of the most beautiful ever to wrap itself around a malt beverage anywhere in this entire country: the Red Fox Ale spout can, from the Largay Brewing Company, of Waterbury, Connecticut.

Our second place spotlight shines on another spout beauty, the can of Old England Cream Ale, from the Old England Brewing Company, Derby, Connecticut.

And our third prize winner is yet again an ale can, but a flat top model: Old Tap Ale, from Fall River's Enterprise Brewing Company.

How about a big hand for all six of our contestants: a bigger hand for our three finalists; and the biggest hand of all for our winner, Red Fox Ale — Red Fox…You Old Fox, You!

Do You Work Hard?

◆

THE MORE THINGS CHANGE . . .

For All You Do...This P.B.'s For You.

Kind of has a familiar ring, doesn't it?

But before I get involved in a suit with Anheuser-Busch (a suit I suspect I'd lose!), let me make it abundantly clear that "This P.B.'s For You" never, ever graced a commercial. There was no such slogan.

Ah, but the concept - of a brew that's just right at the end of a tough, demanding day on the job - that's a different story.

A.G. VanNostrand's Bunker Hill Breweries, of Charlestown, Massachusetts, originated their "Do You Work Hard?" theme to advertise the brewery's P.B. Ale and Lager at least as early as 1909 and used it extensively for the better part of a decade. With TV and radio not yet on the scene, the theme was limited, of course, to print media. Van Nostrand maintained billboards in and around Boston, was a heavy user of newspaper advertising, and made extensive use of what it called "posterettes." These were 10½″ x 14″ in size, printed in striking colors. Each represented a different occupation, with a representation of that occupation drawn exclusively for the brewery by F. Foster Lincoln. The posterettes, and

accompanying dark oak frames, were distributed freely to all dealers who handled P.B. In total there were over fifty occupations represented in Van Nostrand's "Workers' Series."

From barber and baker,
to judge and telephone worker, too...
Do You Work Hard?...
This P.B.'s For You.

The neigborhood baker was but one of over fifty occupations saluted via P.B.'s "Do You Work Hard?" campaign.

January, 1915. *The Western Brewer: and Journal of the Barley, Malt and Hop Trades.* 11

NEARLY EVERY WELL KNOWN TRADE AND OCCUPATION IS ILLUSTRATED IN THE WORKERS' SERIES.

THESE ARE PART OF THE "WORKERS'" SERIES—ALL WERE IN FULL COLORS.

THERE ARE MORE THAN FIFTY DIFFERENT POSTERS IN THIS SERIES.

THESE POSTERS ILLUSTRATE VARIOUS POPULAR SPORTS.

Page from a January, 1915 *Western Brewer* article entitled "Talks on the Advertising of Beer"

When I acquired this magnificent 1895 lithograph fifteen or so years ago, I dubbed it "The Lady in White." All these years later, she's still in white, and the lithograph is still magnificent. What's intriguing is the subtlety involved: only the brewery's calling card is included to let the viewer know that this is, after all, a beer ad.

A Formidable Force

A.G. Van Nostrand warrants attention not just for its well-ahead-of-its-time advertising theme...but because it was a formidable force in New England brewing for very close to a century.

With roots that stretched back to 1821 when it was founded by John Cooper and Thomas Gould, the brewery was purchased by William T. Van Nostrand shortly before the Civil War. Under William T. the brewery prospered, but it was his son, Alonzo G. Van Nostrand, that took it to its greatest heights. Immediately upon graduation from Boston's English School in 1872, A.G. started in at the brewery, and, purposely, at the very bottom of the brewery: familiarizing himself with and working his way through each department. In 1878, at the tender age of 24, he became a partner in the firm. A year later he originated the P.B. trademark for the brewery's ale. In 1886, realizing the success of Bass Ale in bottles, he added a bottling department. Five years later, in November of 1891, A.G. conceded that man (and woman) does not live by ale alone: he constructed a separate lager brewery. And, finally, in May of 1892, A.G. bought out his father, becoming sole proprietor of the Bunker Hill Breweries.

However, what impresses me most are not A.G.'s many achievements listed above, notable as they are. No, what impresses me most is a delightful little booklet put out by the brewery in 1897 to commemorate seventy-five years (plus one) of brewing at 40 Alford Street, Charlestown. While a fair share of the booklet is the usual puff — about the wonder of the brewery's products and its sterling leadership — there's also page after page of views of the brewery, both inside and out. Simply turn the page for at least a partial tour of yesterday.

Oh be jolly!

Circa 1905 P.B. Ale ad

"A Most Convincing Ale"

A.G. was mighty protective of the P.B. name. When he learned of saloonkeepers selling ale other than P.B. as P.B. he hauled them into Massachusetts Supreme Court...and won. The practice stopped.

Four pages of suspense is enough already: "P.B." stood for the Purest and the Best that can be brewed.

ARLINGTON AVENUE—YARD.

The brewery was exceedingly proud of the fact that P.B. Ale was the only malt beverage used in Massachusetts General, Boston City, and Carney hospitals, where it was prescribed for convelescents and others who needed a mild tonic.

Van Nostrand produced a full line of brews: P.B. Ale and Lager, Old Stout Porter, Half and Half (a blend of P.B. Ale and Old Stout Porter); Bunker Hill Lager, Boston Club Lager, and Old Musty Ale. The latter came by its rather unusual (and not too inviting!) name from the old English custom of using such words as "old" and "musty" to connote a very old, heavy, and high alcohol-content still ale. Van Nostrand liked to make clear that "the musty part is all on the outside of the cask, with the cobwebs and the dust."

A FEW BUNKER HILL ADVERTISEMENTS.

MAIN STAIRWAY AND THE "TAP."

MR. VAN NOSTRAND'S PRIVATE OFFICE

A.G. obviously didn't subscribe to the old adage that a cluttered desk is the sign of a cluttered mind!

MAIN FLOOR IN BREW HOUSE

ALE FERMENTING ROOM

Bunker Hill Lager

A. G. VAN NOSTRAND,
BUNKER HILL BREWERIES
CHARLESTOWN, MASS.
ESTABLISHED 1821.

For many years - both before and after the turn of the century - Van Nostrand had the largest output of bottled ale of any brewery in the country. In 1900, which someone undoubtedly figured was a good year to keep exact count, the brewery sold 892,092 bottles of its ale and porter.

Sad to say, but P.B. Ale, Bunker Hill Lager, Old Musty et al would never be made again in Massachusetts after prohibition . . . and all that you survey here would be torn down to make way for a line of the Boston Elevated Railway.

31

Eberhard: This Bud's For You

THE MAN WHO PUT THE ANHEUSER IN ANHEUSER-BUSCH

Before there was Anheuser-Busch and Budweiser and Michelob and Busch and Eagle Snacks there was Anheuser's Beer.

Eberhard Anheuser: from soap to suds.

But today, apart from being the first name of what was America's sixty-first largest corporation the last time I looked, Anheuser gets little billing. There is no beer named Anheuser*. The Cardinals do not play in Anheuser Stadium.

Yet, if it were not for Eberhard Anheuser there would be no Anheuser-Busch. Eberhard was a native German who came to

America and made good - not in beer, but in soap. So successful was his St. Louis soap manufactory, in fact, that Anheuser was able to loan $90,000 - a not inconsiderable sum of money, then or now - to the struggling Bavarian Brewery, also located in St. Louis, in the late 1850s. When the brewery went bankrupt, Eberhard assumed control. Beer, however, turned out not to be the success for him that soap had been: within two years Eberhard owed a goodly chunk of money to a young brewery supply-store owner by the name

E. Anheuser & Co. and C. Conrad & Co.'s Original Budweiser (U.S. Patent # 6376!) bottles, both from the 1870s.

These two bottles tell the story: before there was Anheuser-Busch there was Anheuser; and before there was A-B's Budweiser there was Carl Conrad's Budweiser.

* Although there may be: as of this writing - March, 1988 - A-B is test marketing a lager named Anheuser in New Hampshire and Arizona.

of Adolphus Busch. Busch, the youngest of twenty-one (yes, twenty-one!) children born into a wealthy German family, had come to America to find his fortune in 1857.

And find it he did. The brewery supply debt was cancelled in a memorable way. Adolphus had been courting Lilly Anheuser, one of Eberhard's four daughters. In 1861, they were married. (Actually, it was a double wedding: Adolphus' older brother Ulrich took the hand of another of Eberhard's daughters, Anna, in the same ceremony.) Within two years, Busch was a part owner of the brewery; by 1873 he was a full partner.

Enter Budweiser. In 1876 Adolphus Busch met Carl Conrad, a St. Louis wine dealer recently returned from a trip through Bohemia (now a part of Czechoslovakia). While there, he'd lunched one day in the small city of Budweis, on the banks of the Vltava River. Wine dealer or not, Conrad liked a brew or two with lunch. The monks in the local monastary brewed the local favorite. Conrad tried it, and loved it. So impressed was he, in fact, that he made a beeline for the monastary, where he succeeded in obtaining the beer's formula and rights to brew it in the United States. Conrad named the beer Budweiser.

Connecticut Historical Society

Budweiser - and Anheuser-Busch - is very much in evidence in this circa 1915 shot of Kirk & Eisele's Saloon, 605 Main Street, Hartford. Forget St. Louis and shoot for national distribution was Adolphus Busch's plan. It worked.

Washington Avenue, Portland, Maine
October, 1986

There have been, not surprisingly, many takeoffs on A-B's "This Bud's for You" slogan...including the Cleveland florist who's used it as his slogan since 1983. Sued by A-B, the florist won: Federal Judge Ann Aldrich ruled that it would be "absurd" for anyone to confuse flowers and beer. Closer to home was Edwin B. "Bud" Thurston, Jr.'s bid for a seat in the Maine legislature in 1986. (P.S. He lost).

and instead take Budweiser - in bottles - national. It was a bold move...but one which history has certainly recorded as successful. Today Budweiser is far and away the largest selling beer in the world. And Michelob and Busch are no small potatoes, either. But none of it would have happened if it were not for Eberhard Anheuser and the success of his soap and the attractiveness of his daughter.

Back home in St. Louis, Conrad contracted with Busch to brew Budweiser for him, and it sold well. In 1880, however, some of Conrad's other ventures went sour, and Busch loaned him money to stay afloat.

That same year, Eberhard Anheuser passed away, leaving Busch in full control. Anxious to expand the business, Busch liked what he saw when he saw Budweiser. He decided to try to buy the American rights to it from Conrad. He offered Conrad the elimination of the debt, a substantial amount of additional money, and an executive job at the brewery. It was a most generous offer. Conrad accepted.

Busch was now free to roll...and roll he did. He'd noticed what Conrad had earlier: Budweiser had unique properties that allowed it to keep well when bottled, and it could be pasteurized, further retarding spoilage, with the loss of virtually none of its flavor. Busch decided to go for broke with Budweiser; to forget the local market

Opened in 1970, A-B's Merrimack, New Hampshire plant is small by King of Beer standards (It's the second smallest of A-B's eleven facilities), but is IMMENSE by New England standards. Its 2,700,000 barrel capacity is approximately 117,000 times the capacity of all of New England's other breweries - all micros - combined. As one micro proprieter recently jested, "Heck, they probably spill more in a week than I brew in a year."

March,

From Berlin With Love

◆

LOWELL'S HARVARD BREWING COMPANY

What has been called the home of the modern American factory system and the most important planned industrial community in America, Lowell, Massachusetts, has had but one brewery of any consequence in its 165 years of existence. But that one brewery was a major one. Of perhaps greater interest, however, was the brewery's "German Connection" both before and during World War II. Before we get to all of that, though, let's go back to the brewery's beginnings, back to 1894. In that year a group of eastern New England beer distributors, lead by John Joyce and John Coffey, organized the Consumers' Brewing Company. A name change was made, to the Harvard Brewing company, in 1898, with John Joyce continuing as the company's president.

That Harvard was a biggie, especially by New England standards, was highlighted by the leading trade paper of the day, *The Western Brewer*, in its monumental ONE HUNDRED YEARS OF BREWING, published in 1903. Its glowing write-up of the brewery must have been a source of great pride in Lowell :

> "(The plant) consists of two separate and complete breweries, one for lager beer and the other adapted to the brewing of ale and porter, a mammoth bottling house, magnificent office

CONSUMERS' BREWING CO.

Brewers of

STOCK ○ LAGER

CONSUMERS BREWING CO. LOWELL MASS.

IN THE LOWELL BREWERY

The people of Lowell have an institution in which they may feel proud.

The plant is unsurpassed in facilities, and the product is unequalled by any on the market.

"Regardless of Cost"

The Consumers' Brewing Company as it appeared in a full-page advertisement in the *Souvenir Programme for the Fourth Annual New Year's Eve Concert and Ball* at Lowell's Big 12 Club, December 31, 1894. The statement "The plant is unsurpassed in facilities" was not without merit: nationally known brewing expert Dr. Carl Rach would later state that the Consumers' Brewing Company was constructed "regardless of cost."

building, stables, cooper shops, carriage houses, etc. The annual capacity of the plant is three hundred and fifty thousand barrels.

The products of the company are sold throughout the Eastern, Central and Atlantic Coast States. The plant is the largest of its kind in the New England States, and is considered to be one of the finest and best equipped breweries in the United States."

Open, Harvard

A very common - but handsome nevertheless - piece of breweriana is this bright red pre-pro Harvard opener, meant, of course, to be used in opening "The Finest Bottled Beer In The World" (see next page).

"America's Health Beverage"

Respected for its $1,000 and Green Label Beers, Harvard was also the originator of Pickwick Ale, a name that would be carried to greater glory by Boston's Haffenreffer & Company.

1909 ad for Harvard $1,000 Beer, "America's Health Beverage."

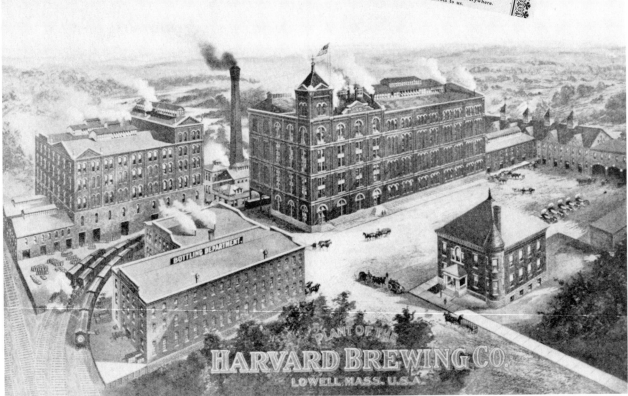

View of the Harvard Brewing Company from BREWERIES OF OTTO WOLF, published in 1906

Circa 1905 Harvard serving tray that is, I think, as beautiful as the woman who adorns it.

Let Them Have Grape Juice

Harvard is known to have tried its hand at ginger ale, root beer, orangeade and, of course, the usual near beer during prohibition...but did it also involve itself in the grape juice business? This brightly labeled bottle - bearing Harvard's name and logo - from the Naboth Vineyards, of Brocton, New York, (way over in western New York, on the shores of Lake Erie), would certainly suggest that it did. No one around Lowell, however, seems to know for sure, and calls to the Brocton Village Clerk's Office, and the Town Clerk's Office yielded no information or recollection whatsoever. A conversation with Ed Kurtz, Town Historian for Brocton's neck of the woods, however, proved otherwise. Mr. Kurtz knows his stuff: told me that Naboth was in business from 1910 or so until the 1940s; that they made wine only once (when a goodly quantity of their grape juice was in danger of going bad!); that they specialized in private label runs of grape and tomato juice, and other products. Mr. Kurtz did not recall Harvard specifically...but opined with me that - searching for ways and means to remain operative during prohibition - Harvard most likely had Naboth make juice for them under contract, and then they, the brewery, distributed it in their own New England marketing area.

The Next Chapter

When beer bounced back in 1933, Harvard bounced right back with it. The brewery had been purchased for $300,000 by New York interests, headed by Erwin F. Lange, in late 1932. Considerable monies were put into the plant and its equipment, with the result that Harvard was in remarkably good shape as it entered the next chapter in its history.

The 1930s were basically good for Harvard. Its brewmaster, Dr. Richard Juerst — himself German-born — would proclaim in late 1933: "Many persons associate the most notable achievements in brewing with Germany. This is far from true. Today, especially, many of the finest breweries in the world are right here in our own country."

Few would doubt that Dr. Juerst included Harvard among those "finest breweries."

Still Proud

Just as was true before prohibition, Harvard was especially proud of its bottled beer and its bottling house.

Liquid Carbonic Corporation ad in the August, 1934 issue of *The Brewer and Malster* magazine.

Taste-Test Package

The brewery came up with a rather novel idea in late 1939: put out a sampler package. The public, reasoned Harvard president Walter Guyette, was very poorly informed as to the types of malt beverages being made by his and other breweries. He designed a package - an attractive one, of course - that held two bottles of each of the company's products...Harvard Export Beer, Harvard Ale, Clipper Ale, and Harvard Porter. And, just to round things out to an even dozen, he included two cans each of Export and Harvard Ale. The result was one heck of a package. Commented *Modern Brewer* at the time: "It was an immediate hit. Salesmen liked it, distributors liked it, retailers liked it. Best of all, the public liked it."

At two six-packs for less than a buck, want to bet they still would?!

Creating publicity for the Taste-Test Package was almost as important as the idea itself. Here's Harvard prexy Guyette (that's he on the right) presenting the very first Package to Boston's Mayor Tobin.

Mayor Tobin Receives First Taste-Test Package From Pres. Guyette of Harvard Brewing Co

The German Connection

At about the same time as the Taste-Test idea was starting to click, Harvard made news in another, less flattering way. One of its employees was arrested for supplying information to the German government. Seems he had been transmitting radio messages from his home on Andover Street in Lowell concerning the local shipping industry.

Worse, German interests had been accumulating Harvard stock, and by the outbreak of war in 1941, controlled a majority interest in the brewery. Concerned that

Harvard profits were finding their way back to Germany, the Justice Department seized control of the brewery under the Alien Custodial Act. It would be well into the mid-1950s — toward Harvard's very end — before the U.S. government and members of the family of Fritz von Opel, of Germany's Opel Auto Works, would resolve what had become a source of major embarrassment to most all concerned.

A Strong Lineup

Pictured here is a mini-collection of Harvard labels and coasters from the brewery's last twenty-five years of operation. Recalls Frank DeCaro, who worked many of those twenty-five years as a truck driver for Harvard Distributors:

"They (Harvard) made some good brew, I tell you. The beer was out of this world. They talk about Budweiser and Coors: that Harvard Export Lager was one of the best. It was known all over New England, I guess. Harvard really had the body. You'd have a drink. And you'd probably have half a glass...put it down and the foam would stick right onto the glass. It had the body. That beer was something!"

Interviewed in his Methuen, Massachusetts home in late September, 1987, the 80-year old hale and hearty DeCaro really got excited when I asked him about Harvard Bock:

"I could drink that bock beer all day ("I used to like that, too" chimed in wife Mary from the next room). A lot of 'em (people) used to wait to get the bock beer. There was a lot of German fellows that I knew in joints I used to deliver to, especially the Bavarian Club in Lawrence. I used to go in there and they'd say 'Hey, Frankie, you got the bock beer today?' It was quite the seller."

Golden Brau and Connecticut Yankee were secondary brands put out by the brewery in its last few years of operation. Golden Brau was brewed from 1951-56; Connecticut Yankee, 1954-56.

Potent Stuff

From 1936 to 1948, Harvard also brewed a super potent product called Clipper Ale. Weighing in at about 8% or so alcohol, "It was made," bantered longtime former brewery employee James Ryan in 1981, "so the Maine Maniacs could get drunk for 20¢."

When The Selling Stopped

Richard J. Riley, 50-year old grandson of long time Harvard brewmaster Dr. Richard Juerst, recalls the brewery's arduous final days:

"I can remember at one point, when Harvard was starting to fail, 1954 or so, they paid all of the employees in silver dollars so that the people in town would know that the payroll was going into Lowell, that the brewery was contributing money to the town.

Did it work? Well, no: it (the brewery) didn't last too much longer. There was sort of a phrase around- 'Give me anything but Harvard' - which was really a bad thing to

WITH HAMPDEN

"It's a Pleasure to be Thirsty"

HAMPDEN-HARVARD BREWERIES
WILLIMANSETT, MASS.

Johnny Hampden

"It's A Pleasure To Be Thirsty"

With the aquisition of Harvard, Hampden changed its name to the Hampden-Harvard Breweries. In a December 1956 announcement, Hampden spokesmen made clear their intention to continue to brew the Harvard brand, and, in fact, to "build up its sales considerably." Such was not to be the case, however. This ad from the summer of 1957 - promoting only Hampden Beer and Ale - probably says it all. Harvard sales languished until 1964, when they stopped completely: the brand name was discontinued.

Harvard Lives On

But wait, Harvard lives on. In Portland, Maine, anyway. There are at least two Harvard back bar mirrors still in place and in use in the "Forest City." One is cracked, but one - in the bar that's part of Pizza Villa, 940 Congress Street, next to the bus terminal - is not.

I talked with daytime bartender Roger Sabin, who commented that people still come in and ask for a Harvard:
"Very frequently people off the Greyhound bus will see that (mirror) and say 'Oh, I'll have a Harvard.' And I'll say 'I'm sorry, but you're about twenty-five years too late.' Then they'll giggle, and realize that it's an old mirror."

I sensed that Roger has a real sense of pride in the mirror (which he refers to as "a unique piece of furniture"). And sure enough, he has. He's even become quite an avid collector of Harvard breweriana in the eleven years since he first laid eyes on the mirror.

As to how it's still there, virtually flawless, thirty-one years after the brewery closed and probably a good half-century after it was installed, Roger beamed as he recounted its "history":
"Yep, it's still here in spite of a few brouhaha's, a few bottles, and a few chairs. You can see some nicks in the mirror where a bottle hit one night, and a chair's hit up there, too. But it lives. It leads a charmed life, I guess."

My only comment: let's hope that charmed life continues. It's a beauty!

Roger and "his" mirror. The full mirror measures nine feet by three feet; the Harvard part of it, one and a half feet by two and a half feet. While "Maine Ale" probably sounds impressive - especially in Maine - there was, in reality, no such animal. It was most likely regular Harvard (or perhaps Clipper) Ale renamed to make it all that much more inviting to Mainers.

say. People didn't show much loyalty. And then there were rumors that the wells which were on the adjacent territory were contaminated by a graveyard or something which was nearby the brewery; that the water going in the beer was supposed to be contaminated. That made things really difficult."

Difficult, indeed. In 1951, Harvard ranked an even 50th in size among America's brewing companies. By 1955, four years later, Harvard had risen in rank to number thirty-nine.
Sound good?

It wasn't. The brewing industry was going through a tremendous thinning out process: the only reason Harvard rose eleven notches was because so many of its contemporaries folded before it did. In reality, Harvard's sales had plummeted those four years, from 278,000 barrels sold in 1951 to 183,000 barrels sold in 1955.

A year later, in December of 1956, Harvard joined the ranks of the thinned out: the brewery and its brands were absorbed into the Hampden Brewing Company, of Williamsett, Massachusetts, with all operations in Lowell ceasing.

41

Give 'em Hull

◆

THE NUTMEG STATE'S LAST OPERATING BREWERY

There are probably few people around New England today who would raise their hand if asked to recall Hull's Export Beer. There are probably fewer still who would raise their hand to say that they recall it fondly.

But my hand would be raised in answer to both questions. Hull's, though on its last legs, was available for seven of the nine years I lived in Connecticut. Quarts went for three for a dollar . . . and I can clearly recall that it was as good as or better than stuff that went for a whole lot more. What would I think of it now? I don't know . . but I sure wish it were still around for me to find out.

"Worth Stopping For!" The problem was that not enough folks did.

Late 1940's Hull's Beer-Ale sign

No Hull at the Helm . . . And a New Home

Hull's pre-prohibition address was 14-22 Whiting Street, corner of State. And their output - until at least 1912, the year lager was most likely added - was solely in the English tradition, ales and porter.

The elder Hull retired from the firm in 1879. The younger Hull ran things until 1912 when he, too, retired from the firm . . . selling out to Michael McGann and George Jacob, whose descendants ran the brewery for the next sixty-five years.

When beer came back in 1933, Hull's was back in business, but not at its old stand. The former Ph. Fresenius' Sons Brewing Company facility at 820 Congress Street was purchased and renovated . . . and became Hull's new home.

1890 Wm. Hull & Son billhead

The Hull story started in 1872 when Col. William Hull and his son William H. founded the firm of William Hull and Son in New Haven. In those grand and glorious days of brewhouses seemingly around every corner, New Haven wasn't a big-time brew town, but it wasn't inconsequential, either: William Hull and Son was brewery number seven in town at the time of its founding. It proved to be lucky number seven . . . for Hull's was to long outlast them all.

The Naugatuck Nugget

It's been over forty years since Frank "Spec" Shea and Hull teamed up, in late 1947, as "Connecticut Favorites." But while Hull is now little more than history, "The Naugatuck Nugget" is still going strong. At age 67, he's Superintendent of Parks and Recreation for his home town . . . which, of course, is Naugatuck (Connecticut). Contacted in Naugatuck, Frank vividly recalls the campaign and gladly discusses it:

> His renumeration for doing the ad? $1,500.
> His recollection of how Hull's tasted? "Pretty good."

and last

> When asked if he had been proud to be associated with Hull's, Frank replied "Sure was."

(Incidentally, Frank - who pitched eight years in the big leagues with the Yankees and Senators - got his nickname of "Spec" not because he wore spectacles, but because his dad did: Frank was called "Young Spec.")

43

Shades of "Great Taste" vs. "Less Filling"

When upstate rival, New Britain's Cremo Brewing Co., closed its doors in 1955, Hull's became Connecticut's sole remaining brewery. It was an honor that it would hold for almost the next quarter of a century.

Matched pair of circa 1940 Cremo Old Stock Ale display signs

Mid-1970's Hull's Export Beer can

Exported . . . But To Where?

Right down to the end the brewery sported what many considered to be a classy label design on its can of "Export Beer."

But to where was Hull's Export Beer exported?! By the brewery's own admission, it wasn't very far. In a special 100th Anniversary Supplement to the *New Haven Register*, November 5th, 1972, the brewery defined its market as "concentrated in Connecticut," with "services to a few wholesalers in New York and Massachusetts on a limited scale." My own view: "limited scale" meant virtually non-existent. Hull's was, in reality, a Connecticut beer . . . with it often being difficult enough to track down even within New Haven's own cozy environs, let alone trying to unearth it in such far off, distant lands as New York or Massachusetts.

Quality, Value, Sex Appeal, You Gotta Be Smart . . . and "Dietetically Non-Fattening," Too

One certainly couldn't fault Hull's for their lack of advertising imagination or skill. I recently found, in a used bookstore in Williamstown, Mass., a run of playbills from the Shubert Theatre in New Haven for the years 1944 to 1953. Virtually all of the playbills featured a most prominent Hull's ad on the right-hand side of the very first page . . . and most all of the ads touted a different theme. Quality, value, sex appeal, you gotta be smart to buy it - you name it and Hull's used it to promote their brew.

Of special interest was their "Dietetically Non-Fattening" theme. This theme - that beer isn't necessarily blubber building - was first utilized by the California Brewing Association, of San Francisco and Los Angeles, to sell its Acme Beer in the mid-1930s. As Acme ad copy explained:

> "Tests show that it (Acme Beer) contains less than 25% of the fattening substances that are in most of the non-alcoholic beverages, and that the carbohydrates contained in Acme Beer are fully fermented and therefore are non-fattening."

Sounds a little wishy-washy, I know, but the Federal Trade Commission - which investigated the claim in 1936 - bought it, and at least a few other brewers, Hull's included, jumped on the non-fattening bandwagon. And remained on it for many years: it wasn't until 1951 that the FTC altered its ruling to add that such non-fattening statements must be accompanied by the qualifying wording:

> "...when taken in substitution for foods of equal or greater caloric value and not in addition to the normally required diet."

In other words, the FTC wanted it made perfectly clear that beer is non-fattening . . . as long as imbibed in place of something else that's equally fattening or non-fattening.

"Satisfaction in All Three": Not at Helen's Place There Wasn't!

But if people couldn't fault Hull's for their advertising, people could - and did - fault it for its taste. And it's smell. As Helen Cronin, who owned and operated a bar called The Bucket, on Wells Street in Hartford from 1966 to 1970, so eloquently put it in an August, 1987 interview: "Hull's had a distinctive flavor. And a smell. It didn't bother me, but my customers didn't like it. They had all kinds of names for it. And they wouldn't drink it."

The question, of course, is: did Helen's customers - as well as the myriad of other beerdrinkers throughout southern and central Connecticut - really think Hull's was terrible? Or were they convinced by the tv and radio and print blitz, which only the big boys could afford, that brews "imported" from Wisconsin or Missouri or New York were that much better? And, therefore, that a beer from down the road was that much worse?

It's a question which no one can really and fully answer. And after 1977 it became a moot point anyway.

Hull ceased brewing.

Circa 1950 Hull's coaster

Hi Neighbor ...
Have A
'Gansett

◆

THE GIANT THAT WAS NARRAGANSETT

"Hi Neighbor . . . Have a 'Gansett": the words seem to yet endlessly roll off billboards and newspapers and magazines. And bus and trolley cards, too. While down at Fenway Curt Gowdy is beaming forth the beginning of another Sox game: "Hiya, neighbor. This is Red Sox baseball brought to you by Narragansett Lager Beer."

But the billboards and the ads and the mass transit cards are gone. Curt Gowdy is gone. And, for most intents and purposes, Narragansett is gone, too. Sure, it's still available. But it's brewed in Fort Wayne, Indiana. Hi neighbor?

It was not long ago, however, that Narragansett was truly "New England's Beer," New England's largest-selling beer. And we're not talking just Rhode Island, either. A 1955 survey, for example, found that 'Gansett was the number one choice among men in Portland, Maine; that it ranked higher than Budweiser and was favored more than two to one over Miller. Try running that one by the folks in Portland today.

German-American Origins

If most New England breweries were built around a tradition of ale — which they were — Narragansett was an anomaly; it was built, in 1890, as a lager-only brewery. Its founding six — Augustus F. Borchandt,

Herman G. Possner, George M. Gerhard, Constand A. Moeller, John H. Fehlberg, and Jacob Wirth (he of Boston fame: see page 123) were all of German-American extraction. Its first brewmaster, direct from Berlin, was George Wilhelm. It wasn't until 1898 that ale was added to the Narragansett roster.

Growth, from the very beginning, was rather phenomenal. In 1891, the company brewed 27,997 barrels; by 1898, it was 80,083; 1900 saw 101,469; and by 1909, with George Wilhelm still overseeing the kettles, output topped the 200,000 barrel mark. Ale, porter, malt extract, and, of course, lager were all produced. It was the largest brewery in New England.

After prohibition Narragansett bounced back, again New England's largest brewery. Otto Henn, who'd replaced George Wilhelm about the time World War I was unfolding, returned as brewmaster. Emil Schierholz, general manager prior to prohibition, once more headed up operations. Both would remain at their respective posts for many, many years; Emil Schierholz until the late forties; Otto Henn into the fifties. While all this experience was invaluable in many ways, it may have been a negative, too. John McNaboe, Narragansett's last general manager, was later to ruminate: "The obituary column caught

Boston Braves' program ad, 1951

newspaper ad , 1946

Hi Neighbor

Clothing styles changed, but the message remained the same: "Hi Neighbor . . . Have a 'Gansett." The 1951 ad is of note: it was the year the Braves celebrated their seventy-fifth anniversary, making them fourteen years older than Narragansett. Both would eventually go west: the Braves to Milwaukee, then Atlanta; Narry to Fort Wayne. Although it still reads "Cranston, RI" on Narragansett labels (a letter sent to Falstaff's Fort Wayne general manager Earl Thompson asking the how and the why of this went unanswered), it's been five years now since any of it's actually been brewed there.

47

up with us. Nobody here ever put on a drive to catch the younger drinker, the 18-to-35s, because we always had the staunch middle-aged Narragansett drinkers." Outdated plant and equipment was a disadvantage, too. While, starting in 1970, Bud and Michelob were being churned out in an ultra-modern plant less than one hundred miles up the road in New Hampshire, 'Gansett lager, ale and porter were still being produced in a facility that remained too turn-of-the-century in its state of the art. By comparison, we "still have to make beer by hand" was McNaboe's way of putting it.

From an estimated 65.5% of the region's beer sales in 1963, Narragansett fell to about 17% by 1980. Being purchased by national conglomerate Falstaff Brewing in 1965 didn't seem to stem the slippage. In fact, it may have aided it. An extensive advertising campaign for the new parent company's own Falstaff Beer only proved

that spending money doesn't necessarily beat a path to success: Falstaff did not catch on in New England; Narragansett continued to lose ground to Bud, Miller et al.

The end came in the early 1980s. Fitfully. Brewery officials announced the closing of the 91-year-old operation in the summer of 1981; this in spite of a $200,000 tax break allowed by the Rhode Island legislature for 1980. The high cost of energy —having to use oil instead of gas, resulting in a beer-production cost of just over $7.00 per 31-gallon barrel in Cranston vs. just over $3.00 in Fort Wayne — was the major reason cited for the shutdown. In January of 1983 the brewery reopened, although on a much smaller scale than previously. And for what turned out to be but a brief period. Within several months it was shutdown day again. This time for keeps.

Both photos, March, 1988

Come Along Inn, Coventry, Rhode Island

Artic Cafe, West Warwick, Rhode Island

Although the familiar Narragansett Lager signs are still very much in view in and around Rhode Island, gone are the days when about every other tap in the Ocean State foamed forth with a 'Gansett. "Those were the good old days," recalled one former brewery employee at the time of closing number one in July, 1981. "When you went to a bar and asked for a draft it was automatically Narragansett!" Added a fellow ex-co-worker, "If you wanted another brand you'd ask quietly for fear of being thought of as crazy."

All photos: March, 1988

Narragansett Today

What was for many years New England's largest brewery today stands idle, an immense patchwork of brick on New Depot Avenue in Cranston, just south of Providence. A billboard announces the coming of "An environmentally planned commercial/residential development" . . . but repeated phone calls to the number given produced nothing but an unanswered phone. One can only wait - and hope (which is, after all, the state motto!) - that it happens. And that the architectural integrity of the almost century-old brewing complex is maintained in the process.

Some Other Rhode Island Brews and Breweries

As impressive as it was, Narragansett was far from Rhode Island's only brewery. Within the last seventy-five years, beer has also flowed from Pawtucket, Warwick, West Warwick, and not at all surprisingly, Providence. Even pastoral Tiverton, on the state's eastern border, reputedly had a brewery, the Tiverton Brewing Company, for a short while in 1914-1915 (although its existence is not supported by tax records: Tiverton town clerk Beverly Lopes was good enough to let me pore through the town's records and I could find no mention of any brewing facility).

On this and the following three pages is a look at a healthy sampling of the Ocean State's more significant "others."

Circa 1910 letterhead, courtesy the Hug collection

March, 1988

The filigree is gone. So's the top floor. But the smokestack's still there, and so is most of the rest of the former brewery, located on Mendon Avenue in the Darlington section of Pawtucket. Note the black smoke in the circa 1910 letterhead view: while such would be considered a sign of pollution today, in those not-so-distant days it was considered a sign of industry and progress.

Hand/Rhode Island Brewing Company

A man of many breweries would've been an apt description of Michael Hand, Sr. Before he, in 1898, founded the Pawtucket brewery that bore his name, he was involved with the Gulf Brewery, of Utica, New York, and then with the Scranton Brewing Company and the Lackawanna Brewing Company, both of Scranton, Pennsylvania. Pawtucket beckoned, however, and Hand (and his son, Michael, Jr.) constructed the 100,000-barrel capacity Hand Brewing Company plant pictured here. Ale, lager, and porter were brewed. The brewery's pride was its Half Stock Ale, proclaimed to be "The Beverage for the Man who works." An ad from 1915 went on to extol it as "Wholesome. Refreshing. Builds the muscle, nerve, and brawn." Who could argue?

Both Hand, Sr. and Jr. passed away prior to prohibition, but the family carried on. In fact, they may have carried on too well: federal authorities raided the premises repeatedly in the early twenties, charging violation of the national prohibition act. Seems the Hands were making the real stuff rather than the near beer for which they had a permit.

In 1930 the brewery fell into the hands of James Lavell, an Irish-born former Providence saloonkeeper and all-around wheeler-dealer. Convicted, in June 1931, of income tax evasion, Lavell served eighteen months in the Atlanta Federal Penitentiary, getting out just in time to pump money - $100,000 is the figure he gave the press - into pre-repeal modernization of the brewery. By September of 1933, renamed the Rhode Island Brewing Company, the old plant was humming again. Rhode Island Beer, Porter, and Ale were all brewed, but top billing definitely went to the ale: Rhode Island Special Ale, "The Brew of Distinction." The humming stopped in 1938, the brewery's last year of operation. The facility is today utilized as a warehouse by Teknor Apex, a manufacturer of chemicals and industrial products.

Circa 1935 Special Ale bottle

March, 1988

Circa 1935 Roger Williams Ale bottle

The reason there's not a better likeness of the man who founded Rhode Island on his namesake-ale label is simple: no one really knows what Roger Williams looked like. There are no known portraits or paintings of him. Surprising, but true.

The Roger Williams Brewing Corp.

Roger Williams was a post-prohibition-only brewery located at 61-71 Troy Street, just off Broadway in Providence. Incorporated in 1933, it was headed by Joseph Bertolaccinni (also variously spelled, incorrectly, Bertolasina and Bertolacini) for all of its seven years of operation. Julius Cabisius, who'd been around since graduating from brewmaster's school at the Wahl Henius Institute in 1895, was brewmaster. Brands were Roger Williams Ale, Westminster Half Stock India Pale Ale, and Down East Special XXXXXX Cream Ale. Today the facility, a former textile mill that was converted to a brewery, has been converted back to the production of "hard goods:" it houses a number of small jewelry manufacturing firms.

Circa 1895 enamel-over-metal Eagle Ales' tray and PROVIDENCE CITY DIRECTORY ad from 1910, a dozen or so years after the brewery had added "Famous Eagle Lager" to its lineup.

The Eagle Brewing Company

Cars and trucks now buzz along where once Eagle Ales dared to soar. The Eagle Brewing Company was born in 1873 as Keiley (also spelled Keily) Brothers. In 1888, Benjamin Keiley became sole proprietor. Only ale was produced until just before the turn of the century, when lager was added. The capacity of the plant, which operated until prohibition, was a noteworthy 200,000 barrels. Today the site, 455-475 West Exchange Street, Providence, is completely obliterated by the Route 10 expressway.

The Park Brew Company

Founded in the fall of 1899, the Park Brew Company manufactured ale, porter, lager, and malt extract ("Chemists find them Clean and Pure" was their motto) for the better part of fourteen years, until late 1913. The facility, utilized by the Eastern Film Company after Park Brew ceased operations, was completely destroyed by fire in the early morning hours of August 23, 1917. Today the former brewery's site next to Roger Williams Park at 1100 Elmwood Avenue (U.S. Route 1), Providence, is occupied by an entrance to I-95.

Circa 1910 embossed Park Brew bottle

PROVIDENCE DIRECTORY ad, 1910

Molter's was a brewery of many names. Officially the Henry T. Molter brewery (Henry bought out his brother in 1897) from 1897 to 1911, it also often went by the wonderful name of the What Cheer Brewery. From 1911 until its closing in 1920, it was known as the Consumers Brewing Company.

Circa 1908 serving tray, courtesy the Hug collection

Different angles: the former brewery then (from a 1903 sketch) and now (March, 1988)

Molter/What Cheer/Consumers Brewing Company

A pioneer among Rhode Island breweries was this plant, which still stands perched above Spectacle Pond on Molter Avenue in Cranston. In the early 1860s, two gentlemen by the name of Kelley and Baker established the small brewery. Andrew Woefel bought out Baker's interest within several years. Then, in 1868, Nicholas Molter bought out Charles Kelley's interest, the business becoming Woefel & Molter. In 1876, Molter - a former sausage manufacturer and butcher - became sole proprietor, and it was he who built the brewery into the success that it became. Characterized as "genial and big-hearted," Molter was also a leader among the Providence area's German-American community. And a good businessman. By the time he passed the operation down to his sons, Henry T. and John N., in 1885, it was a most formidable enterprise . Only lager was brewed for most of the brewery's existence, ale not being added until about 1905. The firm ceased operations with prohibition and never reopened as a brewery.

The original brewhouse was destroyed by fire in 1876 and rebuilt, under the keen eye of Nicholas Molter, the same year. That would make at least the central portion of what is today Ralph Shuster's Scrap Metal a solid 112 years old. Is Ralph impressed? I don't think so: as I was putting my camera away one of his associates came charging out of the building: "The boss wants ta know whadya doin' walking around the building." Aware that I was not going to be asked in for a guided tour, I explained that I was writing a book about New England's breweries. "I don't know if the boss'll like da publicity" was his response.
I assured him he wouldn't get much.

The Kent Brewing Company

Somewhere in this huge, old - constructed in 1871 - textile mill in West Warwick there lurked the Kent Brewing Company, brewers of Kent Ale, for a pair of years in the thirties, 1933-1934. What I like most is the former brewery's address: 2 Bridal Avenue. The word "bridal" comes from the old English custom of creating special ales for special occasions. "Bridal" is a derivative of "bride ale," ale brewed in honor of, naturally enough, the bride.

March, 1988

Rhode Island breweriana collector Ed Theberge and one of his most memorable finds, a PBC lithograph from 1896, the first year of the brewery's new name. Ed, glass of Hope in hand, is one of a growing number of New Englanders who have come to appreciate the beauty of old beer/brewery advertising and packaging.

American/Providence Brewing Company

James Hanley (see page 3) was no dummy. In the brewery that bore his name on Fountain Street, he turned out the best of ales. "Peerless" he dubbed them. But Hanley didn't overlook the popularity of lager, either, and in 1891 he oversaw the organization of the lager-only American Brewing Company (to become the Providence Brewing Company in 1896). Bohemian, touted as both "The Beer of TODAY" and "New England's Finest Beer," was the brand. The audience, of course, was the area's German-American populace, and fully half the brewery's employees were of German heritage (although Hanley, born in County Roscommon, Ireland, was president and John J. Maguire, sounding suspiciously Irish also, was his vp). A porter and Canada Malt Ale were subsequently added, and an additional ale, Nutshell Ale, was introduced in 1913. A malt extract - "Absolutely Pure: The Best for Nursing Mothers" - rounded out the product line. Capacity grew from an initial 70,000 barrels to 200,000 by the time of James Hanley's death in 1912 at the age of seventy. As with so many other breweries across New England - and America - the Providence Brewing Company came to a screeching halt with prohibition, never to reopen.

March, 1988

Bohemian Export Beer ad, Providence Opera House program, 1916

March, 1988

The former brewery, located at the junction of Harris Avenue and Eagle Street on the fringe of Providence's colorful Federal Hill area, presents an imposing sight to this day. As with the Hand/Rhode Island Brewing Company facility, the top floor and ornamental towers have been lopped off. Still, even that which remains towers above the neighborhood, clearly visible from many a Providence vantage point. Heralded by the city's Board of Trade in 1910 as "one of the model plants in the county," the old brewery's central core is today the home of Capital (formerly Green's) Moving and Storage, while the outbuildings are occupied by J & G Auto Repair. When I informed Beryl Rowl, the only employee around and about when I visited Capital, that she was working in a former brewery, she seemed pleased, if not thrilled. "Well, I learned something today," said she.

In Search Of Victuals

◆

THE LANDING OF THE PILGRIMS

Yes, the Pilgrims really did land where they did, at Plymouth, because they were out of beer. It's an oft-repeated tale that happens to be true. Their intended destination was further south, on or near the mouth of the Hudson.

Blame it on the Speedwell

Every American, from pre-kindergarten on up, knows of the the *Mayflower*. But what of the *Speedwell*, the *Mayflower*'s intended sister ship on the now historic voyage? The two sailed jauntily out of Southhampton, England on August 15th, 1620, the *Mayflower* at 180 tons the major craft; the *Speedwell*, at but 60 tons the tag-along vessel. Before land was hardly out of sight, though, the *Speedwell* turned out to be a leaker. Both ships headed back and put in at Dartmouth, in Devonshire. There the *Speedwell* was overhauled and, on September 2nd, both ships once more set sail. You can probably guess what came next: after 300 or so miles the *Speedwell*'s leaks cropped up a second time. It was back to England yet again, this time to Plymouth, where it was decided to abandon the *Speedwell* and go it alone with the *Mayflower*, which set out — this time for real —on September 6th.

The result of all of this time spent patching up the *Speedwell* was an overcrowded *Mayflower*, a disheartened band of saints

(as they generally called themselves), and a semi-spent supply of provisions. Add a long (sixty-five days) and rough voyage, the fact that winter was fast approaching by the time land was finally spotted, plus the very real shortage of provisions, and you can see why Plymouth harbor, although far north of their goal, looked fine to our Pilgrim Fathers. "We could not now take time for further search or consideration, our victuals being much spent, especially our beere," is how one of the band of dedicated souls so clearly put it in a diary maintained aboard ship.

The Pilgrims numbered 102 when they docked at Plymouth, 73 males and 29 females. One of the band, a William Butten (or Button), died during the trip. But there was an addition, too. A baby boy was born unto Elizabeth and Stephen Hopkins while the *Mayflower* was en route. They named him Oceanus.

Let's Call it Pilgrim Ale

What do you do when an event such as the tricentennial of the landing of the Pilgrims comes along — the perfect occasion to launch a new beer (or ale, as it was actually ale that our forefathers — and foremothers, too —were short of) — yet it's prohibition and the land is supposed to be dry? Answer: you delay the launch until the land is wet...and then you go for it. That's just what James R. Nicholson, post-prohibition head of Boston's Croft Brewing Company, did. And he did it with flair. A delegation from Plymouth — that included a number of direct descendants of the Pilgrims, naturally — was shepherded to the brewery, given the royal tour by Pilgrim-dressed misses, treated to a luncheon, and made part of the "official" Pilgrim Ale dedication ceremonies. Such hoopla was, of course, picked up by the media, with the result that Pilgrim Ale was off and running (although it didn't run far: after an initial burst, sales fizzled and Pilgrim Ale was discontinued by 1938).

Pilgrim Ale ads, 1936

"Speak For Yourself, John"

Four decades earlier a Boston brewery of another time had also paid homage to the Pilgrims. The brewery was Habich & Company's Norfolk Brewery. Their homage took the form of a wonderfully illustrated piece of what is now choice breweriana. Entitled "The Mayflower Calendar," its pages recount but a few of the highlights of Henry Wadsworth Longfellow's classic "The Courtship of Miles Standish."

Cover, "The Mayflower Calendar"

In the layout and design of "The Mayflower Calendar," Habich upheld somewhat of a pre-prohibition Boston-area beer advertising tradition: keep the actual advertising message small. Classy. But probably not awfully effective in terms of its real goal, which was to entice people to step up and order — even demand — Habich's IPA, Golden Ale, Extra Stock Porter, Cabinet Export Lager, and/or Bismarck Brau.

No matter, however. Habich & Comapny did ok. Taken over by Edward Habich in 1874, the brewery was solely an ale affair at first, but a sizable one. Its 1879 output of almost 31,000 barrels placed it tenth among Massachusetts' twenty-eight brewers. Lager was added, most likely, in the late 1880s. The brewer was absorbed into the Massachusetts Breweries Company three years after this calendar was put out, in 1900, and closed down in 1902.

Penned in 1858 by Longfellow, himself a direct descendant of Priscilla Mullins and John Alden, "The Courtship" is a 63-page narrative poem that, perhaps most of all, serves as a lesson in how *not* to conduct a courtship. Based on historical and traditional accounts of the time, the poem tells the tale of Captain Miles Standish, whose wife Rose died soon after the Pilgrims departed the *Mayflower*, leaving the good Captain "weary and dreary."

Enter fair Priscilla. Only eighteen, "the lovliest maiden of Plymouth" has been made lonely, too: her father, her mother and her brother have all succumbed to the rigors of that first horrible winter in the New World. Miles is in love with her.

But the Captain is shy. A short man in his mid-thirties, he is the leader of Plymouth's militia, the Colony's military expert, and a veteran of many, many a battle. Afraid of no man, Miles is basically a coward when it comes to woman. "I am a maker of war, and not a maker of phrases," says he as he entreats his best friend, John Alden, to do his bidding for him.

Little appears to be known about Rose Standish, except that she was but one of many weakened by the long voyage across the Atlantic, and that her passing left Miles a lonely, lonely man.

Priscilla (sometimes spelled Priscila) was the daughter of Alice and William Mullins (sometimes spelled Mullines), both of whom perished the first winter in Plymouth. Described by Miles as "an angel whose name is Priscilla," one can only wonder — especially given the heavily male ratio among the group — how many other Pilgrim men secretly pined after Priscilla.

Sturdy and rugged, Miles (also spelled Myles) Standish engaged in many a feat of derring-do, both on the Continent and in America. . . and lived to tell about it. He lead a full life for thirty-six years after the famous landing, passing away in 1656 at the robust old age of 72.

Poor John. He, too, is in love with fair Priscilla. But, true to his friendship with Miles, he calls upon our Miss Mullins and sings the praises of his comrade.

Priscilla is not moved.

"If the great Captain of Plymouth is so very eager to wed me, why does he not come himself, and take the trouble to woo me?
If I am not worth the wooing, I surely am not worth the winning!"

John, although his heart is far from fully in it, persists on behalf of Miles. Finally Priscilla, her own heart at stake, bursts forth with those most famous of all words: "Why don't you speak for yourself, John?"

And they lived happily ever after. Right? Yes, but not before forty-two more pages of poem (which is not to knock Longfellow: I found "The Courtship" to be most enjoyable reading, though most of his better-known poems are, let's face it, long by today's fast/faster/fastest entertainment standards). John feels he's let his friend down; Miles agrees, comparing his now former friend to Brutus. Things calm down only when Miles and his eight-man militia are called away to do battle against the Indians. Miles, alas, is soon after reported killed. John, though still feeling dreadful about things, is now free to woo — and win — Priscilla for himself. Which he does. Their wedding day arrives in good order . . . but who should show up at the very last minute, double alas, but the Captain, alive and well after all. However, he's come to realize his error: that he should have done his own bidding; that John is his friend; that there's no sense in moaning any longer . . . "No man can gather cherries in Kent at the season of Christmas."

The union is blessed. The poem is ended.

P.S. It's nice to report that after poems end life goes on. Captain Miles, presumably recovered from the heartbreak of Priscilla, married a new arrival to the Colony named Barbara (last name unknown) a year later. As for the Aldens, well, they created something of a one couple population explosion by having not one, not five, not ten, but eleven children. John obviously knew how to do more than just speak up.

John, probably the youngest adult aboard the *Mayflower*, was either eighteen or twenty-one, depending on which source you believe. He was a cooper by trade, hired by the ship's company to care for the beer barrels during the *Mayflower*'s voyage, and was not planning on remaining in America. Meeting Priscilla changed all that.

Though included on "The Mayflower Calendar," Elder Brewster and Mary Chilton were, at best, but bit players in "The Courtship of Miles Standish." Actually, I couldn't find Mary — fifteen at the time of the sailing and, legend has it, the first white female to set foot on Plymouth soil — in the poem at all. Elder Brewster is included, but his role in the Colony — and getting the group there — was far greater than his role in Longfellow's poem. In his mid-fifties, William Brewster made the trip to America with his wife Mary and his sons Love and Wrestling. (Those were their names. Honest.) Described as a man of culture, travel, and knowledge, he, more than any other person save Governor William Bradford, was vital in keeping the Colony going during those first lean years.

Israel and George and Ethan, Too

Before we leave Priscilla, John, Miles et al, let's put it down right here in black and white that, not only did the Pilgrims land because there were running short of beer (among other things), but that beer was their basic beverage. "Beer was the everyday drink among the Plymouth people" stated William Elliot Griffis, flat out, in his THE PILGRIMS IN THEIR THREE HOMES — ENGLAND, HOLLAND, AMERICA (Cambridge: Houghton, Mifflin & Co., 1898). Other sources agree. The biggest problem was rounding up the ingredients with which to make it. Barley, especially, was often in short supply. But the stouthearted group overcame that with verve and imagination ... and molasses and oats and corn and pumpkins and you-name-it. As rhymed one of the group:

If barley be wanting to make into malt,
We must be content and think it no fault,
For we can make liquor to sweeten our lips,
Of pumpkins, and parsnips, and walnut
tree chips.

Hops, too, were a problem. They grew wild in New England, but were often lacking in sufficient quantity. In stepped spruce: plentiful, it was found to be a good substitute, both in terms of adding taste and as a preserving agent.

Not Alone

The pilgrims were not alone in their fondness for beer. When John Winthrop, later to be governor of the Massachusetts Bay Colony, arrived in America aboard the *Arbella*, there were "42 Tonnes of Beere" (about 10,000 gallons) on board with him. The future governor obviously knew how to arrive with panache. Diana Karter Appelbaum, in her 1984 book, THANKSGIVING: AN AMERICAN HOLIDAY, AN AMERICAN HISTORY (New York City: Facts on File) writes that "Harvard's early commencements were public revels. Kegs of beer and tables of food were set out in Harvard Yard for guests who came from the furthest reaches of the Colony (Massachusetts Bay Colony) to hear the speakers and drink ale." (sometimes too much of it, she also points out).

"Old Put," Israel Putnam, was a successful Brooklyn, Connecticut brewer and tavernkeeper before he turned his hand to soldiering. A hero of the French and Indian War, he was commissioned a Major General by the Continental Congress in 1775 and served with distinction, most notably at Bunker Hill, in our fight for independence.

The Nutmeg State...and Elsewhere

"Beer was the common drink in Connecticut as elsewhere," says Atwater in his HISTORY OF THE NEW HAVEN COLONY. "A brewhouse was regarded as an essential part of the household, and beer was on the table as regularly as bread."

"Elsewhere" certainly included the rest of New England. In colonial days, brewers and tavern-keepers throughout the region generally enjoyed the highest respect of their neighbors and fellow citizens. More than a few of the most important men of colonial and revolutionary times were brewers or tavern-keepers or both. Among them was Samuel Adams, "The Father of the Revolution," who was the son of a brewer and a brewer himself. Generals Putnam, Weedon and Sumner were all involved with brewing, as was Thomas Chitenden, the first governor of Vermont.

Chitenden and the Allen brothers, Ethan and Ira, were part of the Green Mountain Boys, who liked nothing better than to hoot and holler — while figuring out ways to trounce the British, of course — at the Catamount Tavern in Bennington or Zadock Remington's Tavern in Castleton. It was Ethan, in fact as well as in legend, who carried a barrel of beer up Mount Washington, all 6,000-plus feet of it ... so as to have "proper refreshment" on hand when he reached the summit.

Israel and George and Ethan, too.

OAKDALE TAVERN
OLD HARTFORD TURNPIKE
WALLINGFORD, CONN.
Tel. 513

The Only Inn in New England at which Washington did not Stop!

But We Do Serve
GOOD FOOD
Telephone for Reservations.

1941 ad for the Oakdale Tavern ..."The Only Inn in New England at which Washington did not Stop!"

Try as we might, New England can't claim the Father of Our Country. But he sure spent a lot of time here. More importantly, he loved his porter: in fact, to this day there's a recipe for it — written out in his own handwriting —in the collection of the New York Public Library.

Just Like In Those Good Old Days

◆

THE MICRO BREWERY MOVEMENT IN NEW ENGLAND

In your great-grandparent's day most every town of any consequence in America had its own brewery, its own brew. Beer, for the most part, was distributed locally. Not much cross country or trans-Atlantic stuff.

Well, at least a hint of those days is starting to reappear. Sure, the big five - Anheuser-Busch, Miller, Stroh, G. Heileman, Coors - account for 90% of the beer sold in America. And the chances of that changing much are slim indeed. But an exciting thing is happening. Fueled by the success of imports, by the impressive track record of boutique wineries, and by the legalization of home brewing in 1977, small brewers are dotting America. Most of the dots are in California and the Pacific Northwest, but they're also in Iowa and Texas and New York and Minnesota and fourteen other states. And they're in New England.

Called micro breweries, they, as the name makes clear, are exceedingly small: so small that, if my math is correct, all five of New England's micros put together won't brew in a full year what Anheuser-Busch brews in its Merrimack, New Hampshire plant over the course of just three days. Two of the five, known as brewpubs, sell only on premises. But smallness is part of micro charm. Beer is made almost by hand — lovingly, as each of the beermakers (beercrafters would be a better word) will tell you — and watched over much as if it were a small child.

"Fresh is Best."

So, What's In It For You?

So it's handmade. So what?

So plenty. Local beer is fresh. What location, location, location is to real estate, freshness, freshness, freshness is to beer. Beer gets "tired" from traveling or from sitting. It begins to break down, to lose its "perkiness." As Boston's Massachusetts Bay Brewing Company states so well in its promotional flyer: "Beer belongs in your glass, not on a ship or truck."

As important, micros provide the beer drinker with choice: ales, porters, Christmas brews, headier lagers. Beers, if you will, for the more discriminating palate. Or, so as not to make even the most humdrum beer enthusiast uncomfortable, beers that provide variety for a blah palate. "Beer," as sayeth David Geary of Portland's D. L. Geary Brewing Company, "is one of those things like bread - you can only take so much white bread and then you want rye bread."

Over the next six pages, then, BEER, NEW ENGLAND presents some rye: good local, fresh rye. Plus whole wheat, oatmeal, pumpernickel, etc.

Sorry, no white.

Catamount Brewing Company
58 South Main Street
White River Junction, Vermont

A former 1910 Swift & Company meat packing plant houses Vermont's contribution to micro brewing. And quite a contribution it is: when you're written up in *Time* ("In Vermont, Making Beer the Old-Fashioned Way"; February 23, 1987) during your very first month of operation you know you must be doing something right!

Steve Mason and Alan Davis, a pair of one-time Vermont educators, shared their first brews with the world - or at least Vermont and New Hampshire - on February 1, 1987. It was a goal that was a long time in the making, with seeds that harked back to Steve's home brewing days while an undergrad at the University of Michigan in the mid-1970s. In 1983 he took the goal one giant step further by spending several months as an apprentice at the minute-sized Swannell's Brewery, Hertfordshire, England. From that experience came the basis of the recipes for both of Catamount's "regulars," Catamount Amber and Catamount Gold. Both are ales, naturally. To brighten the Christmas season, 1987, Catamount brought out a special Holiday Porter. In a recent conversation with Steve, he pronounced it most successful, adding that it may become a regular, too.

In naming their brewery and their brews, Steve and Alan wanted to say "local," and "majestic" as well. And "Catamount" did it: a catamount is - or was - a species of cougar that once roamed the North Country of Vermont and New Hampshire. The fact that Ethan and Ira Allen and the Green Mountain Boys used to hang out at the Catamount Tavern in Bennington also lends a nice touch.

For now, Catamount is basically available in the North Country (the brewery's slogan is "Pride of the North Country") and in bottles only, although plans are afoot for expansion into the Boston area and for what many purists consider the real thing, draught beer, too.

Both photos courtesy Catamount Brewing Company

Alan and Steve (second and third from left, respectively) and the rest of the Catamount "brew crew" in front of the brewery.

How wonderfully poetic — given the several instances of former brewery-now-meat-packing-plant — that Catamount is housed in a one-time Swift & Company facility. The conversion to a brewery was not easy, however: an initial capitalization of $425,000 obtained via a combination of an SBA loan, a private stock offering, and a low-interest State of Vermont development loan proved not enough, and Steve and Alan had to go out and round up another $185,000. But round it up they did, the result being a nifty-looking and operating red brick brewery with a capacity of 5,000 or so barrels of ale a year.

May, 1988

Located in a former furniture warehouse, Commonwealth is a joy to behold . . . and an ale lover's heaven. When I stopped by for a taste or two, choices included Golden Ale, Amber Ale, Celtic Ale, Boston's Best Burton Bitter, Classic Stout, plus Shandy (bitter and lemon soda), Snakebite (Amber Ale and cider), etc., etc.

Commonwealth Brewing Company
Merrimac and Portland Streets
Boston, Massachusetts

At 41, Englishman Richard Wrigley is the undisputed king of eastern brewpubs. One of the co-founders of New York's Manhattan Brewing Company, a chic Soho brewpub, Wrigley left the Big Apple to do it all over again in Boston in 1986. His Commonwealth Brewing Company, located across from the Boston Garden, is the result. And the result is good: an abundance of polished brass and copper to look at, a rich selection of English-style (what else?!) ales to partake of.

Production has been about 2,000 barrels a year, all sold on premises. That may change, though: plans are in the works to bottle and sell off premises, too. Plus there's expansion afoot, as well, with brewpubs in New Orleans and San Francisco in the cards.

The brewery has recently begun to bottle some of its ouput. Bottled or draught, as friend and fellow quaffer Clark Adams of Brookline put it: "Even if it's not your favorite style (of beer), slightly sweet or whatever, you can't help but love it."

Gritty McDuff's
396 Fore Street
Portland, Maine

. . . PLUS THERE'S MORE happening all the time. As you read this another brewpub will hopefully be up and running. Twenty-four year old Richard Pfeffer and associates, under the name Brew Corporation, have promised to bring made-on-premises ale, porter, and stout to Maine's first city. State licensing problems appear to have been overcome; the $200,000-$300,000 needed to get going is being raised via a limited partnership; plans are set to order brewing equipment from England in the near future. As to the Gritty McDuff name - which would not have been my first choice - Richard admits to it being completely made up: "We wanted to have somewhat of a British Isles' type lean . . . and we thought it was a fun name."

June, 1988

Richard, left, and his associates Steve Barnes, 25, and Eric Harrison, 27. What got them all to smiling so: Eric's quipping "Pretend we're really going to open."

In addition, Henry Cabot is well along on plans for his brewpub in Waldoboro, Maine (see page 122) and the Hartford Brewery Ltd., lead by Philip H. Hopkins of West Hartford, has promised to bring ale and lager to Connecticut brew buffs by early 1989.

Alan, Karen, and David outside the entrance to the brewery, located in an industrial park on the western fringe of Portland. David credits Alan Eames, a well-respected man about beer, with putting the idea of a brewery into his head. At the time, 1982-83, David was selling medical equipment. Although he liked the concept, he thought the reality of a brewery was, in his words, "a crackpot scheme." But the more he thought about it, the more he liked it. One thing led to another and the result was a business plan ("Karen began it when I was in England in 1984"), funding ("We sold stock privately") . . . and a brewery.

D.L. Geary Brewing Company
38 Evergreen Drive
Portland, Maine

If each of America's fifty or so micros were represented by a dot on the map, then the dot representing Portland, Maine might logically be a little larger than all but one of the others. "Correct me if I'm wrong, but I think we're now, after Sierra Nevada (in Chico, California), the second biggest micro brewery in America," commented David Geary, president of the brewery that bears his name - the D.L. Geary Brewing Company - on the outskirts of Portland. David wasn't bragging, but he was proud, and for good cause: the very week I interviewed him in late March, 1988 was the week his brewery's annual capacity had been boosted from 6,000 barrels to 8,500 barrels.

Defining a micro as a brewery with a less than 15,000 annual barrel capacity, David is probably correct. Geary's is most likely number two. . . not bad for an operation that placed its first brew on the market in the last month of 1986, and that hardly has the most populous state, Maine, as its sales base. "We're getting into New Hampshire now, and we've been in the Boston area for a while," says David. But Maine is the nucleus, with 80% of the brewery's output sold in Vacationland; and 80% of that 80% sold in southern Vacationland, Portland to Kittery.

Geary's is a family affair: David is president, wife Karen is treasurer. Both are fulltime employees (in every sense of the word: "The yeast works through the weekend and so we have to be here, too."). Joining them as the third key to the brewery's success is 28-year old Alan Pugsley, and Englishman whom David met while visiting the UK's tiny

Old Hug Pale Ale. . . Or On Working At The Brewery

Don't look for Old Hug on the shelves of your supermarket or package store. No, to enjoy Old Hug you had to be at the right place, Lorain, Ohio, at the right time, February 27, 1988. Longtime friend and breweriana enthusiast Tom Hug and his sweetheart Alice Hirt ("turning a Hirt into a Hug," the pastor couldn't refrain from pointing out during the service) were getting married. Why not print up some special labels and transform six or so cases of Geary's into Old Hug for the reception, thought I. David said it was fine with him. So I designed a label, which was fun, and had a batch printed up at a printshop in downtown Portland. Easy enough so far.

The appointed day for label affixing - as part of the brewery's weekly bottling run - arrived. I and, more importantly, my labels were on hand . . . only to discover that the labeling machine couldn't handle them. "OK," I said, "I'll put them on myself: one hundred forty-four (six cases of twenty-four) of anything can't be much."

Karen fixed me up with a glue pot and a brush, and I started in, dabbing each label in all four corners plus adding a splotch in the middle for good measure; then pressing the whole mess onto the bottle, holding it there until the glue had taken. Not great fun. And slow: one hundred forty-four of something can be much.

Old Hug: a hit in Ohio. After all the labels were on and I was loading the cases into my car, David remarked, "Well, I guess now you can call yourself a contract brewer."

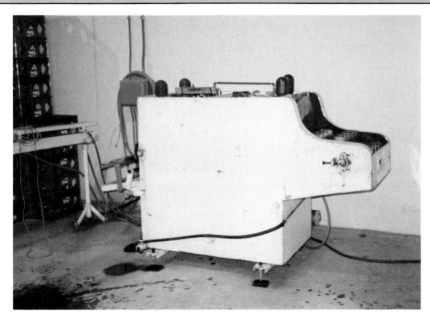

Anyway, I'd probably still be there, glue pot in hand, if Karen hadn't come over to me and asked me if I wanted to switch: "You take my place on the bottling line and I'll put on the labels," she suggested. Sounded fine to me. Her job - which became my job as part of the six-person team - was to take recycled, prewashed bottles out of cartons and load them, upside down, into the rinser, a timeless hulk of a machine fed by a conveyor belt that always seemed to move a little faster than I did. (As the day wore on, however, I learned techniques that made us - the machine and I - about even. Four years of college hadn't been wasted after all.) I found myself getting excited. I'd certainly visited enough breweries, now here I was actually working in one! I found there was a rhythm, both with respect to "my machine" and the bottling line in general. A steady rhythm. Fulfilling, yet monotonous. For excitement, I experimented with filling the four-across conveyor slots in different ways. I found I like the "outside-in" method (fill the two outside slots first, then the two inside) best at first, but later switched to the "inside-out."

By the end of the day they were calling me "speedo."

P.S. Between Karen and myself the labels all got put on (some straighter than others); the Old Hug made its way from Maine to Ohio; everybody at the reception loved it; and the Hugs are living happily ever after.

"My machine": my co-worker, Mark Scease, who took the rinsed bottles and fed them into the filler, had other words for it. He called it "the pain in the ass machine."

March, 1988

March, 1988

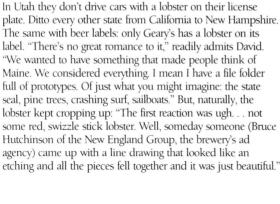

Stacked and ready to go.

In Utah they don't drive cars with a lobster on their license plate. Ditto every other state from California to New Hampshire. The same with beer labels: only Geary's has a lobster on its label. "There's no great romance to it," readily admits David. "We wanted to have something that made people think of Maine. We considered everything. I mean I have a file folder full of prototypes. Of just what you might imagine: the state seal, pine trees, crashing surf, sailboats." But, naturally, the lobster kept cropping up: "The first reaction was ugh. . . not some red, swizzle stick lobster. Well, someday someone (Bruce Hutchinson of the New England Group, the brewery's ad agency) came up with a line drawing that looked like an etching and all the pieces fell together and it was just beautiful."

Ringwood Brewery in 1984. Intrigued by the opportunity to, in effect, start a brewery from scratch, Alan moved to the States in 1986. It's a move he hasn't regretted.

Nor have David and Karen any regrets about beginning the whole thing in the first place. David, 42, a Portland native and a graduate of Purdue University in West Lafayette, Indiana, talks of the joy he felt when he first heard someone (other than himself!) say "Gimme a Geary's" as it started to flow at Three Dollar Deweys (see page 122) in Portland's Old Port in December of '86. Or how he still gets a charge out of seeing a stranger in the supermarket pick up a six of the bottles with the lobster on the label and put it in their shopping cart. Karen, a native of Joliet, Illinois and also a Purdue graduate, recalls the good feeling she felt when, the problems of getting their bottling line going in March of '87 finally resolved, a Nappi (the brewery's distributor, Nappi Distributors) truck pulled up and loaded up: "I can still see the Nappi truck with all its bays filled with bottles of Geary's."

It's, as David is wont to say, "an ancient and noble profession."

63

Massachusetts Bay Brewing Company
306 Northern Avenue
Boston, Massachusetts

March, 1988

Rich, Massachusetts Bay's president and sales force, in front of the brewery. Located in the Marine Industrial Park just past Jimmy's Harborside, Mass. Bay lives up to its name: it's but a Dwight Evans' throw from the Bay. In fact, its space was formerly utilized by a shipbuilding concern. Tours of the brewery are conducted four times a week: Tuesday and Friday at 1:00 p.m. and Saturday at both 11:00 a.m. and 1:00 p.m.

March, 1988

Introduced in the summer of '87, draught sales account for about one third of total. Rich, himself, prefers draught accounts, feels draught "is a better way to serve beer: the keg is a better way of packaging beer than bottles. You don't have to worry as much . . . you know it's going to arrive in the glass in better shape than in bottles."

What do you do when you've traveled a fair chunk of the world and enjoyed good beer . . . then to come back home to the U.S.A. and face basically pedestrian brews? Well, if you're Rich Doyle, you decide to brew your own. "I spent a significant time in Europe and Southeast Asia, in the South Pacific, and I thought: 'there are great beers there. Why is it necessary to have to go to, in some cases, a third world or second world country to get good-tasting beer?' That didn't make a lot of sense."

With old Harvard chums Dan Kenary, 27, and George Ligiti, 32, Rich, who's only 27 himself, set out to change that, to put some sense into things. At least in the Boston area.

Starting in January of 1986, the trio - along with 24-year old brewmaster Russ Heissner -proved just what teamwork can do: money was raised (at backyard barbecues, wedding receptions - you name it), a brew formulated, the name Harpoon decided upon, labels designed and printed, etc., etc. The biggest problem, no surprise to any Boston observer, was finding suitable space. "Real estate was a disaster. There's just not that much commercial real estate in Boston. And we didn't want to be in a suburb. We wanted to be right in Boston. That made a big difference to us. So that was very difficult. And it was a "lowlight" because we really were all dressed up and (had) nowhere to go. We had tanks, we had money, we had a product name. we had labels. We had all that in November (1986) and we didn't move in here until March (1987)."

"Another lowlight was the day we moved in, 500 kegs arrived. The same day! And we had a lot of work to do in here. We had to dig drainage ditches; we had to knock out some walls; we had to build walls; we had to put down carpeting; we had to paint everything. And so one of our party - who will remain nameless - ordered 500 kegs to arrive the day that we got here. March 17, 1987. So we were two months away from brewing anything . . . but we did have 500 kegs. We must have moved those kegs three or four or five times in the next two months, just handing them one to another."

Rich laughs as he tells the story now. As well he should: Harpoon has been selling smartly (he estimates it'll do over 8,000 barrels in 1988), morale among the company's ten employees is excellent, there are a couple of new products in the works, and, on the day in late March that I visited Mass. Bay, it was obvious another spring had arrived in Beantown.

As David Landis wrote of Rich, Dan, and George in the September 4, 1987 issue of *USA Today*: "Ah, to be young and have your own brewery."

You can bet that's a harpoon the man with the hat and the horn is holding. Just who he is (or was, rather) and why he's all decked out, however, is a mystery . . . but a mystery that may soon be unraveled. Rich, George, and Dan are planning a "Name That Man" contest: the first person who correctly guesses the man's identity wins an all-expenses-paid trip to Nantucket or the like. The photo, 80-years old, was discovered by Mass. Bay's freelance designer, Marjorie Millhon. It more or less crystallized things, representing just what the brewery had been looking for: something that stood for New England's tradition of seafaring, and that could also be visually demonstrated.

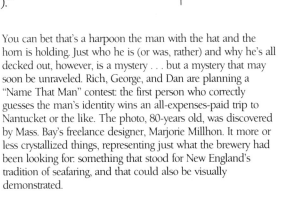

Peter: "I like lagers."

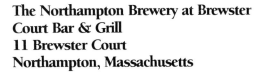

The Northampton Brewery at Brewster Court Bar & Grill
11 Brewster Court
Northampton, Massachusetts

The thing that first struck me about the Northampton Brewery/Brewster Court Bar & Grill is that, from the outside, it looks not unlike a church. The second thing is that, unlike New England's other brewpub and micros, Northampton specializes in lager. "I like lagers, and I guess I just liked the idea of making a smoother beer," explains co-owner and brewmaster Peter Egelston. Peter adds that there was also a desire to be different: "Rather than just be one more micro-brewery ale, we wanted to distinguish ourselves."

Opened in August, 1987, the brewpub is the brainchild of four people: Peter, a 29-year old former Brooklyn, New York school-teacher and longtime home brewer; Peter's sister, Janet Egelston, 26; Cora Drew, 35, former commercial artist and Peter's wife; and Mark Metzger, a 33-year old ex-merch-andiser for rock bands. Peter owns and oversees the brewery end; Mark, the restau-rant end. Mark, who'd ostensibly come to Northampton to go to law school, had spent some time at Santa Cruz, California's Front Street Brewpub, and been impressed with it. When, in December of 1986, he saw a "For Sale" sign on what had been the carriage house for the Brewster mansion - "The thing about it was that it was on

March, 1988

Brewster Court, and a brewster is a female brewer" - the plans for law school were forgotten. It was a real spur of the moment thing. "We just bought it," admits Mark.

Legal entanglements aside, he and the group haven't regretted it. Business is brisk and one senses, especially in talking with Peter, a very real sense of personal crafts-manship. No plans are in the works to sell off premises, both because of legal questions and because all the brew that can be produced in the brewhouse's 1,000 barrels a year capacity is easily sold on premises. But, more exciting, there's a beer garden coming. It'll be where the parking lot is at present, and will have arbors and vines and be, in Peter's words, a "nice little oasis where people can come and sit." Sounds great!

BREWSTER COURT
BAR & GRILL
11 Brewster Court · Northampton

Having to form two corporations - one for the brewery (Northampton Brewery) and one for the restaurant (Brewster Court Bar & Grill) - is just one of the legal hassles encountered by the gang of four. There was the joy of finding out, a week before the grand opening, that the City of Northampton's lawyer would not allow any exterior sign that had the word "brewery" on it. Fortunately, Mayor David Musante came to the rescue on that one. "You can call your place anything you want to; you can call it the Northampton Nuclear Plant if you want," said he.

A delighted customer. Brewster Court has three taps. . . one for its amber (the biggest seller; here being enjoyed by my friend Penny), one for its golden (Peter's personal favorite), and one for its special. Specials, which change about every six weeks, have included a bock, an Octoberfest beer, and, on hand during my visit (and my personal favorite), a porter. Promised for next summer: a wheat beer.

Waiting in the Wings

Waiting in the wings are at least three "contract" brewers. A contract brewer is one who pays someone else to do his or her brewing. As such, of course, he or she is not really a brewer at all, but rather a merchandiser or marketer. None the less, contract brewers have made some very significant contributions to American - and New England - brewing and beer selection. I say "at least three" above because I strongly suspect that there'll soon be more. Connecticut is ripe for either a micro or a contract brew (how about Nutmeg Amber or Nathan Hale Ale - see page 95 - as possible names?). And New Hampshire is due, too (Old Granite State?!). Even western Massachusetts will, I would imagine, have a Berkshire Brau or some such animal before too many more moons have passed.

As of this writing (Spring, 1988), however, there are only three contract brewers of any real consequence in our six states. Each has avowed to build an actual brewery — rather than contracting elsewhere — in the near future. I hope — no pun intended, of course — that they do.

Boston Beer Company

There are probably few people in all of brewland as controversial as Jim Koch (pronounced "Cook"). Did he, perhaps more than any other individual, revolutionize eastern America's beer picture? Or is he just some guy who has a beer brewed for him out in Pittsburgh and then slaps Boston Lager labels - Samuel Adams Boston Lager labels, to be precise - on it and peddles it throughout New England? Is Sammie - as its known in the trade - really the best beer in America, as voted by the attendees at Colorado's Great American Beer Festival in 1985, 1986, and 1987? Or has the Festival been a bit of a sham, where he or she who has handed out the most tee-shirts and/or caps has gotten the most votes?

The verdict is still out on the above . . . but it's in on the fact that Jim Koch shook up a lot of people when he challenged the European big boys with respect to the purity of the beer that they export to America. Jim's "When America asked for Europe's tired and poor, we didn't mean their beer" campaign maintained that Heineken, Beck's and St. Pauli Girl - and many another European import - would not pass the 472-year old Bavarian Reinheitsgebot purity law that decrees that nothing but water, malt, hops, and yeast go into that which is called beer. Adjuncts are in there, too, claims Jim. But they are not in Samuel Adams.

Koch, 38, has a couple of Harvard degrees and was a big bucks consultant with the Boston Consulting Group until he decided, in 1985, to carry on his forefathers' brewing tradition. The result: he raised $400,000 to form the Boston Beer Company (no relation to the brewery in Southie that held title to America's oldest brewery for so many years: see page 17), dusted off an old family brewing formula, hired brewing expert Joseph Owades as his master brewer, and contracted with the Pittsburgh Brewing Company, brewers of Iron City and IC Light, to brew his newly-named Sam Adams. Boston Lightship, a low calorie version of Sammie, was introduced in 1987.

Jim's next step is the one that intrigues me the most: he's starting to roll on the restoration of the former Haffenreffer & Company (see pages 18 & 19) facility in Jamaica Plain. Boston Beer, working with the City of Boston and the Neighborhood Development Corporation of Jamaica Plain as well as with private funding, plans to restore a good half of the buildings remaining in the old brewing complex, and to brew Samuel Adams in Boston rather than "out west" in Pittsburgh. The move is expected to be made sometime in late 1988. (Which means, I realize, that by the time you're reading this, Boston Lager should truly be Boston lager.)

Samuel Adams Boston Lager was introduced to Boston on Patriot's Day, April 19, 1985. Less than two months later, in June, its success was boosted considerably by being voted top honors at the Great American Beer Festival in Denver. Sales are now in the 30,000 barrels a year range.

Maine Coast Brewing

Jon Bove, 36, and Hugh Nazor, 50, got together to form Maine Coast Brewing in 1986. Both had been longtime homebrewers; both wanted to start their own brewery; both lived in Portland. So why not?

Actually, Jon, who bought out Hugh in November of 1987, can give you a lot of reasons why not. His visions of owning and operating his own brewery go back to 1983; yet five years later he is still breweryless. Inability to obtain sufficient financing stalled him at first; a disastrous fire knocked him out of the brewer's box more recently.

Unable to raise enough money initially, Jon - and Hugh - went the contract route in late 1985. Their first Portland Lager, brewed by the Hibernia Brewing Company, Eau Claire, Wisconsin, reached the market in March, 1986. Buoyed by its success, the partners pursued the dream of their own brewery, and were progressing nicely - "The deal was signed and everything settled," laments Jon - toward a move into an historic former textile mill in Lisbon Falls, Maine when, in late July, 1987, fire gutted the building. As a result, Maine Coast is still contract brewing. Operations were moved from Hibernia to the F.X. Matt Brewing Company, whose own brands include Matt's, Saranac 1888, and Utica Club, in Utica, New York in the summer of 1987, in order to lower shipping costs and to allow for greater quality control. Since the move to Utica, Jon has also brought out Portland Lager on draught, and it's now available in a number of places, virtually all in Portland or Boston.

As to present plans for that elusive brewery, Jon's initial words, when I talked with him in late March, 1988, were "We're making some progress, but I'm not willing to make a public statement at this time." When, later in our conversation, I reminded Jon that I'm not exactly the *Boston Globe*, he loosened up a little, amending his words to say that chances are good he'll be able to get something going again toward an actual brewery by the end of 1988.

Distributed throughout New England and an additional eight to ten states. Portland Lager sold in the 4,000 barrel range in 1987.

Jon expects to do about the same or slightly better in 1988. Beautifully reproduced on its label is a view of the almost 200-year old Portland Headlight, a National Historic Landmark located not in Portland, but in Cape Elizabeth, just south of the Port City.

September, 1987

Jon's license plate reflects a major goal: get Portland Lager going on tap. He has.

Hope Lager has, I think, a most attractive label, but I think it will suffer from its name. I know that "Hope" is the state motto, and that's nice . . . but try saying "I want a six-pack of Hope" without wanting to add "and a case of faith" (and a little charity, too?). Even the beer's slogan "Hope . . . for the best!" is as negative as it is positive. I would wish that I'm wrong: it would be mighty fine to see the Ocean State have its own brewery again.

Hope Brewing Company

The Johnny-come-lately to New England's contract brewing scene is Rhode Island's Hope Brewing Company, headed up by partners Richard Fensterer, III, 42, and Stephen Woerner, 37. Hope Lager, brewed by The Lion, Inc., brewers of Stegmaier and Gibbons beers, in Wilkes-Barre, Pennsylvania, made its debut in late February, 1988. Believing that "Rhode Island wants a brewery back," Steve and Dick plan on starting up in Providence before 1988 is out. On board to oversee that everything turns out the way it should is brewmaster Tim Morse, 39, fresh from yeoman service at San Francisco's Anchor Brewing Company as well as a short stint at Commonwealth in Boston.

Sign, I.M. Gan Liquors, Warwick, Rhode Island, March, 1988

Keeping Up With The Joneses

◆

NEW HAMPSHIRE'S BREWER BROTHERS

"Keeping up with the Joneses" was not just an idle expression in turn-of-the-century New Hampshire brewing circles: it was a most difficult task indeed. Dominating Manchester was True Jones; dominating Portsmouth (and scores of other markets, too!) was Frank Jones. The two were brothers, part of a family of seven children born unto Mary and Thomas Jones of Barrington, a small town roughly fifteen miles west of Portsmouth. Frank was the older of the two . . . and it was he who would go on to far and away greater prominence. Little, in fact, is known about True Jones. He appears to have followed Frank (and several other siblings) to Portsmouth, from whence he made his way to the state's largest city,

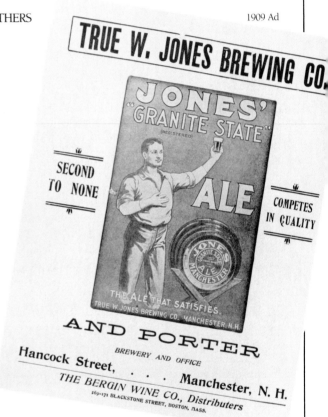

1909 Ad

Manchester. There he, in 1891, gained control of the Carney, Lynch & Company brewery. Changing the name to the True W. Jones Brewing Company, he became king of the Manchester brewing scene. But, then again, that was pretty easy: by the 1890s True W. Jones was the only game in town. He was the only brewer in Manchester. True passed away on October 2, 1899, but the brewery that bore his name continued on until New Hampshire went dry in 1917.

Circa 1910
Tip Tray

TRUE W. JONES, Prest.

M. J. CONNOR, Treas.

Circa 1895
calling card

Circa 1948
Matchbook
Cover

But if little is known about True Jones, lots is known about his older brother. Frank Jones was truly a giant among Granite Staters. Raymond A. Brighton, who chronicled the history of Portsmouth in his THEY CAME TO FISH, devoted an entire chapter to Frank, declaring that, while Portsmouth has had many, many notables in its three-hundred fifty plus years of existence, "none of them dominated their times as completely as did Frank Jones."

Born in 1832, Frank came to Portsmouth - not to be a brewer, but to work as a tin peddler for his brother Hiram's hardware and stove business - at age sixteen. Frank was much too ambitious, however, to merely peddle tin for very long. By 1858 he'd involved himself in the brewery of an Englishman named John Swindells. Within little more than a year he owned it. And once he owned it, Frank Jones set out to make his brewery the biggest and best around. He added a malt house in 1863,

Cont'd. on page 73

IF YOU DRINK ALE
WHY NOT DRINK THE
BEST?

JONES'
"Granite State"
ALE.

Brewed from the Best
Malt and Hops

BY THE
TRUE W. JONES BREWING CO.
MANCHESTER, N. H.

Circa 1910 Ad

COMPLIMENTS OF

FRANK · JONES · BREWING · CO.
LIMITED

PORTSMOUTH, N. H.   BOSTON, MASS.

Circa 1895 Frank Jones advertising art

We've Come a Long Way, Baby

It is said that beauty is in the eye of the beholder ... and males of eight and nine and ten decades ago very often had a lot to behold. In those days, women - as in the case of our pair of snowball-toting girlfriends here - that we would now call hefty (or worse!) were considered all the rage. Thin was not in!

(And yes, Frank owned a brewery in Boston, too. It was known as Jones, Johnson & Company from 1857 to 1877; Jones, Cook & Company from 1877 to 1899; and the Frank Jones Brewing Company from 1889 until its closing in 1903).

Circa 1930 Chamber of Commerce booklet

On the Trail of Life's Mysteries (Or Manchester's Mysteries, Anyway)

Old city directories are fascinating things. While not quite as racy as romance novels, they can certainly be a whole lot more informative. I had recently found a pre-prohibition embossed bottle with the lettering "Dowd Bros./Manchester, N.H./Jones Lager." I'd always thought that both of the breweries associated with the Jones boys were strictly of the ale and porter school, so this came as a puzzler: had one of them actually stooped so low as to make lager? Secondly, many years ago I aquired the Patent Office papers for trade mark #26,276...True W. Jones Bock Ale. The trade mark was duly registered on March 26, 1895...but was it ever really used? Did True Jones ever actually produce a bock ale?

With these questions very definitely the order of the day, I decided to go directly to the source: the Queen City of New Hampshire itself...and its very fine Manchester Historic Association. There I was greeted by the Association's two delightful librarians, Cynthia Gabrielli and Elizabeth Lessard, who really got into the spirit of things. They rounded up an early photo of the True Jones brewery; tracked down a gentleman whose family had purportedly owned the brewery (actually it turned out that his family had owned the Portsmouth Brewing Company, in Portsmouth. But no matter: he, too, was delightful); and, best of all, allowed me full access to their complete collection of city directories.

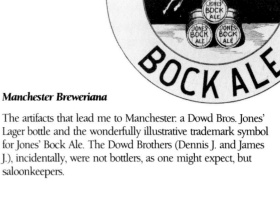

The Queen City

Created as a manufacturing city - to be the Manchester of America - Manchester has lived up to that goal for most of its existence. Its Amoskeag Mills were the largest textile manufactury in the world in the early years of this century. But, even in those heyday textile years, there was also the R.G. Sullivan 7-20-4 Cigar factory, two shoe factories . . . and the True W. Jones Brewing Company.

Manchester Breweriana

The artifacts that lead me to Manchester: a Dowd Bros. Jones' Lager bottle and the wonderfully illustrative trademark symbol for Jones' Bock Ale. The Dowd Brothers (Dennis J. and James J.), incidentally, were not bottlers, as one might expect, but saloonkeepers.

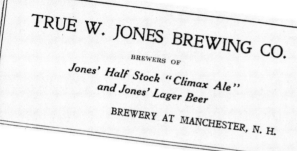

Jones' Lager and Climax Ale

The True W. Jones city directory ad for 1917: advertising Jones' Lager and Jones' Half Stock "Climax Ale." The year 1917 was the last year brewing was legal in New Hampshire until the arrival of repeal.

Lager, Yes, ...Bock Ale, No

My findings: as the end of legal brewing was drawing nigh, the head honchos at True Jones did indeed add lager to the brewery's product lineup. The addition occured between 1910 (when their ad in the city directory makes mention of ales only) and 1915 (when their ad includes "Jones' Lager Beer"). Unfortunately, the brewery decided to save money by not taking a directory ad in the intervening years, so there's no way to pinpoint the exact year lager was added. Jones' Bock Ale, on the other hand, appears never to have been added at all. No mention of it is made in any Jones' ad in 1895 or thereafter, so the patent papers that I'm fortunate enough to possess are all that likely remain of what sounded like a pretty nifty idea.

Carney, Lynch…and Sometimes Conner, Too

Before there was the True W. Jones Brewing Company (1891-1917), there was — at the same address in the Baskerville section of Manchester — Carney, Lynch & Company. Actually, there was a third partner named Daniel Conner, and the brewery was often called Carney, Lynch & Conner…but Dan was slighted in this most attractive series of directory ads from their period as Manchester's reigning brewery, 1879-1888.

1880

1881

188_

1877

1864

But Wait…There's More

The buildings that housed Carney, Lynch & Company, and later True W. Jones, were not, however, Manchester's first or sole brewery. A. (Andrew) C. Wallace — and before that Haines & Wallace — operated the Amoskeag (Amoskeag — Indian for "abundance of fish" — is a most popular name in Manchester) Brewery on Main Street, at the bridge, in the Piscatasquoq section of the Queen City from at least 1864. Even earlier than that, Joseph Wilson is listed in the 1860 directory as a brewer located at 2 Granite Block; Michael Prout, with an address of, alternately, Elm Street and the Marshall Building, is listed in 1856 and 1858; and one R.V. Burt was doing his thing with malt and hops and water on the Wells Block, opposite the City Hotel, at least as early as 1854.

Are old city directories worth reading?
You bet they are!

and a second one in 1879. A new brewhouse was constructed in 1870; in 1878 he added a cooperage department; what were generally believed to be the largest ale and porter storage cellars in the world were built in the early 1880s; and extensive bottling works were constructed in 1900.

What really made Frank Jones a Big Man Around Portsmouth, however, was his outside-of-brewing activities and interests. He was twice elected mayor of his adopted city; served New Hampshire as a two-term Congressman; lost in a bid to become governor by a scant 2,000 votes in 1880; was president of the Boston & Maine Railroad, the Granite State Fire Insurance Company, the Portsmouth Fire Association, and the Portsmouth Shoe Company; and was proprietor of two still extant hotels, the Rockingham (in Portsmouth) and the rather colossal Wentworth-by-the-Sea (in nearby Newcastle).

To again quote Portsmouth historian Brighton: "The man was a legend in his own time."

Frank Jones (1832-1902)

. . . And A Ladies' Man Too

In addition to his many and varied business and political activities, Frank Jones was reputed to be quite the ladies' man, too. In fact, it was the rumor around Portsmouth for many years that the ale that made him famous came about via the romantic route: while Frank was still a tin peddler a smitten-with-him housewife shared her secret recipe for ale with him. He took it from there.

Mrs. Frank

Mrs. Frank was no slouch, either. She was involved in numerous worthwhile activities in and around Portsmouth, was especially active in the Middle Street Baptist Church. Consequently, her husband did many things for the church . . . one of which was to provide warm water - in the brewery's beer barrels - for baptisms. The barrels would be transported through the city's streets directly from the brewery to the church on those Sundays there was a baptism. What a sight that must have been!

The Sidis Institute, donated by Mrs. Frank Jones, Portsmouth, N. H.

Circa 1900 postcard view of the Sidis Institute, one of many charitable activities contributed to by Mrs. Frank Jones

1890's postcard views

Open To The World

As phrases such as "Open To The World" and "Largest Ale Brewers in the World" would indicate, Frank Jones did nothing in a less than fully grandiose manner.
The "Open To The World" statement was undoubtedly true: brewers, then as now, liked to show off their goods . . . their plant, their personnel, especially their product. The "Largest Ale Brewers" claim, however, is somewhat suspect. It may well have been true at some point, but those few historical records that do exist would indicate otherwise. But then again, those few records are all from the late 1870s (when F.J. trailed both P. Ballantine & Sons and the Boston Beer Company in this country alone), before Frank began his full push . . . so no one really knows. It probably makes little difference: Frank Jones was BIG!

73

Those That Tried (To Keep Up With The Joneses)

The Jones brothers did not have a lock on the New Hampshire beer market. There was many an out-of-state brewer who shipped into the Granite State, plus there were several competitors right within New Hampshire's own borders. Chief among these was Portsmouth's Eldridge Brewing Company.

Like Father, Like Son

What became the Eldridge Brewing Company was founded in 1858 by Mssrs. M. Fisher and Herman Eldridge. Originally called M. Fisher & Company, that changed in 1870 when Eldridge bought Fisher out, admitted his son Marcellus into the firm, and changed the company name to Herman Eldridge & Son. This is the son.

When Eldridge's Brewery Was Really Eldridge's Brewery

Eldridge's brewery was still in Eldridge family hands when this wonderfully-pastoral photo was snapped in the wee years of this century. But 'twas not to be so for much longer. Marcellus had sold out to his brother, H. Fisher Eldridge, in 1891, who in turn would sell out to a group headed by Fred H. Ward in early 1913.

After Repeal: "The Ale With The Creamy Head"

In late September, 1933 - in what was described as a "gala celebration" - Eldridge re-opened for business. But it did not re-open at the same location. With former Portsmouth mayor Albert Hislop at the helm, the Eldridge Brewing Company found itself located in what had been the Frank Jones Brewing Company plant prior to prohibition. Ale still flowed from what had been billed as the home of the "Largest Ale Brewers in the World" . . . but it was Eldridge Portsmouth Ale.

William J. Wilson, Brewmaster

Does this man look like a brewmaster? Well, he was . . . and quite a reknowned one at that. The son of a brewmaster (at the J & A McKechnie Brewing Co., Canandaigua, New York), William J. literally grew up in the business. A graduate of Hobart College and the National Brewers' Academy in New York City, Mr. Wilson was considered one of the ale brewers par excellence in this country, was a 32nd degree Mason, and was also known for his ability to dazzle many a fellow golfer on the links at the Portsmouth Country Club.

Original Secret Formula

However, in what was about as close to poetic justice as you can get, after-prohibition Eldridge Portsmouth Ale was really none other than pre-prohibition Frank Jones Ale, as evidenced by this right-after-repeal ad.

"As of Old"

In 1937, in what must have seemed musical chairs to many a bemused Portsmouth-area beer drinker, the Eldridge Brewing Company - doing business, of course, in the former Frank Jones' plant, anyway - switched its name to . . . the Frank Jones Brewing Company. As Frank Jones the brewery remained in business until 1950, when financial difficulties caused it to cease all operations.

Circa 1940
Frank Jones coaster

ARTHUR HARRIS, President   W. F. HARRINGTON, Treasurer
L. J. HARRINGTON, Vice President

Portsmouth Brewing Company

BREWERS OF

HALF STOCK

XXX' Cream and Sparkling Ales

India Pale Ale

Old Brown Stock

And

Portsburger Lager

BREWERY AND OFFICE

64 Bow Street   Portsmouth, N. H.

MANCHESTER BRANCH

P. HARRINGTON SONS, 17-25 LAKE AVE.

A Double Cheeseburger and a Portsburger, Please (Or, On Second Thought, Make That a Double Portsburger and . . .)

The Jones' other sizable New Hampshire competition was the Portsmouth Brewing Company, founded in 1870 by Arthur Harris as A. Harris & Company. In 1875 the name was changed to the Portsmouth Brewing Company. Ale was the brewery's pride and joy. How could it have been otherwise: Arthur Harris, himself, was an Englishman, and his brewmaster, Thomas Leary, was a native of Ireland! Inspired by the Eldridge Brewing Company's success with lager (Eldridge started brewing lager in 1878, the first Portsmouth brewer to stray from ale), however, Portsmouth Brewing did add lager to its output in 1897; by 1901 it accounted for 16% of the brewery's production. And the brewery chose a great name: how could anyone resist ordering a Portsburger?!

The Harringtons were the other ruling family when it came to the Portsmouth Brewing Company. A descendent recently recounted why the brewery never reopened after prohibition: seems that when one branch of the family did indeed go to reopen it they found that a member of another branch had, during prohibition, stripped the insides, selling off all the equipment, piping, etc. The brewery never did reopen . . . and members of the one branch of the Harrington family did not speak to members of the other for years thereafter.

1913 MANCHESTER CITY DIRECTORY ad for the Portsmouth Brewing Company

Courtesy the Hug Collection

Embossed bottle from when New Mountain Spring ruled the Walpole/Bellows Falls brewing world. Today all that remains of the former brewery is the old engine shed.

Good Old What's Their Name

The smallest of the Granite State's turn-of-the-century breweries was located in the Cold River section of Walpole, smack dab on the Vermont line. In fact, the company, organized in 1876 as Walker, Blake & Company, was headquartered in Bellows Falls (Vermont). The brewing, though, was done in New Hampshire.

The brewery, five stories high, was built after a model on display at the Centennial in Philadelphia. It burned down in both 1882 and 1905, but was rebuilt both times.

Apart from the distinctive name of its lager - Cruiser - and its two-state identity, the brewery was most characterized by its seemingly constant changes in name. Shedding Walker, Blake & Company in 1879, there followed Fall Mountain Lager Company (1879-1886); Bellows Falls Brewing Company (1886-1893); Mountain Spring Brewing Company (1893-1895); New Mountain Spring Brewing Company (1895-1900); Crescent Brewing Company (1900-1902); New Mountain Spring Brewing Company again (1902-1904); L.J. Vetterman Brewing Company (1904); and, last but not least, the Manila Brewing Company (1904-1907), owned by old friend Selig Manila (see page 163).

Lager: It's A Word That Doesn't Get Around Much Anymore

◆

THE WORD NO ONE KNOWS . . . YET EVERYBODY DRINKS

Stroll through your friendly supermarket or package store. Check out the beer display...and see if you can find the word "lager" anywhere. You'll find lots of premium beers, a banquet beer (Coors), draft beers, and, of course, the usual supply of light/lite beers. In my search (in Portland), I did find three American beers that still state "lager" on their label - Narra-

Circa 1875 lager bier postcard

For its bier, bier, bier
That makes you want to
Chier, chier, chier

Early uses of the word lager often spelled beer as it was — and is — spelled in Germany . . . bier. Beer or bier, Americans — especially those living in the territories west of the Hudson — loved it.

Today, well over 90% of America's malt beverage output is lager: Bud, Miller, Stroh, Coors, Old Style, Lone Star, Pearl, Dixie, Iron City, Schaefer, Schmidt's, Pabst, Michelob, Sterling, Old Milwaukee - plus Heineken, Moosehead, Beck's, Corona, too . . . They're all lager!

gansett, Portland Lager, and Samuel Adams Boston Lager - but such examples are certainly the exception rather than the rule. And try walking into a bar and asking for a lager: the response you get might prove interesting.

I was quite surprised, moreover, to find during some recent interviews that many people nowadays are even unsure of how to pronounce lager (there's a strong tendency to want to say "lay-ger" as opposed to the correct "log-ger."), let alone know what it means.

Such was certainly not the case a scant three or four generations ago: lager was on most everyone's tongue, literally as well as figuratively. It was a word you saw often: were apt to use often.

"Lager" is a German word meaning to store, to age. As with fine wines and Scotch whiskey, it needs to be aged to really do itself justice. Long popular in Germany and Czechoslovakia, lager was not introduced into "The New World" until 1840 when, legend has it, a Bavarian immigrant named John Wagner brewed up a batch of it in a primative-at-best brewhouse he'd constructed in his Philadelphia backyard. Pleased with the results, he undoubtedly shared it with family, friends, neighbors; maybe even threw a block party. Whatever, Wagner's backyard creation sparked what would become a revolution in our nation's rewing. America's beer drinkers were aptivated by lager's effervescence, tang, nd lighter, less-bitter-than-ale taste. The act that over 1,350,000 German immirants - who already knew and loved their ager - arrived on our shores between 1840 nd 1860 didn't hurt either. Places like rooklyn, Cincinnati, Milwaukee, St. Louis even San Antonio - soon had hefty German-American populations, with secions of town nicknamed "Little Germany" r "Over the Rhine" or the like.

ut places like Boston and Providence and Worcester and New Haven did not. Sure, here were German-American settlements in New England, and German-American populations in most of the major cities, but they were small potatoes compared with those further west.

Take this lack of a large German-American population to embrace lager, add a climate that often benefits from hearty food and drink, throw in New Englanders' natural instinct to stick with what's working ("don't fix it if it ain't broke") . . . and you get the idea that lager didn't catch on in New England to nearly the same extent that it did elsewhere.

It didn't.

Lager Comes To New England

The honor of brewing the first lager in Boston, the first lager in Massachusetts, and - for that matter - the first lager in all of New England...all such honors, awards and prizes go to the same man, John Roessle, who erected a small brewhouse in Roxbury in 1846. Such awards, had they actually been bestowed upon our pioneer lager brewer, would've probably taken up almost as much space as his brewing equipment: his operation was that small. Output was less than 300 barrels a year...an entire year.

But lager had a way of catching on even in slow-to-accept-it New England - and, in the thirty-nine years before his death in 1885, John Roessle had the satisfaction of seeing that first tiny brewhouse expanded many times, and his beer achieve sales that placed him right up among the top Boston brewers. In 1879, a year for which complete statistics are available, his 42,800 barrels sold placed him third, behind Boston Beer Company (77,232 barrels) and the Suffolk Brewing Company (44,083), but ahead of Rueter & Alley (40,300), G.F. Burkhardt (39,382), and Van Nostrand & Company (37,912). Of these, the Boston big six, Boston Beer brewed, ironically, only ale, as did Rueter & Alley and Van Nostrand, while Suffolk brewed both ale and lager. Roessle and Burkhardt were alone in brewing lager exclusively . . . which meant, of course, that Roessle was the largest lager brewer in Boston (and, just as when he'd started in 1846, the largest lager brewer in Massachusetts, and - for that matter - the largest lager brewer in all of New England, too!).

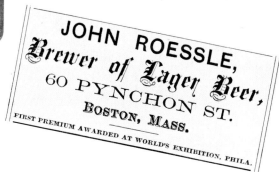

Clockwise, from upper left: a woodcut of the Roessle Brewery, located at Pynchon Street and Columbus Avenue; a 1909 postcard with sentiments - Our Country, Right or Wrong - that smack of much more recent times and agonies; an 1883 "Brewer of Lager Beer" ad from the MANCHESTER (New Hampshire) CITY DIRECTORY; 1914 view of one of the fleet that delivered "The Master Brewer's Master Brew;"

and, in the center,

a nifty ad from the program for Boston's Tremont Theatre for the week of May 10, 1915, a week in which Roessle was in especially good company . . . playing at the Tremont was D.W. Griffith's classic THE BIRTH OF A NATION.

"Help" . . . It Came From Near and Far

In spite of the very substantial efforts of John Roessle, George Burkhardt and others, lager was not really the province of New England's brewers. Looking again at 1879 - and its complete set of statistics - we see that only four of New England's top dozen brewers brewed lager exclusively. Two brewed both lager and ale, while six (including the two that were far and away the biggest, Boston Beer and Frank Jones) brewed ale only.

But if New England's own brewing fraternity was mostly into ale, outsiders - from both near and far - were only too happy to step in and help our region's malt beverage enthusiasts enjoy this thing called lager.

Although well known for her own ales, New York's capital city of Albany had a number of brewers who specialized in lager, and who shipped it into and over the Berkshires. Represented here via a magnificent turn-of-the-century advertising tray is the Beverwyck Brewing Company and, via a hodge-podge of items, the Hinckel Brewing Company. Hinckel, especially, eyed New England's lager market . . . going so far as to print Manchester and Boston on their label (which was misleading, if not downright dishonest: they brewed solely in Albany) and to open a 'Gentlemen's Cafe and Restaurant', which they duly proclaimed to be 'Boston's Finest,' right in the heart of the Hub. Called The Albany, it was a tied house: owned by the brewery, operated by the brewery, and with only the brewery's beer sold.

Circa 1900 Beverwyck Famous Lager tray

Way west of the Hudson, of course, was the real 'lagerland.' The four shipping - or national - brewers prior to prohibition were, from St. Louis, Anheuser-Busch and Lemp and, from Milwaukee, Pabst and Jos. Schlitz. Schlitz appears to have been the most aggressive with respect to New England, especially in and around Boston where they had, starting in 1872, a heavy duty agent - or representative - named Joseph Gahm. His bottles, in fact, are still relatively commonplace (at least at antique shops and old bottle shows) in eastern Massachusetts today. Embossed J. Gahm, 10 Bow Street, Charlestown, Mass on one side, and Milwaukee Lager Beer on the other, they point up how much Milwaukee stood for lager...and how much Schlitz stood for Milwaukee.

Schlitz also established at least one Palm Garden in New England. Modeled after the mother Palm Garden in Milwaukee, and located in the heart of all the happenings at Nantasket Beach, on Boston's South Shore, the Schlitz Palm Garden was a resplendent restaurant, dance hall, and beer parlor all rolled into one. It was, in short, a place where folks could have themselves a jolly good time...and Schlitz could sell them a lot of its Milwaukee Lager.

1878 ALBANY CITY DIRECTORY ad for Frederick Hinckel and his Cataract Brewery; circa 1880 Hinckel Export Beer bottle; ad for The Albany in the program for the Castle Square Theatre, Boston, for the week of March 4, 1895.

Ad from the programme of the Park Theatre, Boston, for the week of November 20, 1893; front and back of circa 1900 embossed J. Gahm Milwaukee Lager bottles; two early 1900 postcard views of the Schlitz Palm Garden, Nantasket Beach, Massachusetts.

Here's a pair of enamel advertising trays, one from the Hartmann Brewing Company, Bridgeport; the other from the Eagle Brewing Company, Providence. Such trays - enamel over metal, much as your kitchen sink before the coming of stainless steel - were fairly common promotional givaways from New England and upstate New York breweries in the very early years of this century. They seldom show up from brewers further west. The Hartmann Brewing Company, Charles S. Hartmann, proprietor, was the successor to a firm that started in 1852. Of special note is the fact that for many years Hartmann's major brand was Rheingold . . . one of at least half a dozen U.S. breweries that once likened its brew to gold from the river Rhein.

Keeping Lager Alive

But, going back those scant three or four generations, people would walk into a bar and ask for a lager. Or an ale. Or maybe even a porter. And bars would make it clear which they served, or - since they probably served all three - which they preferred to serve. Breweries, likewise, would do much the same: show in their advertising and on their packaging what they were all about.

The point to all this: prior to prohibition - and especially prior to the turn of the century - "beer" was an umbrella word that stood for all types of malt beverages, with a very clear distinction being made between those types...lager, ale, porter, stout, etc. Now, while beer is still an umbrella word that stands for all types of malt beverages, it is a word that has come to stand for lager, too. "Lager" has become superfluous...and is, indeed, a word that doesn't get around much anymore. But we're keeping it alive - or at least for the next several pages we are - with an inviting array of pre-prohibition lager-iana that would, hopefully, cause even braumeisters Roessle and Burkhardt to beam with delight.

Not to be outdone by "kitchen sink" giveaways, the New London Brewing Company favored its accounts with solid brass trays advertising its ale, porter, and lager. But it didn't favor them for long: New London Brewing was in business for but four years, 1899 to 1903. Founded by Fall River, Massachusetts' Rudy Haffenreffer, Jr., the firm seems to have been as well known for its Winthrop Spring Hygeia Ice output as for its brews. In 1903 the company's name was changed to the American Brewing Company; in 1905 to the Thames Brewing Company; and, finally, in 1906, to the Pequod Brewing Company. Operations appear to have ceased in 1907. There was talk of a comeback in 1933. A syndicate from New York City purchased the property - labelled in "bad shape" by *Brewers News* - but never did start it up again. Nothing remains of the brewery today.

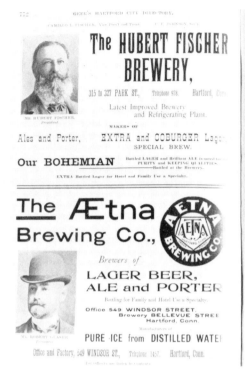

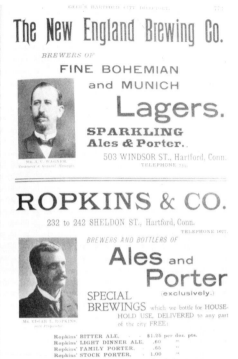

Think of hubs of brewing activity and Hartford, Connecticut is not likely to pop into mind. But in the early 1900s, right up through prohibition, Hartford had four breweries that held their own very nicely. Presented here, exactly as they were postured in GEER'S HARTFORD CITY DIRECTORY for 1906, are all four.

Hubert Fischer was an Austrian who came to America in 1865. He was co-owner of the Fischer & Eppig Brewery in Brooklyn for a decade, eventually moving to Hartford and acquiring the seven-year old brewery of George Sichler in 1886. Fischer added ale and porter to his product roster a year or so before this ad, but lager was always his speciality and his great love. Idle during prohibition, the plant was rumored to be ready to open, under the direction of Camillo Fischer, in 1933, but it never did.

The word Aetna, which undoubtedly connotes life insurance more than beer, takes its name from a volcano on the eastern coast of Sicily. Still active, and the highest volcano in Europe, Mount Aetna (also spelled Etna) was believed in ancient Roman times to be the home of Vulcan, god of fire.

Closer to home - back in New England - Aetna was Hartford's longest-lasting brewery. Or at least it was a part of it: the brewery changed hands and names quite a few times. Founded as the Charles Herold Brewery in 1865, it became the Herold Capitol Brewing Company in 1879, the Columbia Brewing Company in 1896, and - finally - the Aetna Brewing Company in 1900. As Aetna it brewed lager, ale and porter until prohibition. Cereal beverages were tried for a time in the 1920s, but basically the brewery wasn't used for much of anything until repeal arrived in 1933 and it reopened and

operated, again as the Aetna Brewing Company, until 1939. In that year one last name change was made, to the Dover Brewing Company, under which name it remained in operation until forced into bankruptcy by creditors in 1947.

The New England Brewing Company was a latecomer: it was incorporated in 1897 and placed its first beer on the market the following summer. From the first - and right down to the last - both lager and ale were brewed. After prohibition, the brewery was overhauled and outfitted with new equipment. Capacity was brought up to 300,000 barrels a year, the largest in Connecticut. Inspired, perhaps, by Cambridge's New England Confectionary Company and its Necco wafers, New England Brewing came up with Nebco as the name of its beer and ale. It also came up with a rather novel leadership candidate in one J. Harold Murray (more on him in "There's Always..."). New England Brewing was re-organized in 1940; became a branch of the Largay Brewing Company, of Waterbury, in 1944; went out of business in 1947.

Ropkins & Company was the sole member of the Hartford Four that produced ale only...a fact they were wont to stress in their advertising. Founded in 1874 as Shannon & McCann, the brewery went through several changes in ownership before Englishman Edgar L. Ropkins bought it in 1892. As with Hubert Fischer before him, Ropkins came to Hartford via Brooklyn, where he'd been associated with that city's Streeter & Dennison Brewery. Ropkins built the brewery up, from a capacity of but 2,000 barrels a year to over 35,000. Prohibition, of course, put an end to all that. Ropkins did not reopen when brew came back.

P.S. Love those prices!

Collecting trade cards - given away to promote household goods, retail establishments, and the like - was a popular pastime in pre-radio/pre-boob tube days. Here's a trio of circa 1890's Connecticut cards that boost lager . . . one of which even uses it to sell men's clothing!

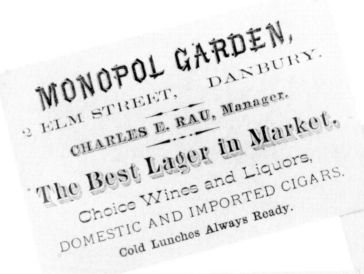

MONOPOL GARDEN,
2 ELM STREET, DANBURY.
CHARLES E. RAU, Manager.
The Best Lager in Market,
Choice Wines and Liquors,
DOMESTIC AND IMPORTED CIGARS.
Cold Lunches Always Ready.

DON'T YOU FORGET IT!

—THAT

Miller's Garden.
No. 15 CHURCH ST.
Is the Best Place to get your

Wine AND Lager

JOHN MILLER,
PROPRIETOR, HARTFORD, CONN.

YOU'LL NEVER MISS THE LAGER TIL THE KEG RUNS DRY.
COPYRIGHTED, BUFFORD, BOSTON.

Grand Opportunity to procure
Winter Suits & Overcoats
AT VERY REDUCED PRICES
At the GREAT SALE now going on at
BAUM & BERNSTEIN'S
Palace Block Clothing House
MERIDEN, CONN.

I billed this as an inviting array of lager-iana, so let's end with the most inviting.

I know that if I were hanging around Springfield in 1900 I'd have headed straight to the nearest set of double doors and partaken of some of Highland Brewing Company's Thick Mash Lager. But it's not 1900. I've missed my chance. And, since "mash" in this day and age sounds more like bourbon (or a certain TV show/movie we've all enjoyed), I called friend and local brewer David Geary, and asked him what thick mash lager might be. His best guess: a beer with more malt per volume of brew, which would lead to a higher-than-usual gravity, which translates to a beer with a higher-than-usual alcoholic content plus some additional sweetness. Regardless . . . David agreed that thick mash lager sounded mighty inviting!

(Note: Further research, in Springfield, discloses the fact that Highland's Thick Mash was a true food beer: very high in nutriments and very low in alcohol. Which means that David and I would have guessed incorrectly. Nevertheless, Thick Mash still sounds mighty inviting!!)

HIGHLAND BREWING CO.,
SPRINGFIELD, MASS.
BREWERS OF LAGER BEER.
THICK MASH LAGER A SPECIALTY.
STOCK ALE, STOCK PORTER.
GOLDEN ALE, CREAM ALE
P. O. Box 675, SPRINGFIELD, MASS.

Highland Brewing Company, Springfield, ad in the OFFICIAL HISTORY, FIRST REGIMENT, CONNECTICUT VOLUNTEERS IN THE SPANISH-AMERICAN WAR, published in 1900

81

Mabel!
Black Label

◆

TWO DECADES OF BREWING ON THE SHORES OF LAKE COCHITUATE

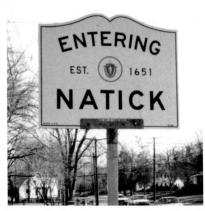

Natick, generally thought to mean "Place of hills" in Algonquian, is basically a Boston bedroom community. At one time a center of shoe production, its best known manufacturing concern prior to Carling's arrival was probably the Whipple Company, makers of Grandmother's Mincemeat.

Carling's coming to town in 1956 was not the biggest day in Natick, Massachusetts' 300+ years of history...

Harriet Beecher Stowe, whose husband was South Natick native Calvin Stowe, forever immortalized Natick in her OLDTOWN FOLKS, written in 1869, and its sequel, FIRESIDE STORIES, written in 1871. Both attempt to "interpret to the world the New England life and character"...with Natick and her citizens the setting.

In 1872, "The Natick Cobbler," Henry Wilson, was sworn in as vice-president, the second highest office in the land, under Ulysses S. Grant.

Local boy Elmer Bent pitched baseball's first "drop ball" and "jump ball," curves that broke sharply downward and upward respectively, in an 1885 game in which a Natick area team knocked off previously undefeated Harvard, 3-1.

Native son Piper Donovan brought fame to the town when he set a new world's record for the hundred yard dash in 1895. It ran in the family: his uncle, Dinso Donovan, once ran fifty miles in five hours, a record that stood for years.

Then there was the time, in 1898, when the town's hook and ladder team set a world's record, connecting and running hose two hundred and twenty yards in 58 seconds.

Horatio Alger, Jr., of "Ragged Dick" and "Tattered Tom" fame, was the son of a Natick minister and lived the last years of his rich life in South Natick, where he died in 1899.

No, Carling's coming to town was not the biggest day, but it was up there. To be the home of New England's first new - spanking new - brewery in more than forty years was, indeed, something to write home to mother about. And it was a dream brewery, ultra modern in every respect, located on a 32-acre park-like setting on the shores of picturesque Lake Cochituate just eighteen miles from Boston.

Cont'd. on page 84

From Cars to Carling's

A lot of rather wacky things happened as a result of the Great Depression. Companies ceased to do business. Companies changed their business. Take the case of the Peerless Motor Car Company, located in Cleveland. A manufacturer of quality automobiles since 1900, Peerless was facing extinction by the early 1930s. Beset by brutal competition from the big three, Ford, GM and Chrysler, plus lackadaisical auto sales in general, its prospects looked bleak.

What to do? James A. Bohannon, Peerless president, thought and thought. And then came up with the answer. Beer. Stop making cars and start making beer. Bohannon's Board of Directors was less than thrilled with the idea but, given the likelihood of repeal coupled with Peerless' slim pickings in the automobile business, had to admit it made sense.

1916 Peerless Motor Car Company advertisement

Years later, Bohannon recalled the next step:

> Having lived in Detroit, right across the river from Canada, I always had a proper respect for Carling's. On a quality basis I associated it with Cadillac, Steinway, and Tiffany. So when at Peerless we had a chance to acquire the American rights, formulas, and technical assistance of Canadian Breweries, Ltd., brewers of Carling's Ale, we were quick to take advantage of it. We had a big, modern plant and lots of ambition, and they had the name. It was a natural.

And it was. Remodeling of the former auto plant was begun in the fall of 1933, with brewing operations getting underway in March, 1934. The newly-renamed Brewing Corporation of America (changed to Carling Brewery Company in 1954) was in business.

The Peerless was aptly - if not modestly - named. With Barney Oldfield doing the driving, the then zero-to-fifty-miles-per-hour record was set in 1904 in a Peerless Green Dragon. And the following year, with Oldfield again at the wheel, the world's first thousand-mile nonstop run was made in Brighton Beach, Brooklyn. In a Peerless, of course.

Carling management was proud of their brewery on the shores of Lake Cochituate, billing it as "a see and tour must for thousands of New England visitors."

Circa 1952 Carling's Red Cap Ale magazine ads

Ad in 1956 Red Sox program

The years leading up to Natick were highly successful ones for Carling. The coveted 1,000,000 barrels sold mark was topped for the first time in 1953 . . . and celebrities the likes of Ethel Merman, Arthur Fiedler and Lucille Ball sang the praises of Red Cap, the brewery's ale. Lucille wasn't Lucy yet, of course, but she was working on it. Her radio show, MY FAVORITE HUSBAND, would soon make the move to the tube . . . and become the basis of the legendary I LOVE LUCY.

Under construction since 1954, the plant had an initial capacity of 600,000 (later expanded to 1,000,000) barrels a year, and was at the core of Carling's continued move into the vital - vital to their very definite goal of becoming one of THE giants of American brewing - eastern market.

Natick, however, turned out to be toward the top of Carling's climb. As much clout as the Mabel! Black Label gang had, it was no match for the really big boys of the day: Anheuser-Busch, Jos. Schlitz, Pabst and, later, Miller, Stroh, and Coors. In an effort to be more competitive, Carling merged with Baltimore-based National Brewing Company in 1975. It wasn't enough: in 1979, Carling National was itself bought up, by the G. Heileman Brewing Company.

By that time, though, most folks around Natick probably couldn't have cared less. In February, 1976, Carling management had advised all 200 employees in the plant that it would most likely close. "Preliminary studies indicate that it may be in the economic interest of the company to close the Natick plant" is how the *Natick Bulletin* ("Published Weekly Since the Civil War") delicately phrased it in its February 11th issue. The official notification of closure came less than a month later. April 15, 1976 was the last day worked.

Nobody remembered to bake a Happy 20th Birthday cake.

P.S. Established fifty-eight years before the coming of Carling, the Whipple Company is still in business in Natick. I stopped by on my way out of town to pick up some of their justly-famed Grandmother's Mince-meat. Noticing a portrait of a distinguished, obviously nineteenth century woman hanging in the office — and mindful of the impact of OLDTOWN FOLKS on the history of Natick — I commented "I guess that's Harriet Beecher Stowe." "THAT'S Grandmother Whipple," I was promptly and very properly informed.

Circa 1960 postcard

Carling's spiffy new plant was both an industry and area showcase. "The brewhouse is a beautiful sight to behold," penned *Modern Brewery Age*. "Solid panes of glass, two stories high, encase the lower part of the building, offering a picture-window view of the glittering stainless steel vessels within and, conversely, acres of green sod and landscape."

Modern looking then and modern looking now is about all I can say for Carling's former brewery. Now called Prime Park, it is the corporate headquarters for Prime Computer, Inc., a manufacturer of general purpose superminicomputers, with research and manufacturing facilities throughout the world, and 1986 revenues of $860,000,000. It is big business.

Prime Park, December, 1987

Circa 1947 Brockert's Black Label label. Black Label was a secondary Brockert's/Worcester Brewing Company brand. For more on Worcester's only post-pro brewery please see pages 148-155.

Circa 1940 label from the Medford Brewing Company. In operation until 1948, Medford was a typical small town Wisconsin brewery. Capacity was but 10,000 barrels. Its primary brand was Medford Lager, shown here.

Those Three Little Words

"Black Label Beer" has a nice ring to it. Carling's thought so: they introduced it to their American public in December of 1934.

At least two other U.S. breweries thought so, too. The Medford Brewing Company, Medford, Wisconsin, produced a beer they called Black Label from 1936 to 1943. And, right here in New England, Worcester's Brockert Brewing Company/Worcester Brewing Company brewed up Brockert's Black Label for the better part of a decade, from 1940 to 1948.

Circa 1952, "Mabel' six-pack carton. Catchy and oft-heard, the Hey Mabel . . . Black Label jingle was a symbol of Carling's glory years in the 1950s and '60s.

"Not To Be Used"

NEW ENGLAND AND PROHIBITION

the late twenties:

> Mother's in the kitchen
> Washing out the jugs;
> Sister's in the pantry
> Bottling the suds;
> Father's in the cellar
> Mixing up the hops;
> Johnny's on the front porch
> Watching for the cops.

Before we get to the roaring twenties - and what made them roar - however, let's step back and trace the roots of what would become "The Noble Experiment."

When a summer, 1987 antiquing expedition across New Hampshire netted the prohibition-era malt extract/malt syrup labels that bedeck this page, I couldn't help but laugh. On each label is carefully stated "NOT TO BE USED FOR MAKING BEVERAGES CONTRARY TO LAW." I mean, who was fooling who? If one believes the contemporary accounts of the years 1920-1933, just about anything and everything imaginable was used as a base for bathtub or basement booze. Malt mixtures certainly qualified and then some, as witness a rhyme in vogue in

Circa 1925 malt extract/malt syrup labels from the Blue Banner Malt Company, Lawrence and Boston

New England Beginnings

As is the case with so many chapters in America's history, the roots of prohibition can be traced to New England. In Boston, in February of 1826, was formed the American Society for the Promotion of Temperance. Generally called the American Temperance Society, this group is considered to be the first American anti-drink organization of any real consequence. Headed up by Justin Edwards, pastor of the Hub City's Park Street Church, the Society was supported by the likes of Rev. Timothy Dwight, president of Yale University, and Rev. Francis Wayland, the first president of Brown University. Within the short period of three years, the A.T.S. could claim a solid 100,000 members.

As Maine Goes . . .

At first the temperance movement advocated just that: temperance. Moderation. But as the movement gained steam its members increasingly advocated total abstinence. The state that, far more than any other, bought the whole prohibition package was Maine.

Lead by Neal Dow ("The Napoleon of Temperance") and his almost militant Maine Temperance Union, Maine went dry in 1846. And, but for two periods of varying "wetness," remained dry until 1933. The "Maine Law," as it came to be known, became the model for many of the prohibition statutes that followed.

But while the "Maine Law" was a model, it was not a success. Maine was a hard-drinking state, so much so that a statistician of the day calculated that Mainers spent on liquor, over the course of every twenty years, an amount equivalent to the net worth of all the property in the entire state. There were also loopholes in the Law. For example, it was forbidden to sell alcohol, but it was not forbidden to give it away. Result: grogshop proprietors would charge a hefty price for a pickle or a slab of cheese . . . and supply the drink free. Bootleggers and "kitchen speak-easies" abounded, with bad booze commonplace, decent malt and spiritous liquors difficult to come by. In an article entitled "The Prohibition Crisis in Maine," observer Robert J. Sprague wrote in the September, 1911 issue of *New England Magazine*: "It is often reported that there is much drunkenness in Maine, and this certainly is true; at

some points in the State there is more than I have ever observed anywhere else in America."

In short, prohibition in Maine was a flop, a flop that should have alerted the rest of the nation to the dangers of enforced dryness. But it didn't. Fueled by strong anti-German sentiment during World War I (the lion's share of America's brewers were, of course, of German extraction) and a constant barrage of "Behind every social ill lies alcohol" temperance propaganda, America just seemed that much more determined to prove its righteousness by passing national prohibition. The 18th Amend-

Ten Nights in a Barroom

Illustration from T.S. Arthur's TEN NIGHTS IN A BARROOM (published in 1854; subtitled "What I Saw There"), a powerful if somewhat melodramatic anti-alcohol narrative that was also adapted for stage use.

PROTEST AGAINST PROHIBITION
THE MORE THE LEGISLATORS HEAR FROM YOU, THE LESS YOU WILL HEAR OF PROHIBITION.
PROTEST.

OUR ALLIES ARE SOME FIGHTERS
THEIR FIGHTERS AND WORKERS INSIST ON BEER. WHY TAKE IT AWAY FROM THE LABORING MEN WHO MUST WIN THE WAR FOR AMERICA?
ASK YOUR LEGISLATORS!

Circa 1917 beer bottle neck labels

Protest Against Prohibition

During and even before World War I the U.S. Brewers' Association encouraged its members to stir up anti-prohibition support among the beer-drinking public. Bottled beer neck label messages such as these were one result. It was to do little good.

ment - Prohibition - was submitted to the states by Congress on December 18, 1917. One by one the states ratified it, until January 16, 1919 when Nebraska became magic number 36: with the necessary three-quarters of the then 48 states having endorsed it, prohibition became - effective one year later - the law of the land.

What's a Brewer To Do?

As of January 17, 1920, the manufacture, sale, transportation and/or consumption of any beverage exceeding ½ of one percent alcohol became illegal. The beer business was out of business. In New England - and nationally - brewers had no choice but to turn to other pursuits. The most logical was near beer, beer from which all but the allowable ½ of one percent alcohol had been removed. Boston's Suffolk Brewing Company had been experimenting with a non-intoxicating brew they called Uno. Hartford's Aetna Brewing Company tried its hand at cereal beverages, as non-alcoholic beerlike beverages were also called. Pickwick Pale was advertised far and wide in the Northeast. Soft drinks were also produced by many an ex-brewer. Lowell's Harvard and Lawrence's Diamond Spring both produced a full line of bottled sodas. The former Meriden Brewing Company, of Meriden, Connecticut, became the Silver City Beverage Company (although there are those who say it was just a front for Jack "Legs"

No Kick

This postcard, bearing an April, 1922 Natick, Rhode Island postmark, pretty much sums up how most folks felt about near beer: drinking it was not an exciting event!

Near Beer is like kissing your own Wife No Kick.

Diamond and Waxey Gordon and the manufacture of bootleg beer!). Some breweries, as with the plant of the Ph. Fresenius' Sons Brewery on Congress Street in New Haven, were converted to the manufacture and storage of ice. The large Dawson's plant in New Bedford was utilized by both an ice company and dairy. Some were converted to far less glamorous uses: the old Kutscher Brewery facility in Bridgeport was turned into an auto salvage operation; the major part of the American Brewing Company in Roxbury became a laundry. But being idle - i.e. basically sitting and rotting - seemed to be the eventual fate of most of New England's breweries during the thirteen-plus years of national prohibition.

"This man was born, lived, drank and died", On a tombstone were these words inscribed. He might have been strong, hearty and hale, If he had insisted on Pickwick Pale.

The one safe and satisfying drink in these flourishing days of bootlegging

Sold at
The Jigger Shop   The College Shop

Distributors
Miner, Read & Tullock
91 State St., New Haven
Wholesale Distributors

Pickwick Pale   Pickwick Stout

"The one safe and satisfying drink"

Most near beer sales fizzled a few years into prohibition. One brand that held its own to at least a fair degree, however (and wisely kept the Pickwick name before the buying public), was Haffenreffer & Company's Pickwick Pale. Here's a cute 1925 *Yale Record* ad that extolls one of its more dramatic virtues: that you could partake of Pickwick Pale without fear of having to have your stomach pumped out . . . or worse!

Circa 1925 Diamond Spring soda bottle

From Suds to Sarsparilla

Lawrence's Holihan Bros. was just one of several New England brewers who gave soft drinks a try when they were legislated out of the beer business.

What's a Beer Drinker to Do?

New England's beer drinkers generally fared better than her brewers. Folks who enjoyed their beer prior to prohibition usually just kept on enjoying it, one way or the other. The proximity of Canada offered an option. Recalls my stepfather Ray Audibert, who came of age in Fort Kent, on the Canadian border, during prohibition: "We'd just cross the river and get it (beer). It was Canada; all you had to do was cross the river, the Saint John River." Or you could elect to take a "booze cruise": many a liner became a party ship on which, out past the three mile limit, you could drink - legally -to your heart's content.

Then there was always the neighborhood speakeasy. Not every town and every neighborhood had a speakeasy, of course, but finding one was usually not very difficult. Finding a speak with decent liquor, however, was often another matter. All kinds of rotgut and poisonous and semi-poisonous liquids were sold in the name of alcohol. In 1923, U.S. Surgeon General Hugh S. Cumming ordered government chemists to analyze samples from confiscated bootleg booze. They found that most all of it

Portland (Maine) theatre card, 1926

1920 song sheet

Three Miles Out

Prohibition's reach extended but three miles off shore, a fact that was made merry in both song (with lyrics co-written by George Jessel, no less) and on screen (THREE MILES OUT, starring Madge Kennedy, shares the bill with the legendary Rudolph Valentino in this 1926 theatre card).

If Only It Were Beer

Prohibition-era cards such as this are fun, but actually beer - as well as virtually all other forms of alcohol - was far from difficult to obtain.

One man, Massachusetts' millionaire Delcevare King, was so upset by it all that he sponsored a contest in 1923 to come up with a new word to describe - and to shame - the millions of his fellow Americans disobeying the dry laws. Over 25,000 entries were received. In January of 1924 King announced the winning word: scofflaw.

contained one or more of the following: wood alcohol, phenol, mercuric chloride, sulfuric acid, hydrochloric acid, pyridine, benzol, aniline, iodine. All are poisonous. In the single year of 1927 deaths attributed to bad alcohol totaled 11,700.

A safer bet was to concoct your own home brew. You had plenty of help: there were an estimated 100,000 malt and hops shops throughout America, plus 25,000 or so outlets that sold home brewing equipment. By the late 1920s the national production of malt syrup was approaching 900,000 pounds a year . . . enough to make over seven billion pints of beer.

Anyway you slice it, America did not take well to the 18th Amendment with its "thou shalt not" provisos. We had become, ruefully noted one federal judge, "the most lawless country on the face of the earth."

Needle Beer

If you were too lazy to make your own beer, you could always buy near beer, add pure alcohol (obtainable via a doctor's prescription or, in a pinch, a visit to your local bootlegger), and end up with what came to be known as needle beer.

Now That's What I Call Good Beer

Just about everything under the sun was used to make alcohol or what resembled alcohol, including many things - such as soap and prune juice? - that shouldn't have been. As summed up by newspaper magnate William Randolph Hearst, himself an avid dry, in 1929:

"I think it can truthfully be said today that any man who wants a drink can get one; and about the only difference between the present condition and the condition preceeding prohibition is that a man who wants a mild drink is compelled to take a strong one; and a man who wants a good drink is compelled to take a bad one."

Legal Beer Comes Back

At one minute after midnight, April 6, 1933, legal beer came back to the majority of the country. Twenty states and the District of Columbia - representing over half the nation's population - turned on the taps and popped the caps. An unbelievable one and a half million barrels were consumed in beer-is-back's first twenty-four hours, a period fondly dubbed New Beer's Eve and New Beer's Day by the press. New England, alas, had to wait to join in the festivities: none of our six states had re-legalized beer as of the magic date. All six were soon to do so, however. Maine, not too surprisingly, was the last, waiting until July 1st to hop aboard the beer bandwagon.

Portland Press Herald, July 1, 1933

City Edition

Portland Press Herald

See Maine List

VOL. 71 ... Weather ... PORTLAND, MAINE, SATURDAY MORNING, JULY 1, 1933 ... PRICE THREE CENTS

Rivers, Lakes, Aye, Oceans Of Beer, Flow In Maine

Cruiser Raleigh Will Arrive This Morning For Legion Activities

Registration Booth For Legionnaires And Special One For Public To Be Opened In Chamber Of Commerce

As The Governor Of North Carolina Said ---

Jack Diamond's Widow Is Killed In Her Apartment

Body Discovered By Building Superintendent On Floor Of Living Room

BULLET WOUND FOUND IN HER RIGHT TEMPLE

Police Express Belief That Shooting Was Preceded By Quarrel

All Possible Methods Of Transportation Used To Distribute Brew

BEVERAGE IS SOURCE OF EMPLOYMENT FOR MANY

Both Bottled And Draught To Be Available After 6 A. M. — Sale Without Permits In Possession Forbidden

Quick Approval Of New Cotton Mill Code Is Indicated

Offer To Increase Minimum Pay $2 Wins Johnson's Praise

President Standing Pat Until True Levels Are Reached By Currencies

Shot To Death

Executive Council Confirms Nominees For Beer Board

Governor Will Rename Trio Today To Avoid Any

Organized Baseball May Return Here

TWO CONTROVERSIAL ISSUES INTRODUCED

"Oceans of Beer"

Talk about a great headline!

Mainers could finally do it: drink beer - legally - along with just about all of the rest of the nation. And do it they did. More than one million bottles of beer were on hand for opening day. Even the weather pitched in: it was one of those 90° scorchers when a brew or two tastes especially good. Newspapers throughout the state brimmed with both large and small beer ads and announcements. Included in the Press Herald on the day of its "Oceans of Beer" headline were advertisements for Pickwick Ale, Narragansett, Genesee, Elizabeth Brew, Aetna Special Dinner Ale ("Aetna Special is a real he-man drink - yet so delicate in flavor - so delicious in body - that women prefer it too"), Utica Club Pilsener, Trommer's Malt Beer ("has many enthusiastic friends and you'll surely be another after once sampling it"), Jacob

Ruppert's Knickerbocker, and Diamond Spring Ale. Goldenrod Lager promised in a full-page ad: "At last - the thrill you've been waiting for!" In the crush of excitement, Ebling's (a relatively well-known Bronx, New York brew) came out spelled "Eberling's", and Molson ended up being "Malsom." There was even an ad, and a large one at that, for a beer that never appeared: "Coming! Next Week!" ran the announcement heralding Old Stuyvesant, "America's Finest Mellowest Old Aged-In-The-Wood Beer." But next week never came.

Prices ran the gamut from $3.50 for Old England, to $3.80 for Edelbrau Lager, to $4.00 for Goldenrod. A case.

The Press Herald's page twelve headline summed it all up: "Happy Days Are Here Again!"

Old Breweries Never Die

◆

OR AT LEAST SOME OF THEM DON'T

Poking around the nooks and crannies and back streets of New England, from Portsmouth to Bridgeport - with thirty-three other former brewtowns in between - I found a surprising number of old breweries still standing. Leaning a little, perhaps, but still standing. Here are a few that smiled for my camera.

Note: for glimpses of other yet extant former New England breweries please see chapters B, H, M, P, S, U and X.

Hampden/Hampden-Harvard/Piel's
45-95 North Chicopee Street
Willimansett (Chicopee), Massachusetts

This, one of the largest more-or-less fully extant brewery complexes in New England, is a combination of old and, mostly, newer buildings. I took photos of only the old.

The brewery's site has lead a checkered life. Brewing started here, on the banks of the Connecticut River, in 1868 when Englishman William Briley built a small but highly successful brewhouse...so successful that within six years he was able to take the profits and retire back to England. The property was leased to a Mr. Crosley, who converted it to a dye plant. All was back to ground zero, though, when a fire completely demolished the facility two years later.

Things lay dormant until 1884, when a government study concluded that Hampden County - home of both Springfield and Chicopee - had the purest water in all of New England. A pair of ambitious Irishmen, John Coyne and Thomas McNierney, took note, decided to build a brewery in the county

. . . and ended up selecting the exact same site as William Briley had chosen sixteen years earlier. Ale, of course, was their only product. They, too, were successful and, in 1890, sold the enterprise to one Thomas Flanagan, and retired wealthy men. Flanagan, a native of Holyoke, honored his hometown by renaming the operation the Holyoke Brewing Company. The name by which the brewery is best known, Hampden, finally appeared in 1894: the company was incorporated as the Hampden Brewing Company, the name it kept even after being absorbed into the Springfield Breweries Company in 1899. For more on that - and Hampden's subsequent history - please turn ahead to pages 160-171. It's all there.

The former Megan's Cafe, 890 block of State Street, Springfield, November, 1987

November, 1987

Most of the former brewery is now occupied by Encon, Inc., riggers and haulers of heavy equipment. A lesser portion is utilized by Kellogg Brush Manufacturing Company.

"Locked Up"

"If you went to a bar and they had four taps there was Hampden Mild Ale, Hampden regular ale, Hampden Lager, and Hampden Porter. If they had three taps, we had three taps. We had 'em all locked up. The whole area."

Daniel Buckley, salesman for Hampden/Piel's from 1937 to 1975

Tucked away in an outbuilding is what almost certainly was the original Hampden Brewery building sign...all forty or so feet of it.

Cremo
John Downey Street at Belden Street
New Britain, Connecticut

What became the Cremo Brewing Company first saw life as the John Zunner Health Beer Company, also known as the Consumers Brewery. It was founded in 1903 by John Zunner, of Hartford. After fourteen months of operation, during which lager, ale, and porter were all brewed, the enterprise folded. In stepped John F. Skritulsky. Born in Lithuania in 1860, Skritulsky came to America in 1880, and New Britain in 1895. It was he who formed Cremo in January of 1905, and it was he who guided it, as president, through to prohibition and its successful re-opening after repeal.

Idle during prohibition, Cremo was completely modernized in 1933, opening anew to great fanfare in September: over 5,000 people turned out to tour the brewery and enjoy some of its product. The thirties saw good times at Cremo. Oscar G. Brockert, certainly one of New England's more experienced hands (see page 153) was brewmaster; sales were good; and the physical plant was expanded several times. The year 1938

January, 1988

was especially rewarding: a new bottling house was constructed, canning equipment was installed and, in a moment of late August drama before a crowd of over 1,000 wellwishers, John Skritulsky lighted a candle and burned the brewery's mortgage. Newspaper accounts the next day reported that "the entire gathering emitted a cheer that resounded throughout the neighborhood."

The early and mid forties weren't bad for Cremo either. Income passed $1,000,000 for the first time in fiscal 1944, with sales of 56,011 barrels, up from fiscal 1943's 36,058 barrels. The years 1945 and 1946 were good, too, but by 1947 most of the news out of the brewery concerned union difficulties and on again/off again strike threats. Management met union demands in August of 1947, but 1949 was a different story: a seventeen-day walkout that throttled the brewery in June was settled only when the state stepped in to arbitrate. Infighting within the corporation in the late forties and into the fifties - with various minority shareholder groups openly criticizing management - didn't help either. By the early fifties, Cremo was losing money steadily. By November, 1955 it was $135,000 in debt, losses were $6,000 a month, and the City of New Britain had a tax lien on the brewery's property. The company's stockholders voted overwhelmingly to dissolve.

Since 1956, most of what used to be Cremo has been utilized by Capitol Farms/Hartford Provision Company as a meat packing plant. Hot dogs, salami, bologna, sausage, frozen entrees, veal . . . you name it and if it's meat or poultry it's most likely processed at the former brewery, set in an almost pastoral location on the east side of town. I took a number of photos, talked with a couple of Provision employees, and was in my car about to drive off when out came Bob Knowlton, literally on the run. Word had somehow spread within the plant of my mission (good news spreads fast?!): Bob wanted to tell me that Capitol Farms is still using one of the original Cremo compressors, and that some of the old beer vats are still upstairs, too. More important, he told me about Marty's: "You oughta go up to Marty's Cafe. They still have a couple of full Cremo bottles," he advised me.

I was on the way. Marty's isn't hard to find. Located on Church Street not far from the brewery, it's a lively spot . . . even at 2:30 on a Thursday afternoon. Eight, maybe ten, people were congregating. There wasn't a Cremo bottle or piece of breweriana in sight, however: seems the former owner had taken it with him when he sold the place. Patron Ronnie Mele fixed that: "I've got a Diplomat bottle at home," offered Ronnie, at 47 a retired lieutenant in the New Britain Fire Department. "That was their top brand: the brand they sold in New York."

He was right. Diplomat was developed as Cremo's top of the line product in 1949. The extra profit per unit helped. But not enough.

Ronnie and his Diplomat bottle outside Marty's. When he went to get it, he asked me if he should shave for the photo. I told him, "Naw, you look great the way you are." And he does. And so does the Diplomat bottle.

Derby and Ansonia/Old England
324-332 Derby Avenue
Derby, Connecticut

"Not beautiful, but basic" is how the notes read from my Old England photo-taking session, January, 1988. Looking at the photos that resulted I'd agree with that assessment.

Founded by Herman Metzger in 1897 as the Derby and Ansonia Brewing Company, the firm's specialty was lager, with ale and porter brewed on a smaller scale. Brewing continued until 1920, when things ground to a halt.

The facility appears to have been used by the Southern New England Ice Company, Inc. during prohibition. It was purchased in the spring of 1933, for a price that was reputed to be in the range of $40,000, by Adolph Gosch, of Stratford, and renamed the Old England Brewing Company. Gosch, who served in the dual capacity of president and brewmaster, had been the pre-prohibition brewmaster at the Home Brewing Company in Bridgeport. His reign at Old England was short: in March of 1934, Henry Comen and Maurice Bailey, both of New Haven, purchased the brewery. They added lager to the ale and porter that Grosch had been brewing. Operations ceased in 1941.

Derby and Ansonia Brewery,
H. METZGER, Proprietor.

Real Genuine Wurzburger

BREWED OF THE BEST CANADA MALT
AND BAVARIAN HOPS ONLY.

AND BREWERS OF

Extra Fine ALE and PORTER

BOTTLED FOR FAMILY TRADE ON THE PREMISES.

328 DERBY AVENUE, DERBY, CONN.
TELEPHONE 347.

An ad, from the 1911 ANSONIA, DERBY, SHELTON AND SEYMOUR DIRECTORY, for Derby and Ansonia's "Real Genuine Wurzburger" . . . and a bottle, with embossed horseshoe and fancy script lettering, from which some of it presumably flowed.

The former brewery is today occupied by Sealand Environmental Services, Inc., a transporter of hazardous materials, and Bob's Canteen, a vending service. A sign on the front of the facility says that the buildings, in remarkably fine condition, were renovated in 1981.

The home that Herman Metzger built for himself still stands, too, looking resplendent across the street from the brewery, at 329 Derby Avenue. (and it's for sale, too . . . or at least it was when I took this photo in late January, 1988.)

The can that held Old England's Cream Ale, circa late 1930s, is now a favorite in my collection. The brewery's slogan for most of its eight-year after-prohibition existence: "It Satisfies All Thirsts."

94

Essex Brewing Company
Haverhill, Massachusetts

I have come to think of Essex as New England's phantom brewery. I've never, in over a quarter century of collecting, seen so much as a single, solitary piece of Essex breweriana. Absolutely no mention is made of it - or Haverhill, either - in ONE HUNDRED YEARS OF BREWING, the classic 718-page tome published in 1903 that purportedly gave a description of every American brewery then in existence. And the better part of a day beating my way around "The Queen Shoe City of the World" (or at least what used to be "The Queen Shoe City of the World," before imports flooded the market) produced almost nothing but frustration. With an address of "Railroad Br," I at least figured out that the "Br" stood not for "Bridge," but for "Bradford": the brewery had been in the Bradford section of the city, across the Merrimack River from Haverhill proper. But had it been on Railroad Avenue or Railroad Street? Bradford has both. The folks on Street said that it must've been on Avenue. And the folks on Avenue said that it must've been on Street. No one knew anything about it. Or wanted to know anything about it. Or wanted to claim it.

George to the Rescue

I finally called my old rhythm and blues' record collecting buddy, George Moonoogian. "Help," I said. And George, a lifetime Haverhill resident, came through! He talked with his mother, his father-in-law, and others. He prowled around Bradford, where he had himself lived as a kid. And he finally concluded that the very building in which he'd played war as a wild and wooly urchin was all that was left of the former brewery.

The Only Problem

Ralph Paul, George's father-in-law, is positive that the brick structure George played in marks the spot. That that's where Essex was after prohibition. And Ralph should know: in his early seventies, he's been a Havrillian (or "Hillie," as Haverhill High's teams are known. "Haverhill's built on seven hills, just like Rome," George told me over an ale after our field work was done.) all his years. Plus, all those years have been spent in the exact neighborhood as the phantom brewery. The only problem is that the building he swears by as having been Essex is not supported by what other information is available. But George believes Ralph. And so do I. I suspect that "Ralph's building" was an outbuilding, a warehouse or truck storage facility, or the like. But part of the brewery complex. Besides, for all his efforts for the good of the book, we had to have something for George to pose in front of!

What Is Known for Sure

What is known for sure is that the brewery that became Essex was founded by Karl E. Schlossstein in 1899. It became the Essex Brewing Company in 1901, with George W. Smith and William Smith, Jr. as proprietors. William, Jr. passed out of the picture in 1905; only George W. is included in corporate ownership listings thereafter, through to prohibition.

George W. Smith — Wm. Smith, Jr

ESSEX BREWERY

Ale, Porter and Lager Beer Brewers

HAVERHILL, MASS.

OFFICE, 168 MERRIMACK STREET.   N E. Tel. 121-3.

In its seventeen years of pre-prohibition life, Essex splurged for an ad in the local HAVERHILL AND GROVELAND DIRECTORY but once, in 1903. This is it.

Essex, which fell into a bad state of disrepair during the 1920s and early thirties, was slow to re-open after repeal. It wasn't until the summer of 1935 that things hummed again. After a very brief period when Howard M. Jenness headed up the operation, local dairyman Elmer G. Butrick (proprietor of Butrick's Pure Milk Dairy: "Dairy Products That Satisfy") took over. Brewmaster was John, usually known as Big John, Ebersold, who'd been on the brewing scene in Europe and the U.S.A. since 1899, including a twenty-year stint with the Hubert Fischer Brewing Company in Hartford. Lager, ale, and porter, all with the Essex name, were brewed. Capacity was 50,000 to 60,000 barrels. Management was especially proud of its well, 365 feet deep, and the purity of the water it provided. In spite of much puff ("See how the famous old Essex ale and lager is made and why it will be the most popular brew in Essex county and eventually place Haverhill foremost in the minds of the rest of the world as it did in days of old," proclaimed a 1935 invitation to come on out and see the brewery; "Nothing Better Can Be Brewed" rang a 1938 ad), Essex never really got far off the ground after prohibition. George's mother, 82-year old Marie Sapareto, may have the answer why: she will tell you that the beer Essex made before prohibition was "the real beer; the later stuff was bad." Elmer Butrick gave up in 1936. George A. Adams, general manager since the operation had re-opened in '35, took over as president for what turned out to be the brewery's last year of operation. The company went bankrupt in late 1937; the buildings and equipment were sold - for $30,000 to the sole bidder - at a receiver's sale in April, 1938.

January, 1988

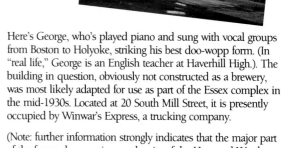

Here's George, who's played piano and sung with vocal groups from Boston to Holyoke, striking his best doo-wopp form. (In "real life," George is an English teacher at Haverhill High.). The building in question, obviously not constructed as a brewery, was most likely adapted for use as part of the Essex complex in the mid-1930s. Located at 20 South Mill Street, it is presently occupied by Winwar's Express, a trucking company.

(Note: further information strongly indicates that the major part of the former brewery is now the site of the Hoyt and Worthen Tanning Corporation on Railroad Avenue, and that all or virtually all of the brewery's buildings were demolished in 1968.)

95

Portsmouth, New Hampshire

Two of Portsmouth's three former breweries still stand, although time and the wrecking ball have taken their toll. The third, the original Eldridge Brewing Company, 24-26 Bow Street, is completely gone. On its site is now the parking lot for the Thomas J. McIntyre Federal Building.

The Portsmouth Brewing Company

Altered considerably, much of the former home of Portsburger Lager, 62-64 Bow Street, was converted into the Theatre By The Sea in 1978-79. The major alteration, a rather remarkable architectural feat, was the removal of the six steel columns that held up the entire load of the brick building - all 1.8 million pounds of it - in favor of a support system which would afford playgoers an unobstructed view.

March, 1988

After eight years of off and on success, Theatre By The Sea is, as of this writing (late March, 1988), at least semi-dormant. No plans, however, are in the works to convert its space to anything else. Other portions of the old brewing facility are occupied by the Theatre Inn, and residential condominium units. An upper level, affectionately known as "the great ranch house in the sky" in local real estate parlance, was added some years ago, as was, of course, the glassed-in theatre lobby/ticket office on the right.

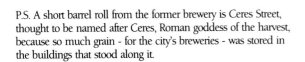

P.S. A short barrel roll from the former brewery is Ceres Street, thought to be named after Ceres, Roman goddess of the harvest, because so much grain - for the city's breweries - was stored in the buildings that stood along it.

Across the street and over some from the former brewery - about where I stood when I took my photo - is a church parking lot. And in that portion of the lot reserved for the church's clergy is this sign. I couldn't resist snapping a photo of it.

Frank Jones (and After-Prohibition Eldridge) Brewing Company

A glance at the "Open To The World" and "Largest Ale Brewers in the World" postcard views on page 73 will give you a good idea of how much the former Frank Jones' complex, at Cate and Islington Streets, has been thinned out. Today's focal point and tallest structure (directly to the left of the clock tower in the postal views) was little more than a stepchild during the brewery's heyday. And yet, while the clock tower (with its forever unfurled flag) and many other buildings are gone, the complex still gives one a sense of sprawl. And immenseness. You find yourself thinking that, if the brewery's area appears this huge now - after so much of it has been demolished - what must it have been like eighty or ninety years ago when it was in full tilt?!

All photos, March, 1988

The buildings that remain have various uses. The largest portion is home to Schultz Meats/New Hampshire Provision Company. Other sections are used by National Discount Mattress, and the Department of Public Works for the City of Portsmouth. And the old malthouse has recently been converted into the Malt House Exchange, a series of shops that includes the Malt House (see page 128), a restaurant and bar that, appropriately enough, features a nice selection of ales.

Meriden/Connecticut Valley
137-157 South Colony Street
Meriden, Connecticut

Alex Gryga, 82, has lived across South Colony Street from what used to be the Meriden/Connecticut Valley brewery for the better part of his life. He recalls the brewery's beer well: had it in kegs - eight of 'em - at his wedding, back on Thanksgiving Day, 1934. (Note: Alex had a little difficulty remembering the year of his marriage when I chatted with him. But he had no trouble at all in recalling the eight kegs!). "It was a good beer. Better than today's beers," he'll tell you.

Looking at what remains of the brewery, it's hard to imagine much of anything tasty coming out of it. Much of the facility is deserted, looked after now only by pigeons. Part of it is used by a welding company. But the words "Connecticut Valley Br" are still clearly legible atop the railroad tracks' side of the old building. That was enough to get me excited.

Much of the former brewery is today abandoned, in bad state of disrepair. The part that is maintained is the home of Storts Welding Company, Inc.

January, 1988

1900 ad included within the pages of the FIRST REGIMENT, CONNECTICUT VOLUNTEERS' OFFICIAL HISTORY, SPANISH-AMERICAN WAR

Meriden Brewing Co.

Ales   Lager
Porter   Beer

GOLDEN PALE ALE
CANADA MALT ALE
EXTRA PORTER
PALE EXTRA
LAGER

ALL BOTTLED AT BREWERY AND SOLD AT MODERATE PRICES
TO THE TRADE.

MERIDEN,   CONN.

(Note: there was a much earlier, nonrelated Connecticut Valley Brewing Company that operated from 1898 to 1915 in Thompsonville, Connecticut (part of Enfield), a town so small that it isn't even included on my trusty Exxon map. No remnant of that Connecticut Valley brewery exists today. Where it once stood there is a Connecticut Light and Power plant.)

The Meriden Brewing Company was founded in 1887 by J.H. McMahon, P.W. Wren, J.A. Hurley, and W.E. Green. Within the space of three years, on October 1, 1890, it was merged into the Connecticut Breweries Company, a corporation consisting of Meriden Brewing and the Albert Wintter and Co. brewery in Bridgeport. Though corporate headquarters were in Bridgeport, operations on South Colony Street appear not to have been much changed. Average output was 35,000 barrels, with ale, porter, and lager all brewed, and sold - according to the 1900 ad reproduced here - "at moderate prices."

At some point, seemingly soon after the turn of the century, the company started using "Nutmeg" as the brand name for its ale and lager. (It's a name I still consider superb for any hearty and flavorful malt nectar that might be brewed in Connecticut. The state deserves its own micro. And Nutmeg Amber sure sounds good to me. Nathan Hale Ale has a nice ring, too.) Other, less quixotic, brand names used prior to prohibition included Munchner and Ideal (both lagers) and Royal (which was an ale).

During prohibition, or at least during the latter part of it, the former brewing facility was utilized by the Silver City Beverage Company. Some say, however, that Silver City was controlled by notorious gangsters Waxey Gorden and Jack "Legs" Diamond, and that whatever soft drink output there might have

been was merely camouflage: that bootleg beer was what was really going on behind those old brick walls.

In February, 1933, Silver City Beverage was purchased by the newly formed Connecticut Valley Brewing Company for $51,000. Thomas E. Coleman was the new company's first president. By June of 1934, however, he'd already stepped down - becoming secretary-treasurer - to make way for Otto Thieme as prexy of what *Brewer's News*, in its June 14, 1934 issue, called "a refitted and reconditioned plant," with a capacity estimated at 100,000 barrels. To more speedily package their brews, Connecticut Valley Ale and Beer, the company invested in a new and large bottling line in the early months of '34.

It was money poorly spent. Before 1934 was out, Connecticut Valley was in bankruptcy; by the end of 1935 they were out of business.

Meriden also had a second, much smaller, brewery. Begun by Charles Schabel in 1892, it appears to have specialized in the manufacture of weiss beer, and to have passed through several changes in proprietorship before closing its doors in 1912. No remains of the brewery, located cross town from Meriden Brewing in South Meridan, survive.

Weiss - or wheat - beer was a relatively popular American malt beverage through the early years of this century. The Weiss tradition is today carried on by at least two of America's smaller brewers, August Schell, New Ulm, Minnesota, and Fritz Maytag's Anchor Brewing Company, San Francisco.

Rex/Staehly and Quinnipiac/Yale

I once lived in Connecticut for nine years, and Connecticut cities yet conjure up certain images for me. Waterbury reminds me of wonderful times with my sons watching Eastern League baseball; Bridgeport reminds me that not everyone in Connecticut is rich; Hartford brings visions of traffic jams; Norwich makes me think of potential; Stonington, beauty. Ah, but New Haven: it makes me think back to the wonder of rhythm and blues vocal group harmony. It was all there in the Elm City, 1952 or so right through the early sixties; the Nutmegs (Story Untold; Ship of Love; Whispering Sorrows), Wes Forbes and the Starlarks (Fountain of Love), Ruby Whitaker and the Chestnuts (Love Is True; Forever I Vow; Who Knows Better than I?), the Scarlets (True Love; Dear One), the Pyramids (Okay, Baby), and the Academics (Too Good to be True). If none of these songs rings too many bells, there's one that will. Recorded in the basement of St. Bernadette's Church in East Haven on a two-track recorder in 1955, it has gone on to become THE classic fifties' love ballad: (I'll Remember) In the Still of the Night, by the Five Satins.

1950's rock 'n roll was far, far more than just electric guitars and Fats, Chuck, Elvis, Little Richard and the other single artists of the day, as good as they were. It was also, especially for me, the mellow sound of four or five voices singing in sweet harmony, a harmony to which New Haven's groups so richly contributed.

With some of the old sounds in my head - and my heart - and a Natco Street map of New Haven in my hand, my son Curt and I set out to find what all remained from the city's reigning days as king of Connecticut's brewing centers.

First stop, of course, had to be Hull's, the state's last operational brewery (please see Give 'em Hull, pages 42-45). Although it's been but eleven years since Hull's brewed its last batch, nothing at all remains of the brewery. On the 800-820 Congress Street sight is now a rather bleak two-story housing project. That pretty much set the tone for most of the rest of the day.

Around the corner, at 369-376 Davenport Avenue (named for John Davenport, whose band of Puritans settled New Haven three and a half centuries ago), we did find Rex/Staehly, a very short-lived after-prohibition-only operation. It was hardly a gem, but at least it was there. That's certainly more than can be said for our next stop. Wehle (the Weidemann Brewing Company before prohibition), in operation through 1943 at 1131 Campbell Avenue, West Haven, is completely gone, replaced by a Railroad Salvage discount store and a McDonald's.

Next was George A. Basserman's Rock Brewery, located at 21-57 Rock Street near East Rock Park. Since Basserman went out of business away back in 1891, we didn't really expect to find much. And we didn't: all that's there now is a wooded slope.

We had even worse luck with our next two targets: the Weibel Brewing Company, listed alternately at 322 Oak Street and 270 Legion Avenue, and Elm City, 14-22 Whiting Street. After almost giving up several times - with all its one-way streets, to find any given address in New Haven you end up seeing substantially more of the city than you'd ever imagined in even your wildest dreams - we took a gas station attendant's advice. "Go to the fire station three blocks up: they know everything and they have a huge map, too," he said. He was right: at the station, Captain Robert Callahan set us straight. "No use looking for Whiting Street," he told us. "It doesn't exist anywhere." Seems the street and all its structures - including old breweries -had long since been done in, replaced by the New Haven Coliseum and a host of other relatively modern buildings. No respect. Legion Avenue is still there (we never did find Oak Street), but that's about all you can say, at least along the stretch where Weibel's ("New Haven's Old Time Brewery") used to be. It's now occupied by a large expanse of cleared land.

By this time in the day it was getting late. I was beginning to think that my title for this chapter was a misnomer: old breweries do die. Plus the ones that I'd been finding yet extant were far from architectural award winners. But suddenly there it was. I fairly shouted "Curt, it's a brewery, it's a brewery!" I couldn't believe it. And what a brewery: with but one sweeping look it restored completely my faith in the beauty of those old time brick edifices from which ale and beer and porter flowed. If BEER, NEW ENGLAND could've had a centerfold . . . this would've been it!!

Built to last forever, old breweries often end up as storage facilities. Such is the story with the former Rex/Staehly brewery. With a capacity of 42,000 barrels, the Rex Brewing Company opened for business in 1933, destined for a short, short life. It closed in 1934. Two years later, Emil Staehly, owner of the Staehly Bottling Works in West Haven, gave things a second shot. He operated the facility as the Staehly Brewing Company, also destined for a short, short life. It closed in 1937. Most of the former brewery is today occupied by the Orchard Storage Company, agent for National Van Lines.

What would win my still-standing New England Brewery Beautiful Award - hands down - was founded in 1882 by Peter Schleippmann and William Spittler. They called it Schleippmann & Spittler. In September of 1885, after fire had ravaged much of the plant, the enterprise was reorganized as the Quinnipiac Brewing Company (When John Davenport and his band of Puritans settled New Haven in 1638 they didn't name it New Haven: they named it Quinnipiac - "long water people" - in honor of the Indian tribe that used the area as part of their hunting ground. "New Haven" was adopted in 1640.). While Quinnipiac was headed by absentee president William Northwood of Detroit, Spittler stayed on as secretary. The big three of ale, porter, and lager were all brewed, with lager the specialty. About 1895, N.W. Kendall, the son of a hop farmer, bought out Northwood's interest and became president. Kendall, who'd been Quinnipiac's treasurer since its inception, was a mover and shaker. He served the U.S. Brewers'

Association as both president and vice-president, and it was he who organized the once-important Connecticut Brewers' Association. And, in July of 1902, he guided the corporation through another change in name: to the Yale Brewing Company. With Kendall at the helm, Yale brewed until prohibition, then produced a non-alcoholic beer.

In August of 1933 the facility was purchased by the newly-organized New Haven Brewing Company, headed by powerful Newark, New Jersey brewer Christian Feigenspan. No beer, however, appears to have ever been brewed after repeal. In fact, the next use for the former brewery seems to have been as a Civil Defense storage center during World War II, followed by life as a National Gypsum factory. Bottom was seemingly reached when the grand old edifice became a storage depot for used tires. Worse yet, the brewery's area in the Fair Haven section of the city, which once laid title to oyster capital of America, had fallen on hard times, too, with the brewery site more or less the neighborhood garbage dump.

All photos: January, 1988

"A lot of angles" is what Curt noticed most about the former brewery, located at the confluence of Ferry, Pearl, and River Streets, overlooking the Quinnipiac river. He admired the workmanship of the stonework, too. We both agreed that the buildings, Romanesque Revival in style, had been most assuredly crafted for beauty as well as for function.

Rescue

When all appeared as good as lost, in stepped a trio of Cambridge, Massachusetts firms that, working together, specialize in the conversion of historic 19th century industrial and commercial structures to modern-day use. With the help of New Haven's first Urban Development Action Grant, they, starting in 1983, poured $16 million into what was named Brewery Square. The results: 104 apartment and twenty-seven condominium units. And a neat place to live. Commented Inget Gruttner, who's lived at "The Square" since the first units became available in 1984, "You don't even need heat in the winter or air conditioning in the summer: the old brewery's built that well!"

LOOK
WHAT'S
BREWING IN
NEW HAVEN

BREWERY SQUARE

One Brewery Square, New Haven, CT 06513
(203) 776-4456

We can thank the Cambridge Development Corporation, Bruner/Cott and Associates, and the Shoreline Corporation, working with the City of New Haven, for the grandeur that is Brewery Square. And, I'm delighted to be able to say, it's a venture that has turned out profitably for everyone concerned. Sales and Rental Manager Mary Ellen Squeglia reports that but a very few units remain unspoken for; that all is well on the banks of the Quinnipiac.

101

Paris of the Naugatuck Valley

◆

A TALE OF WATERBURY'S TWO BREWERIES

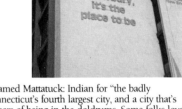

Waterbury (originally named Mattatuck: Indian for "the badly wooded region") is Connecticut's fourth largest city, and a city that's now blossoming after years of being in the doldrums. Some folks love the growth, feel it's long overdue; others decry it, feel it will erase the city's character and family atmosphere.

When my older son, Carl, was about four, he and I drove through Waterbury on Interstate 84. I, in a fatherly tone, said, "Son, this is Waterbury." He, in a childly tone, said, "Where's the water?" Noticing for the first time — and I'd driven in and about Waterbury scores and scores of times —that there really wasn't any, or any that was readily visable, I beamed. "What a bright child I have," thought I. In a fatherly tone, of course.

Well, Carl's now twenty-three, and the city that Charles Monagan called the "Paris of the Naugatuck Valley" in his September, 1987 *Yankee Magazine* article "Will the Real Waterbury Asert Itself?" is still lacking any highly visable body of water, though obviously the Naugatuck is out there somewhere. But what Waterbury doesn't lack, as you've probably already surmised, is a worthy brewing tradition.

A beer they could call their own came to Waterburians in 1874. In that year Frederick Nuhn set up shop at 358 Bank Street, in what was then known as Nuhn's Grove. But the output of his lager-only Naugatuck Valley Brewery was limited. Business was slow until Martin Hellman and Michael Kipp purchased the operation in 1881. Under their leadership both sales and capacity were increased. In 1891 operations were moved to 1090 Bank Street, in the Brooklyn section of the city. Ale was added in 1895.

Martin Hellman, who bought out his partner Kipp in 1889, died in 1892. His widow, Sibilla, proved more than capable of carrying on. Under her guidance the brewery was incorporated as the Hellman Brewing Company in 1895 and brewed Pallida Lager and Alpha Ale, among others, until the unwelcome arrival of prohibition in 1920.

Enter George H. Largay, who might rightly be called a brewer's brewer, and whose introduction to the world of brewing was right out of Horatio Alger: the brewmaster of the Star Brewing Company in Boston happened upon him unloading a carload of coal one day — obviously with great vigor — and in effect said, "Hey, kid, how'd you like to work for me?" That was 1897. George was eighteen, in search of a career. He found it in brewing: so impressed was he that he decided to save $2.00 each week (out of his total pay of $7.00 for a 63-hour workweek) toward the $500.00 it took to attend the National Brewers' Academy in New York City. It took five years of

Two 1880's views of the brewery during its Hellman & Kipp days. Hellman ran the business side of things; Kipp, who was trained in Germany, the brewing end.

HELLMANN & KIPP'S LAGER BEER BREWERY.

An advertisement for Hellman from the 1903 WATERBURY AND NAUGATUCK DIRECTORY. The adjacent Hygeia Ice Company plant, erected in 1901, was under the same ownership as the brewery.

I don't know about in real life, but on bock beer posters and calendars goats always seem to have such personality. I recently ran across this gem of a circa 1900 poster in a northwestern Connecticut antique shop, and was I ever delighted.

saving, but he made it, graduating in 1902.

From 1903 to 1908 our future Waterburian honed his skills, serving as assistant brewmaster in New Hampshire (True W. Jones, Manchester) and Virginia (Consumers' Brewing Company, Norfolk), then headed for the greater glory of Montreal and an assistant brewmaster post with Molson's. Next came his first full brewmastership, with A. Keith & Son, in Halifax, Nova Scotia. From 1918 until prohibition, he served as brewmaster for C.H. Evans & Sons, of Hudson, New York, brewers of the widely reknowned Evans Ale.

Prohibition gave George Largay a good chance to reflect...and to realize that he'd like to operate his own brewery. And if one brewery is good, he must have reasoned, two is probably better. He ended up buying both the former Harry F. Bowler Brewery in Amsterdam, New York (which he operated as the Amsterdam Brewing Company from 1933 to 1940) as well as, of course, this chapter's feature brewery: the former Hellman brewery in Waterbury. Were it not for the honor of a gentleman, however, the

Cont'd. on page 106

Vin Largay in front of one of the several red fox portraits that adorn his office, January, 1988.

A Brewer's Son Remembers

When I approached Vin (Vincent) Largay, at 57 the Chariman and C.E.O. of Buell Industries, a manufacturer of car parts and a major Waterbury employer, he was somewhat hesistant. "This is the first time I've discussed the brewing industry in fifteen or twenty years," he cautioned. But he warmed to the task, ended by commenting that he guessed he knew considerably more than he'd thought. Yes, Vin, you do. Thanks.

On Growing Up Part of a Brewing Family

It was a very intimate thing. I think that it was an extraordinary thing that we were very much a part of: the business part of it. Because my father would come home for lunch every day and whoever happened to be there — a salesman or a customer or a visitor — he'd bring him home. And even as young people seated around the table we would hear them discussing things. So I think that probably the entrepreneurial spirit was fostered by those kind of discussions. He had nine boys — seven of his own and two adopted — and eight of the nine ended up being heads of their own companies.

On Working in the Brewery During the War

I had worked there (at the brewery) part time during the war when they were manufacturing a lot of beer and shipping it to the troops overseas. The beer was packaged in double cases of bottles with recycled metal for metal caps and sawdust around the bottles. They would strap two of these cases together with adhesives and strapping, and the idea was, when you came to a military port that had limited dock space, they could push these beer cases over the side and float them into shore. I don't think a case of beer ever saw the water. Munitions, maybe yes. But not beer.

On the Tearing Down of the Brewery

The Redevelopment Agency in Waterbury wanted to acquire it (the site). And unfortunately at that time they didn't have the foresight to rehabilitate facilities like they do today and just decided to put a ball to the whole thing.

On Mazeika's Cafe...and Being Thirsty in Waterbury

I don't remember that one specifically, but I do remember that just on Bank Street there must have been fifteen or twenty bars. Each neighborhood had a couple. There was no chance of anyone dying of thirst in this town. (note: it would have been difficult for Vin to remember Mazeika's: it was strictly a pre-prohibition establishment, in operation from 1906 until 1920...long before Vin was even born.).

Circa 1915 Mazeika's Cafe advertising poster

On How Red Fox, the Brewery's Primary Brand Name, Came To Be

When prohibition was repealed, he (my father) had a meeting one day with my uncle (Mark Gallagher), who was actually a clothes designer, but he was a marketing type, and he said, "George, what would you like to call your beer?" and he (my father) said "Red Fox." He'd always had a fondness for the red fox as an animal. He was a great sportsman. A hunter and a fisherman and an outdoorsman, and the red fox had always particularly fascinated him. He respected it.

But he (my father) said how could you ever get a slogan that would be appropriate? And my uncle said, "That's very simple: 'Just What You've Been Hunting For.' " I think that it was as simple as that. And they actually did use that slogan. (Note: a check with Ken Ostrow of Newton, Massachusetts, a New England breweriana collector and historian, reveals that Red Fox was not a brand name that was new with Largay: it was used prior to prohibition by Massachusetts Breweries, a Boston combine (see page 105). Ken also pointed out that Largay used Black Fox as a brand name as well, although not nearly to the extent that it used Red Fox.)

Red Fox Light Beer label from 1940 or so . . . long before "light" became pretty much a synonym for low calorie.

Waterbury Republican photo

Two views of George H. Largay from those happy days when beer came back . . . and the dream of his own brewery (actually, breweries) came true.

Red Fox when it was a name used by Massachusetts Breweries. This delightfully-worded ad is from the souvenir program of Newburyport, Massachusetts' 50th anniversary as an incorporated city, June 24-26th, 1901.

On His Father's Consumption - Or Non-Consumption - of Beer and Other Alcoholic Beverages

He never drank. He would taste the beer, swish it around in his mouth, and spit it out. He had a very acute taste; could taste the competitive beers and tell you, with unmarked labels, whose beer was which and so forth. But he never drank any.

On Why His Father Settled on Waterbury

My guess is that he heard it (the brewery) was a good facility and a good deal, and decided it would be a good place to raise his family. But that's speculation on my part.

February, 1966, Waterbury Republican photo

June, 1967, Waterbury Republican photo

Although looking as massive - and almost as majestic - as during its heyday, the former brewery's months were numbered when these two shots were taken.

Waterbury deal would not have gone through. Vin Largay, youngest of George Largay's eleven children, reminisces: "I recall the story of him buying the brewery. He bought it from Judge Hellman (Charles M., presumably Sibilla's son) over in Meriden. He went over to see him and told him who he was and what he wanted to do and made an offer. The gentleman said fine, and he stood up and shook hands. My father asked if he wanted a deposit. The gentleman said, 'We just shook hands.' A few hours later someone came in and offered him a very substantial premium above what my father had offered him, and the gentleman said, 'I'm sorry, I have a contract.' And the other man said, 'Well, is it a written contract?' And the Judge said, 'No, we shook hands on it.'"

Brewery in hand (no pun intended, of course), George set out to make it as up-to-date and modern as possible. And he did. "We have a remarkably fine plant and we will put out a wonderful glass of beer," George was quoted as saying in the April 22nd, 1933 issue of the *Brewing Industry*, a trade paper of the day. And, again, he did

just that — put out a wonderful glass of beer — as many an oldtimer around Waterbury will gladly attest to.

It was not enough. As rugged as life increasingly became for all of New England's small brewers (Largay's capacity, at peak, was 150,000 barrels. Toward its end, it also owned and operated the larger New England Brewing Company, of Hartford, but the two still added up to a pittance compared with the nationals), the proximity of New York City made things that much worse for Connecticut's brewers. There was simply no way to match the muscle — and dollars — of the Big Apple's Jacob Ruppert (Knickerbocker), S. Liebmann's Sons (Rheingold), Schaefer, or Piel's. As early as 1933, in fact, the Connecticut Brewer's Association complained that the Nutmeg State had "become a dumping ground for the products of out-of-state breweries."

It got worse. Vin Largay again: "The introduction of television and mass marketing really hurt. We probably had a couple hundred billboards around the state. And I don't know what the advertising budget was. We had taken our present business there (at the Bank Street facility) and grown it to the point where it was very inefficient to

The William V. Begg, Jr. Apartments January, 1988

After the brewery's closing, Vin's older brother John (who I was privileged to meet in 1975) used the facility to launch what is now Buell Industries, but was then Connecticut Screw and Rivet. Sold to the Waterbury Redevelopment Agency in 1967, the 76-year old complex was demolished later that year. On the site now stands the William V. Begg, Jr. Apartments, an eight-story senior citizen's home.

The Waterbury (and Eastern, too) Brewing Company was obviously no stranger to matchbook advertising. Represented here are several of the brands they produced during their short after-prohibition existence.

Looking resplendent on the occasion of its second birthday: Eagle as it appeared in a 1903 WATERBURY CITY DIRECTORY advertisement. Riverside Park was a section of the city, touted as "for residences of the better quality," that was being developed at the time.

EAGLE BREWING CO.,

BREWERS OF CHOICEST

Lager Beer,

Ale and Porter.

Riverside Park,

WATERBURY, CONN.

operate in that facility. It would have meant a massive investment in new plant and equipment to compete. We were faced with competition out of the New York markets from television and advertising and, I guess, (we had) limited resources. I believe there was a difficult union situation involved, too, with the Brewery Worker's Union. Also, my older brother John had worked for the War Production Board at the end of the war (World War II): he had been in the grain allocation end of it, and I guess saw the firepower of the Budweisers and the Millers and those type of people."

Given all of the above less than blissful circumstances it's no wonder that the Largays decided to pack it in. Ruppert made them an offer in 1947 — for the Largay brand names and equipment only, not the brewery — and they accepted.

Eagle/Waterbury/Eastern Brewing Company

The second of Waterbury's two breweries lead a short, but colorful to say the least, life. Founded in 1901 by Thomas Finnegan and Paul Suese as the Eagle Brewing Company, the ownership semi-changed hands almost immediately: Thomas H. Hayes replaced Suese as co-proprietor in

1902. In July of 1903 the firm, with a capitalization of $25,000, was incorporated. Hayes, an Irishman who'd come to America to seek his fortunes as a teenager, was president, while Finnegan served as treasurer. In April, 1913 Hayes died and - almost as a sequel to Sibilla Hellman, in a scenario that could be entitled WATERBURY AND HER WOMEN - his widow, Ellen, took over as head of the brewery and remained

his dad at the brewery, was more or less general manager (under his mother) in the years preceeding prohibition. Daniel J. Leary, born in Waterbury in February of 1892, was educated in the city's public schools and Waterbury Business College. After various local positions, he started as an accountant at Eagle in January, 1911, rose to treasurer within a few years, and was the brewery's president during all of its

In Happier Days

Waterbury Republican photos

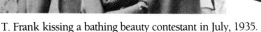
T. Frank kissing a bathing beauty contestant in July, 1935.

His Honor in May, 1938, two years and ten months before he became #14,563 at Wethersfield State.

And, below, his trusty comptroller, also May, 1938, two years and ten months before he took off for parts unknown.

You've probably heard the one about the guy who went out for a corned beef sandwich and the sandwich came back but he didn't. Well, that's about the way it was with Dan Leary. On the evening of March 6, 1941 - the day his conviction was upheld by an Appeals Court - he told his family he was going downtown and would "be back after a while." "After a while" turned out to be six years: it wasn't until February of 1946 that Leary - who insisted that he was James Donovan, a religious goods salesman - was found in Chicago and extradited back home to start his prison term.

at the helm until prohibition.

How To Describe T. Frank Hayes and Dan Leary?

Enter the Frank and Dan Show. T. Frank Hayes was Ellen and Thomas' son, born unto them in July, 1883. He worked with

fairly short after-prohibition life.

But both men had goals that transcended brewing. T. Frank Hayes used his family's extensive real estate holdings as a springboard into politics. Beginning with an appointment to the Board of Charities in 1922, he progressed to the Board of

Education, state senator, lieutenant governor (two terms under Wilbur Cross), and mayor - for five terms - of Waterbury. Dan Leary's record was not unimpressive, either. Appointed a member of the Board of Finances in 1921, he became an alderman in 1928, and was elected city comptroller, under Frank Hayes, from 1929 until defeated in 1937. That defeat - by a scant margin of 37 votes - triggered an investigation into Waterbury's finances that would rock the city for years to come.

How to describe T. Frank Hayes and Dan Leary? Powerful? Amibitious? Mischievous? How about guilty: that's what the Supreme Court of the State of Connecticut found them in 1939 in the locally-infamous Waterbury Conspiracy Trial: guilty of attempting to defraud the City of Waterbury out of millions of dollars. Twenty-three persons in all were convicted, with Hayes and Leary receiving far and away the most severe sentences: ten to fifteen at Wethersfield State Prison. Hayes eventually served six years, Leary seven.

The brewery? It made its way through the thirties, 1933 to 1938 anyway, as the Waterbury Brewing Company. Being on the same team as the ruling political machine had some obvious benefits. Vin Largay laughed when I asked him what he knew of Largay's competitor: "They had interesting marketing programs, I understand. Like if you didn't stock their beer in your tavern the water or gas didn't come into your place. Things of that sort. It was very direct."

With the Conspiracy Trial, which was about the biggest show in town from 1937 through 1939, in full swing Leary changed the name of the brewery to the Eastern Brewing Corporation in late 1938. But he remained as prexy.

It mattered little, however. With its political clout gone the brewery was almost history. It closed in late 1939.

The former brewery, located at 100 Eagle Street just up from Brewery Street, has certainly fared better than its old rival. No housing project here. Most of the facility is now occupied by Prolastomer, Inc., manufactuers and distributors of pelletized plastic products.

January, 1988

January, 1988

On that street, Brewery Street, where old friends - and brothers - meet. Here are my two sons admiring the view of the still impressive (don't they look impressed?) former home of Eagle/Waterbury/Eastern. That's Carl on the left, Curt on the right.

109

Quintessential They're Not

◆

BUT GOOD THEY ARE: IN PURSUIT OF NEW ENGLAND'S
BEST BEER-DRINKING BARS

My idea of the quintessential — containing all the elements of perfection — bar would include two or three ales, a porter, and two or three lagers. All on draught. All preferably American made. And all at circa 1958 prices.

No video games.

A degree of age, since age so often gives character.

Maybe some interesting older photos or the like on the walls. Baseball is best. Football and basketball and boxing count. But not for much. Wrestling doesn't count at all.

The jukebox - of course there'd be a jukebox - would include the Moonglows,

Nutmegs, and Heartbeats, and Fats and Chuck, as well as Bob Seger, plenty of Rolling Stones, plus a goodly dose of country and western, the real plaintive, tearjerk kind.

There'd be good
sounds on the juke box

Plus there'd be mouthwatering food at cheapie prices, witty and charming and friendly personnel, smoke free air, a good - but not overwhelming - mix of patrons, etc., etc., etc..

With the above in mind, my friend Penny — fresh from her assistance at the Northampton Brewery (see page 65) — joined me. Not in search of the quintessential bar. Not even in search of New England's best beer-drinking bars. (That would come later: see pages 117-131). No, we decided it would be more meaningful - not to mention more manageable! - if we researched a number of bars, attempting to develop helping hints so that you - yes, you - could seek out your own "quintessential" watering hole(s).

We decided to pick one target city. Small enough to be do-able; large enough to offer some variety. And, to minimize pre-conceived notions, we decided it should be a city to which neither of us had ever been.

We chose Burlington, Vermont.

Founded in 1771, Burlington (population 37,700) is Vermont's largest city and the economic, cultural and social hub of the state.

Vermont's Queen City

Burlington is a hot town. Rand McNally's PLACES RATED ALMANAC calls it the second best small city in America. *Playboy* ranks the University of Vermont, located in the heart of the city by the lake, as the number four party school in the country. Folks who visit what is nicknamed "Vermont's Queen City" rave about it.

We drove up on Saturday, December 26th, the day after Christmas, secured lodging . . . and set out, Bar Information Sheets (hereinafter referred to as BIS; see page 116) in hand.

The Tour: Evening/Night One

Our first stop was not especially notable. We parked our car and walked along the city's historic Church Street Marketplace, a four-block pedestrian main street mall. It was beautiful, but the weather had turned biting cold and we were feeling much the same. The **QUEEN CITY TAVERN** (103 Church Street) looked fine. Bud, Heineken and Lite made for an unexciting draught selection. The place was smoky; the football game on the TV above the bar too loud. But everyone - employees and patrons alike - was friendly . . . and appreciative of our mission. Jim (Fraser: "It's not French, it's not German . . . it's Scottish"), the bartender, was especially appreciative. Noting that things might be slow with the area's five colleges all on Christmas break - "Come back in a few weeks when the students are all back!" - Jim still romanced a good six or eight places. We headed out.

The **DAILY PLANET** (15 Center Street) looks like it sounds: sort of modernistic deco. An antique toy car and Red Baron plane suspend from a nouveau pressed tin ceiling. The ladies' room is purple and green. The Redskins were beating the Vikings on a soundless TV.

I passed on the impressive draught selection - Guinness, Bass, John Courage, Molson Golden, Michelob, Lite - to try my first bottle of Catamount (Vermont's "state" brewery: see page 60) Holiday Porter. I was not disappointed. Nor were we disappointed in the food. The Planet's bar fare included burgers, nachos, Chinese noodles, burritos, salads, and soup of the day. Actually, soups of the day: cream of mushroom and Manhattan clam chowder (I came to Burlington, Vermont for Manhattan clam chowder?!). We settled on the cream of mushroom, which was so good (Penny: "Exquisite") that we almost lost sight of our real research mission. Fortunately, we caught ourselves in time.

The **DEJA VU CAFE** (185 Pearl Street) came highly recommended. "You'll love their beer selection," Jim had told us. We did . . . but I didn't much care for the atmosphere. A large tent-type sign outside the entrance that read "Tea Time 4-6:00" made me feel somewhat uneasy, and portended what was to come. Still, sixty-nine beers from twenty-two countries in bottles, plus John Courage, Molson Golden, Coors, and Michelob Light on tap, is nothing to sneeze at. Deja Vu, which bills itself as "A contemporary French bistro," is beautiful. Penny was impressed. With its exposed brick, polished woods and charming holiday decorations of small white lights with pine boughs, how could she not be? Still, the Deja Vu's drinking area can best be described as bar-surrounded-by-restaurant. Worse, every three minutes or so our bartender, a large-ish and formal woman who did not exude much warmth, turned on a pressurizing steamer for one of the establishment's obvious specialties, winter warmer drinks, giving the place all the atmosphere of a Boeing 747 at take-off. We concluded that the Deja Vu, while probably a fine choice for beer with dinner, was not a good place to come for beers alone, at least not at the bar.

After the Deja Vu, The **PUB** (71 Church Street) seemed a welcome relief. No formality here. Just a long, narrow twenty-two stooler (plus nine booths). Photos of softball and basketball teams lined the walls. "The Pub" t-shirts could be bought for $7.00 each. It was approaching 9:00 and the place was getting jammed with, as Penny put it, a "young and interactive" crowd. Friendship was evident and conversation was good. And loud: on the blackboard above the bar was chalked "If you don't answer by the 4th gong your (sic.) gone." The draught selection was Lite, Labatt's 50, and Pabst. I had a Pabst - at 90¢ a pint a good value - and a Shenandoah, which translated to a white meat of turkey and melted Swiss sandwich accompanied by a one-ounce bag of chips, all served in a red plastic basket. If not completely yum yum, it wasn't bad and, at $3.60, was good value, too.

111

CARBUR'S (115 St. Paul Street) is part of a small northeastern chain. "There's six of 'em" was about all our waiter - who hardly looked old enough to legally drink himself - could contribute. Carbur's decor is what I would call Old General Store. Some great stuff. Signs and posters and objects d'advertising. As at Deja Vu, the beer selection - bottled beer selection, anyway - is so extensive that a Beer List is on hand. Included are eighty-two brews from twenty-three countries, plus Heineken, Lite, Molson's Golden, and John Courage (which, we were told, has taken the city by storm the past year or so) on tap. Carbur's also sponsors a Beer Club. "Visit" each of the twenty-three countries represented on their Beer List - by sampling one of each country's brews, naturally - and you'll receive - "as a tribute to your Bon Vivanty and Connoisseurship" - an AROUND THE WORLD IN 80 BEERS t-shirt. Sample all eighty-two beers (no more than three per visit) and the sky's almost the limit: you and yours will be treated to lunch . . . plus you'll be rewarded with your very own "plush hooded sweatshirt emblazoned with a colorful seal testifying to your accomplishment in trekking AROUND THE WORLD IN 80 BEERS."

We did not join the Club.

"Boston comes to Burlington" is how one observer of the local bar scene described **SWEETWATER'S** (Church and College (Streets). "A fern bar" is how another characterized it. Set in a high-ceiling former bank building, Sweetwater's is definitely a place to see and be seen. Mauve and grey decor is accentuated by bartenders in Oxford blue button downs attending to clusters of outgoing and youngish (ages 25 to 32) upscale professionals. It was 11:15 and the place was packed and abuzz with conversations. TV's - with no sound - and tapes - with very definite sound - added to a noise and activity level that bordered on upset to the nervous system.

For such an obviously trendy watering hole we found Sweetwater's draught lineup to be rather pedestrian: Heineken, Bud, Coors, Lite, Michelob Light. Catamount, Bass and Portland Lager, among others, were available in bottles.

While we were surveying the scene from our at-the-bar vantage point, the head Oxford blue took notice and asked if we were doing a review. When told it was for a book about beer he promptly turned, most disinterestedly, away.

I wished we'd have said we were from the Globe or the Times.

To Beer or Not to Beer

Beer is not a soft drink, and should not be treated as such. It is an alcoholic beverage. It can get you drunk. It will impair your senses and your reflexes.

Do not drink and drive. Driving under the influence can get you in an accident, arrested, or dead. Plan your tour so it can be done on foot or via public transportation. If your route is spread beyond the means of public transportation, take a cab or arrange to have a designated *non-drinking* driver.

Repeat: Beer is not a soft drink. **Do not drink and drive.**

Our first night's last stop was a quickie. The **DOCKSIDE CAFE** (209 Battery Street) features a modest bar within a nautical decor restaurant. One may beer and dine on an outdoor terrace overlooking Lake Champlain during the warm months. John Courage and Budweiser comprise the draught choices. What I will remember most about the Dockside: the bartender's flippant remark "Beer is beer."

We decided to head home for the night.

The Tour: Evening/Night Two

Our second evening/night started out in a conservative mode. We dropped in at *JAKE'S ORIGINAL BAR & GRILL* (1233 Shelburne Road, South Burlington), another of our friend Jim's recommendations. Jake's is part of a new complex called Lakewood Commons, located about a mile south of the Burlington line. It has that suburban look to it. In fact, "Suburban Plush" is how I described it on my BIS. But it's not offensive. The bar area, a large, nice and open square set-up, is a mix of Old General Store (much of it, unfortunately, Reproduction Old General Store) and Generic Country. A lot of browns and dark greens. While looking the place over, our bartender, Winn Curren, served my Bass Ale in a mug. Ugh. And a mug that was frosted. Double ugh. But he was most gracious when I requested that he salvage things as best he could by re-serving it in a room temperature thinner-lipped vessel.

Bud and Lite, in addition to Bass, were the draught selections. Basically, Jake's is a spacious and nicely appointed beef and seafood restaurant with a separate spacious and nicely appointed bar area. Its one major weakness: it doesn't carry Catamount (although Winn agreed that they should.).

From Jake's it was up to North Street. Herb Durfree, a 25-year old native Burlingtonian we'd met and talked with during the day, had referred to the North Street area as "the melting pot of Burlington." His friend, 27-year old Mary Lou Peduzzi, was more explicit. "Bring your gun" she advised.

North Street is the main drag of the untrendy side of town. Blue collar all the way. We hit the *COZY NOOK* (23 North Street) first, just a little after 5:00. Things were slow. A couple of guys playing pool in the back room (which is actually a lot bigger than the front room, where the bar is). Two customers and a bartender up front.

After ordering up a Genny (at 75¢ a large glass a good value), we looked around. And there's a lot to look around at in the Cozy Nook. For starters, there's the largest collection of Genesee plastic signs I've ever been privileged to view. There's shuffleboard (the real, old-fashioned, knock-the-pins-down bowling shuffleboard). There's a matched pair of globe-type nut dispensing machines, one for peanuts and one for pistachios. A "No Profanity" sign beams down from behind the bar. And the matchbooks advertise not the Nook, but "Collect Stamps: 1,000 Stamps for only $2.95" (a good value, I again reflected). My favorite item was a game named Big Choice . . . for 25¢ you get a chance to wrap a claw-like device around (and to keep!) a pink or a lavender or a turquoise stuffed animal. Penny played "All My Ex's Live In Texas" on the jukebox.

We loved it. (It was at about this point that Penny turned to me and said "Heck, I might go into the book-writing business. This is fun!"). Any place that has a jukebox with a good mix of heavy country and western plus the likes of "Sweet Little Sixteen" by Chuck Berry and "Party Doll" by Buddy Knox and the Rhythm Orchids has to be ok. Ordering up another couple of Genny's (served on Bud coasters), I made note that the Nook's few other patrons were drinking Bud out of the bottle. "It's the morning crowd that mostly drinks the Genesee," explained Bruce Hardy, the Cozy Nook's manager.

Asked where the best close-by place for a little food was, Bruce - and patrons alike - strongly suggested the Steer 'n' Stein, up the street a few blocks. "Great fried perch" was the consensus, though, being Sunday evening, they warned us that the S'n'S's kitchen might be closed.

It was. Every Sunday, from 6:00 to 10:00, live country and western music comes to the **STEER 'N' STEIN** (147 N. Winooski, corner North Street) and the kitchen closes. No fried perch for us (although we went back the next morning and had an order for breakfast!). The band, a five-piece combo called Back Forty, was great. ("been playing here about a year: the last band had to quit because their lead singer landed in jail," Gordon at the next table over informed us.). We danced to "I Got The Highway 40 Blues," "Smoke, Smoke, Smoke That Cigarette" and a real rocking version of Bob Seger's "Old Time Rock & Roll." Genny and MeisterBrau

Beer/Bar Tour Hints 101

1 - **PLAN AHEAD** Plan your tour - or at least the rudiments of it - in advance. See what places, neighborhoods, towns look interesting ahead of time. Properly conducted Field Research will pay off every time.

2 - **NO SHIRT, NO SHOES, NO SERVICE** Dress for the occasion. Be yourself, but show respect for where you are, too, Don't wear $300.00 threads or your best mink to a down home place, or your old sneaks and long-faded jeans to Le Taverne Ritz. If you're planning on a variety of places, middle of the road dress is probably in order.

3 - **NO FROSTED MUGS PLEASE** Don't be bashful about the type — or temperature — of the drinking vessel of your choice. If you want a thin-lipped glass, say so. If you want it room temperature, say so also.

4 - **TOUR WITH A GROUP** Go with friends. If touring is fun as a single or as a couple, it can be more fun in a group (but not a gang: you don't want to overwhelm). Organize your own threesome or foursome or whatever. If you really want to do it up big, write the Bar Tourists of America (c/o Jack McDougall, 12 Sylvester Street, Cranford, N.J. 07016). The BTA, as it's known, is a dedicated bunch that conducts bar tours all across the county, New England included.

5 - **EAT** A bar tour should not preclude food. Have a good stick-to-your-ribs meal before heading out and/or eat as you go. Bar food may not always be what AAA or the MOBIL GUIDE would recommend, but a surprising amount of it isn't bad. And definitely avail yourself of any on-the-house munchies: peanuts, pretzels, and especially popcorn.

6 - **REMEMBER YOUR MISSION** Don't overindulge. It's tough to be objective when you're sloshed. It's no fun, either. Enjoy a small draught - or no draught at all - at each place. Soft drinks and coffee are perfectly acceptable. Remember your mission: to see what each place has to offer . . . without necessarily feeling the need to partake of it.

7 - **DON'T DRINK AND DRIVE** There's nothing wrong with drinking, as long as it's enjoyed in moderation. There's nothing wrong with driving. But the two definitely do not mix. **PLEASE . . . do not drink and drive.**

were on tap. We stuck with the Genny. When the band took a break, so did we . . . and headed back to The Daily Planet.

Places often don't seem as good the second time around. The Daily Planet did. The only thing missing was the cream of mushroom: it was not one of the day's soups of the day. That was more than compensated for by the sparkle of the fill-in bartender, Tim Welch, doing his thing in a turned-inside-out sweatshirt. Plus, just as I was digging into a pint of Bass and Penny into a plate of chicken and cheese burritos, who should walk in but Jim (Fraser), our Burlington bar mentor from the Queen City Tavern. "How you'd do? Where'd you go?," he was anxious to know, pleased at our progress. Before we left, I couldn't resist asking a question myself: what brought Jim to The Daily Planet on his time off? His answer could probably serve as a summation of the Appeal Of Bars Everywhere: "I like The Planet. I come for a few beers and a burger . . . and to meet my friends."

From there it was on to **ESOX** (198 Main Street), a place we'd discovered doing Field Research during the day: I'd spied this wonderful-looking alligator with beer mug in hand (claw?) on what turned out to be the Esox' awning. My only question was whether it was, indeed, an alligator. Or was it a crocodile? Proprietor (and Sunday night bartender) Richard Blum resolved that one: "Supposed to be a northern pike . . . but it doesn't look like it." An esox, we were told, is a type of salmon. (Note: I'm sure it is. But it must be a rare species: my READER'S DIGEST GREAT ENCYCLOPEDIC DICTIONARY goes directly from "esoteric" to "esp.". There is no stop for "esox.") "I like it," mused Richard re his bar's name. "Sounds like a baseball team for those that don't know fish."

From fish to darts. Burlington is darts country, and nowhere in our travels was this more evident that at the Esox. A case filled with darts and dartiana - sort of a one-stop dart supply shop - is strategically located between the comfortable bar up front and the back - or dart - room. "The place back here is packed when they have dart games," part-time employee Mary Cannizzaro assured me. And they have them quite often: Esox sponsors five teams - three men's and two women's - in the various City Leagues, with matches made that much more enjoyable, we suspected, by the Esox' admirable draught selection: Genesee, John Courage, Molson Golden, Heineken, and Bud Light.

The **SHEIK** (41 King Street) was another place we'd noticed in our daytime Field Research. I was especially taken with the logo on their outside hanging sign. Featuring live music, mostly acoustic, two or three nights a week, the Sheik is also big on video games. An unwalled-in room directly off the bar fairly dazzles with "Big Event Golf," "Future Spy," and the biggie while we were there, "Laser War" (with Digital Stereo!). Dazzles, that is, if you like video games. I don't.

The draught selection wasn't great, but the price was. "We have a special on pitchers tonight," the cheery woman behind the bar told us. "$2.05 for domestic" (Coors or Bud) "and $3.00 for imported." (Heineken or Labatt's 50). Very good

value. Still, it was late. We settled on a glass each (Penny, Coors at 85¢; myself, Labatt's at $1.00) and were just into our first sip when who should appear but one of the hazards of a tour: a person you've chatted with earlier in the evening who now wants to tell you his/her life story. In this case it was a "her" that we'd exchanged about eighteen words with back at the Cozy Nook . . . but who had apparently come to think of us as long lost best friends in the ensuing time span. We (mostly Penny) listened until what appeared to be a not-too-rude break in the word flow . . . and then we made our escape.

A gathering at the Esox. Left to right: Mary Cannizzaro, Chris Little, Herb Durfee, Mary Lou Peduzzi

115

As we made a beeline across the street to the **CHICKENBONE CAFE** (43 King Street) I think we thought that - just perhaps - we'd saved the best for last. Jim had touted the Bone, as it's locally known, as "the most unusual place you're going to find around here." "Trust me," he'd said when we asked what made it so unusual.

Actually, we had tried to get in the Bone Saturday, but had found too long a line outside the door. Tonight was better, but not much. Saturday night at Sweetwater's was crowded… this was mobbed. About every 21 to 25-year old student that hadn't gone home for the holidays must have decided to make it to 43 King Street. And shout: above the four TV's, above the throbbing (but good!) rock music, and above everyone else. Penny's reaction: "It's so noisy, I'm calm."

One of the back walls - and the Chickenbone is a big place - was bedecked with a fine collection of sepia and black and white photos of Lou Gehrig, Ted, The Babe, Yaz, and more… if you could fight your way through the crowd to get to them (we did). We also fought our way up to the bar - or near it, anyway - to check out the draught selection: Heineken, John Courage, Bud. And to grab a great big bowl of free popcorn (a good value, I once more observed.).

We shouted with the best of 'em for awhile, then decided we were at a point of diminishing return: we were tired, and it was time to pack it in.

End of evening/night two. End of tour.

This is the Bar Information Sheet (BIS) we used. Broken type and all. Feel free to copy it. Or develop your own. It'll make any bar touring you may do that much more fun. And "official!"

```
                    BAR INFORMATION SHEET

                         Name _____

                         Address _____

                                 _____

                                        Date _____
                                        Time Arrived _____
                                        Time Departed _____

      Recommended by _____

      Appearance of Neighborhood _____

      Outside Appearance _____

      Inside Appearance/Decor _____

      Draught Selection _____

      Bottle Selection _____

      Prices _____

      Accoutrements:

            TV _____              Programming _____

            Video Games _____

            Pinball Machines _____

            Jukebox _____   Type of Selections _____

      Personality of Personnel _____

      Mix of Crowd _____

      Food _____

      Other Notable - or Non-Notable - Features _____
```

Beering it in Burlington: Wrap Up

We "did" thirteen bars (no superstitions here!) over our two evening/night stint in Burlington. What did we learn that isn't included in Beer/Bar Tour Hints 101? Well, we learned that being a bar critic is demanding. But fun. We learned that a bar tour can be a good way to better know a friend, probably even a spouse.

And we got to know a strange city rather well, rather quickly, checking out areas that we might otherwise — mistakenly —have overlooked.

Most important of all, however, was the chance to meet some pretty good people, folks that we most likely would not have normally met. And to talk with them. Socially interact, if you will. In the November/ December, 1987 issue of the *American Breweriana Journal*, Fil Graff wrote that a bar hopper or bar tourist can justly be considered "a keen observer of the social interactions of the 20th century American consumer sub-culture in that venerable institution, the tavern."

Fil's words and tongue were, I'm sure, somewhat in cheek, but still . . .

One-Hundred Ninety-Two of the Best: The Oldest/Largest Selection/Most Intriguing Beer-Drinking Bars in New England

What to do about the rest of New England?

My initial plan had been to merely mention a few other obvious picks, such as Jacob Wirth's in Boston and Three Dollar Deweys in Portland. Then I thought why not write to fellow breweriana buffs to see what good places they know of. Tap their knowledge, as it were. This netted a number of recommended spots. My next thought was to cover some of the major cities myself, which I did...and it proved to be addictive. It's not, I found out, difficult to slide into a role of gadabout and bar critic!

Before I knew it I was heading out on all sorts of field trips. The results follow but, prior to jumping into them, I should make clear that, as much field research as I did, the one-hundred ninety-two places included over the next fifteen pages are not meant to be all-inclusive. Cape Cod is not covered. Nor is northern Maine, Nantucket, Martha's Vineyard, etc., etc. Plus I'm sure I've missed some goodies even in those areas I did attempt to cover. Also, places chosen reflect my likes (I'm a sucker for anything old: old buildings, old graphics, old songs, old prices) and dislikes (I'm not a big fan of malls or large chain operations, what with their almost universal sterility and sameness).

The one-hundred ninety-two were chosen on the basis of (a) beauty - with old beauty counting for more than new beauty - and/or (b) good beer/ale selection - with draught counting for more than bottles - and/or (c) character. This, the last selection factor, was the most difficult to define, yet was the most important: did the place stand out from the ordinary? Did it have warmth? Heart?

There are no Holiday Inns or Sheraton Taras here. Don't look for many ferns. And, while some of the places are truly gracious, some are definitely not. They run the gamut . . . just like beer drinkers.

There are no quintessential bars here . . . but there are some darned good ones!

Connecticut

A half a day spent roaming around **BRIDGEPORT** unearthed four places worthy of note. I suspect there may be a lot more. My first find was actually a rediscovery: I'd enjoyed dinner at the **OCEAN SEA GRILL** (1328 Main Street) back in the late 1970s, but had forgotten its deco beauty. Both its red and pale green facade and its graceful bar are treats to behold. Bite the hand of anyone that ever tries to change it. **PJURA'S** (121 Wall Street) maintains much of its original 1926 lustre: its dining room is beautiful, its bar attractive. Notice especially the etched "The Lady" mirrors over the bar and the Connecticut Chop House (Pjura's original name) reverse painting on glass by the front entrance. Probably the trendiest place in town is the **AUSTIN STREET CAFE** (417 Myrtle Avenue). Opened in 1885, Austin Street is an eclectic mix of old and new; part "new wave" (as my waitress, Joanne, dubbed it), part Grover Cleveland. Last - and definitely least - is **DOLAN'S CORNER GRILL** (Middle and Golden Hill Streets). "Dine in Comfort/Booths for Ladies" it says outside Dolan's. Comfort, maybe yes, but hospitality, don't count on

it. "I'm here to sell whiskey and beer, not to answer questions," was the reply of the bartender (who I'd bet was also the proprietor) when I inquired how old the place was without making a purchase. When I explained I was writing a book and a little publicity couldn't hurt, he scowled "Nah, I don't need guys just comin' in and looking." Regardless, it's an attractive older - circa 1935 - bar worth a look. Tell Mr. Personality I sent you.

The **PULASKI CAFE** (46 Main Street) in **DANIELSON** has an interesting art moderne exterior, although inside it's just another bar. Less than one hundred paces away is one of my favorite finds: the **DANIELSON RESTAURANT** (Main Street), with a comely pressed tin walled barroom and a sparkling little dining room - featuring tall wooden booths and yet more pressed tin walls - that you're not likely to forget.

When I asked Scott Sutter, the Danielson's congenial barkeep, if he had any business cards or matches, he hunted around and came up with something far better: this stylish letterhead from a half-century or so ago, when the Danielson was as much a hotel as it was a bar/restaurant.

April, 1988

The Stork Cafe; The Stork outside the Stork Cafe; The Stork, with patrons Dick Coffey and Lou Oliwa, inside the Stork Cafe. How does The Stork sum up forty-two years in the business: "Very good; very educational; very friendly."

Jack McDougall (he of Bar Tourists of America reknown: see page 114) gives plundits to the **POST TAVERN** (839 Boston Post Road, U.S. Route 1) in **DARIEN**. Says Jack: "The place is great clutter; you name it, it's on the walls and ceilings. Anything and everything." Jack thinks that underneath it all there's a tin roof but no matter, it sounds just fine the way it is.

Tiny. But lovable. That's **STORK'S CAFE** (124½ Hawkins Street), tucked way away on a side street in **DERBY**. But ask enough people how to get there and you'll find it, with a Genny neon and a row of trophies in the window and the stars and stripes flying just to the left of the neon. The Stork has been run by Anthony ("Stork's been my nickname since sixty-eight years ago: I'm 73.") Mastrianni since 1946. That's forty-two years! It's a great little place, with wainscoting on both the walls and the ceiling, an adorable marble corner sink (yes, sinks can be adorable), and Genny for 25¢ a glass: "The last of the quarter beers," laughs Stork. Also worth a look, mostly for its facade, is the bar attached to the **KING CITY CHINESE RESTAURANT** (106 Main Street). It's a case of contrast: the bar, with its 1940's large cream and black glass blocks, dwarfed by the bright red, green, and yellow Oriental motif of the restaurant immediately next door.

If you're ever around **ESSEX** be sure to stop in at the over 200-year old **GRISWOLD INN** (Main Street) strongly recommends Jerry Otrin, a breweriana collecting friend from Westbrook, who loves the atmosphere. States Jerry unequivocally, "The Gris is the best!"

Places with names such as Peaches and Apricots and Shenanigans usually have all the tang and originality of your local laundramat, but **SHENANIGANS** (Bushnell Plaza, corner of Gold and Main Streets) in **HARTFORD** is an exception. Built around a streamlined former diner - the Phillips Diner, which occupied a place of honor on Route 6 in Woodbury, Connecticut from 1946 until 1978 - Shenanigans features a good beer list, a nice menu, and live local musical talent nightly. For just plain old time warmth and personality it would be difficult to top the **MUNICIPAL** (485 Main Street). Opened in 1924, the Muni - as it's known

locally - presents almost a postcard view of the past with its high tin ceilings and wonderfully comfy original wooden booths. Toss in a delightful melange of oldish Hartford photos and a jukebox with the likes of "Sincerely" by the Moonglows, "Gee" by the Crows, "Blue Moon" by the Marcels, and "Burning Bridges" by Jack Scott and you have a grand place to enjoy a fine beer selection. Also in Hartford, the **ARCH STREET TAVERN** (85 Arch Street) is a lively gathering spot; the **RUSSIAN LADY** (191 Ann Street) is most attractive; and the **MARBLE PILLAR** (22 Central Row; not open evenings) looks as if it stepped out of 1940.

Follow Route 7 from New Milford to West Cornwall and you're in for a delightful ride along the Housatonic River, complete with covered bridges, waterfalls...and the **BULL'S BRIDGE INN** (U.S. Route 7, Bull's Bridge) in **KENT**, a most relaxing stopover for lunch, dinner and/or a drink.

Charming and quaint - much like **LITCHFIELD** itself - is the **VILLAGE RESTAURANT**. Told "it's been there forever" by folks in Watertown, I headed on up, only to find what looks for all the world like a coffee shop from the outside. Inside, though, is a very pleasing 1890 tap room, with Ballantine Ale and three others on draught. Moral - as you might've guessed! - you can't always judge a bar by its cover.

The **ADAMS MILL RESTAURANT** (165 Adams Street) in **MANCHESTER** is set, not surprisingly, in the old Adams Mill, an 1880 former paper manufactory. Today it's a quite posh and very lovely restaurant, with cuisine that *Connecticut Magazine* calls "varied and imaginative." I would agree... plus there's Watney's and Double Diamond on tap.

MERIDEN's contribution to good, homey bars is **MILNER'S CAFE** (521 Broad Street). And Milner's is homey, with four draught choices, friendly clientele, a very nice sandwich menu ("and the kitchen's always open," proprietor Linda Johnson didn't hesitate to tell me), and at least a fair share of its pre-prohibition warmth retained. Also in the "Silver City" and worthy of mention for its more-or-less art deco interior is **DESANDRE'S CAFE** (26 Britannia Street).

Four score ago you'd have gone there to admire a Stevens - Duryea ("A gentleman's car of excellent quality") or a Waverly Electric ("The best Electric runabout made for ladies' or gentlemens' use") or maybe even a Cadillac ("The most popular and best low priced Touring Car in America"), but today you'd go there to admire lunch or dinner and/or a choice of six beers/ales on draught and thirty-four more in bottles. "There" is **CAULKINS** (Main and Washington Streets) in **MIDDLETOWN**, a handsome bar and restaurant located in the built-in-1905 former F. W. Caulkins' automobile showroom. From automobiles to show biz: less than a handful of blocks from Caulkins is the **MIDDLESEX OPERA HOUSE RESTAURANT** (600 Plaza Street). Opened in 1892, the Middlesex has seen and heard President Taft, John Philip Sousa (and his 150-piece band!), Lionel Barrymore, Douglas Fairbanks, Sr. and a whole lot more. Closed as a theatre in 1960 and stripped of its auditorium via demolition two decades later, the Middlesex's lobby and foyer were wonderfully transformed into a lounge and restaurant in 1985. The look is almost Mediterranean; the effect is almost dazzling. (Not to forget the impressive beer list: five draught and a solid - as in good - dozen bottled choices.)

Friendly staff, good food and good beer: that's how I'd characterize **BANQUERS** (132 Main Street), deep in the heart of downtown **NEW BRITAIN**.

With its several porch-bedecked Victorian former inns and its surrounding hills, I find **NEW HARTFORD** to be one of Connecticut's more delightful villages. **YESTERDAY'S** (Route 44 and Bridge Street), located in one of the former inns, is quite delightful itself. Airy and with an historical decor, Yesterday's features five beers on tap, a sizable bottled selection, and a tasty lunch and dinner menu.

In **NEW HAVEN, KAVANAGH'S** (1166 Chapel Street) has a warm atmosphere; **DEMERY'S** (1 Broadway) is an informal college hangout with an impressive draught selection; the **OLD HEIDELBERG** (1151 Chapel Street) has been serving food and brew since 1757; the **GREENERY CAFE AND RESTAURANT** (954 Chapel Street) would be better if it didn't have that cheap steakhouse look; and, my favorite, **RICHTER'S** (990 Chapel Street), radiates wonderful old world charm beneath a ceiling that's a joy to behold ("original restored," volunteered the bartender between pages of Stephen King's SKELETON CREW). Then there's **PEPE'S** (157 Wooster Street), where the service is slow (nonexistent?) but the pizza, washed down with a pitcher of Genesee, is great.

For a smallish city (population 29,000), **NEW LONDON** presents a remarkably tempting array of brew spots. In the order in which I happened upon them, there's the **LIGHTHOUSE INN** (6 Guthrie Place), which offers superb dining and five draught choices in a wonderfully majestic mansion overlooking Long Island Sound; the **DUTCH TAVERN** (23 Green Street) with pitchers (Schmidt's or PBR) for $3.50, a stamped tin roof, two-tier card tables (one tier for your cards, one for your beer glass), and just a splendid time-honored atmosphere. Plus, bartender Chip Miller proudly told me, the Dutch, opened in 1933, was a favorite haunt of Eugene O'Neil during the famed playwright's many sojourns in New London; the **HALF KEG** (647 Broad Street), a circa 1947 Quonset hut with a cozy, almost diner feel and a score of glossies of ballplayers of yesteryear (including Waterford native and ex-Giant, Oriole, and Senator secondbaseman Billy "Shotgun" Gardner); **YE OLDE TAVERN** (345 Bank Street), a richly-wooded bar and grillroom with stuff - old sporting prints, Winnie Winkle and other comic strips, a large nude oil, even beer trays - hanging everywhere; and **CARLO'S CAFE** (465 Bank Street), an adorable little woodboothed Italian corner restaurant with circa 1945 Schaefer decals flanking the entranceway.

In what was a trip back through time for me, I revisited **YOUNG'S HOTEL** (now the **TRACKSIDE CAFE AT YOUNG'S HOTEL**, 10 Railroad Street) in **NEW MILFORD**, a place I'd enjoyed on a number of occasions in the 1970s. It was gratifying to find it looking as good as ever, with original 1902 back bar, tin ("with about ten coats of paint," notes proprietor Ronald "Rocky" Richter) roof, and wonderful green and white facade.

A rather charming spot for a meal and/or a beer is the **HAWKS' NEST PUB** (Route 44), located in **NORFOLK** in what is undoubtedly the biggest and most ornamentally wonderful old brick building (anyone who loves breweries loves old brick buildings!) for miles around.

One of Connecticut's cozier spots - Bid's Tavern, 631 North Main Street - recently closed, but **NORWICH** still chips in with **BILLY WILSON'S** (78 Franklin Street), downtown next to the *Norwich Bulletin*. BW's, which features a lineup of six strong draught choices and has a heritage that dates back to 1893, is a little like a carnival, with video games, a coin-op basketball toss, huge screen satellite tv, and rock music nightly.

The **COPPERMINE INN** (162 Coppermine Road, one hundred or so yards off Route 34 just over the Stevenson Dam) in **OXFORD** can claim scenic dining/drinking overlooking Lake Zoar. During the summer, when their outside lounge is open, is an especially fine time to drop by.

On the **PORTLAND** side of the Connecticut River someone has handpainted a large invite to "Come On Over." I did, and discovered the **PORTLAND RESTAURANT** (188 Main Street). Set in a 107-year old smallish brick building, the Portland has what one might call a weathered grace. You'll especially like its bar and backbar.

SULLY'S CAFE (441 Howe Avenue) in **SHELTON** is an attractive blend of old and new. What makes it is the 1897 back bar and the four commanding carved lion's heads that frame the top of it.

The **HOP BROOK** (77 West Street) in **SIMSBURY** features beautiful dining and an extensive beer and ale list in a restored 300-year old former grist mill.

Along **STONINGTON**'s wonderfully picturesque Water Street are **HARBORVIEW RESTAURANT** (Cannon Square) and adjacent **SKIPPER'S DOCK** (66 Water Street). Under the same ownership, the view of Block Island Sound is better from Skipper's, but the beer and ale selection - Bass, John Courage, three others on tap - is better at Harborview. Its tap room excels, too: it's a beauty, with richly paneled walls and a handsome bar and back bar.

If a cozy restaurant and bar, loaded with old town photos and warmth, appeals, you'll definitely appreciate the **VI-ARM'S RESTAURANT** (76-78 Main Street) in **THOMASTON**. The "Vi" comes from Vito and the "Arm" from Armand, first names of the original proprietors. "It was a short term - one year - partnership," explains Lydia DeFiore who, with husband Armand, owns and operates the Vi-Arm's, "but we never changed the name because our son's name is Victor." I'm glad. Because if they changed it they'd have to change the good looking sign out front, too. And that would be a pity.

After I'd recovered from the shock of a maitre'd who answered my request for a pint of Bass, which they have on tap, with the reply "What's a pint?," I found the **YANKEE PEDLAR** (93 Main Street) in **TORRINGTON** to be an acceptable place. Service was slow, but food and drink were ok.

Bring together a peach of a 1911 corner bar and restaurant, nine beers and ales on draught, and a most congenial

Opened the year before Fenway Park, the Old Corner's original proprietors were Philip Behlman and Edward Fahey, and they called the place, naturally enough, Behlman and Fahey...a fact still celebrated on the tiled-floor entrance.

April, 1988

"I love it. I love anything old, so it's the cat's meow for me," is how John responded when I asked him how he feels about owning the Old Corner. That sense of love, happily, reflects itself in the care and warmth of the 77-year old landmark.

proprietor and, voila, you have the **OLD CORNER CAFE** (178 North Main Street) in **UNION CITY** (Naugatuck). There's a beautifully inlaid tile floor, gorgeous bar and back bar, original fans, tin roof and walls, and a men's room you won't believe. Ask John Woermer, who's owned the Old Corner since 1972, to show you the wall match striker, the gas jet at the bar for lighting cigars, and some of the venerable establishment's other marvelous features. John loves the Old Corner, and loves to share its beauty and history with patrons and guests. Order up a Double Diamond or McSorley's Ale and relax. And enjoy! Also in Union City is the **VICTORIA INN CAFE** (23 Union Street). Far less elegant than the Old Corner, the Victoria does boast a nice back bar.

A gem - if an unpolished one - of an old corner saloon, complete with tin roof, tin walls and magnificent back bar, is

*P.S. Add **McGRATH'S CAFE** (866 Baldwin Street), **WATERBURY**, to the list: a recent *BTA* newsletter rings out with praise for it.

WACKIE'S (431 West Main Street) in **WATERBURY**. On the same block is **NO FISH TODAY** (457 West Main Street), an old-bar-converted-to-fancy-restaurant that serves excellent food . . . and has an original Old England Ale & Beer neon hanging from its former days. **ACROSS FROM THE HORSE** (26 North Main Street) is a lively gathering spot. And **DRESCHER'S** (25 Leavenworth Street), located in a 1904 building that was moved two hundred feet to its present site in 1982, serves a nice glass of Guinness.*

Many a bank, from depression days on, has been converted into a restaurant, but rarely are the results as attractive as they are with **HEMINGWAY'S** (545 Main Street) in **WATERTOWN**. Bass on draught, plus frequent bottled beer specials (Anchor Steam was featured when I was there), add to the attractiveness.

Although their beer selection could certainly be better, the **VICTORIAN LADY** (877 Main Street), **WILLIMANTIC**, has a comfortable atmosphere and some nice 1940' s beer and soda (mostly soda) signs. While there, check out the splendid deco entranceway to the Hotel Hooker (that really is its name!) a block away.

A good idea or an idea ahead of its time: that was the question as I drove into **WINSTED** to watch a movie (BILOXI BLUES) and drink some beer at the **GILSON CAFE AND CINEMA** (354 Main Street). Formerly the Strand Theater, owners Al and Robin Nero converted it to a restaurant and theater in 1986, feature three tiers of tables and chairs, a light fare menu, and, unfortunately, a light fare beer selection. But I enjoyed myself and, apart from the server showing up with the check at a most crucial point in the movie, found the concept - of mixing beer and cinema - to work fine.

Although I found some of the decor on the tacky side, there's nothing at all tacky about the view from the back deck/dining room of the **BRITANNIA SPOON COMPANY** (296 Church Street, Route 68) in **YALESVILLE**. It's magnificent. If drinks (six choices on tap) and/or dining overlooking a waterfall in a restored former spoon manufacturing plant appeals, Yalesville could be the place for you.

Maine

In spite of its rather inane name, NO TOMATOES (36 Court Street) in **AUBURN** is an interesting nouveau bar and restaurant in an old building.

Probably the best place in **AUGUSTA** for a brew is the **RIVER GRILLE** (333-A Water Street). There's lots of brick, entertainment nightly, and a choice of eighteen bottled beers.

Far and away the best selection in **BANGOR** is at the attractive **WHIG & COURIER PUB & RESTAURANT** (18 Broad Street). Named in honor of a defunct Bangor newspaper, the W & C has five beers on tap (Geary's, Bass, Guinness, Coor's, and Michelob) plus another thirty-five or so, including some good stuff, in bottles.

In **BELFAST**, with its grand late 19th century brick buildings wending their way down to where the Passagassawaukeag (Indian for "passage to the sea") River joins Penobscot Bay, I dropped in at the Chamber of Commerce's information booth. There, Margaret Bowen and Phil Rackliffe advised me to head immediately to both **DARBY'S RESTAURANT AND**

PUB (105 High Street) and **ROLLIE'S CAFE** (37 Main Street). Were they ever right! Rollie's sports a back bar from the 1860s ("came off a schooner from Boston," 35-year old proprietor Randy Jenness didn't hesitate to tell me.) plus a cooler that's been around since Silent Cal Coolidge was at our nation's helm. Rollie's, which plays host to an abundance of families with its pizza/sandwiches/burgers and video games, has five taps running (though it's an uneventful five) plus quite a few others in cans. If Rollie's was a find (and it was: pre-pro bars are tough to come by in the Pine Tree State), Darby's was a downright discovery . . . a most attractive restaurant with an exquisite back bar - small but most ornate, with gilded columns, stained glass (the top part of which, patron Damon Lobel pointed out, appears almost to be a Tiffany shade cut in half), and a marble base - and one of the loveliest tin ceilings I've yet viewed. The wood/metal base stools (there're seven of them) and the polished brass footrail - plus Bass, Bud, and Moosehead on tap, eight others in bottles - round out things very nicely.

During the summer season the **BOOTHBAY HARBOR** area abounds with fine places to enjoy an alfresco brew. My favorite would be the **LOBSTERMAN'S WHARF** (Route 96) in East Boothbay. But the best selection (three tap; eighteen bottled) may be "inland" a block or so at the **BOOTHBAY SCHOONER** (74 Townsend Avenue) in Boothbay Harbor, located in the 1894 former Pythian Opera House. Plus, a must: **ROBINSON'S WHARF** (Route 27, Southport Island), where the selection is pedestrian is best, but the view and wonderfully relaxing outdoor atmosphere more than make up for it.

Although **CAMDEN** and most of its shops are too cute for my tastes, **CAPPY'S CHOWDER HOUSE** (Main and Commercial Streets) is an ok place. Seafaring and rustic in decor, Cappy's features a nice seafood menu, Geary's and Bass on tap.

Tucked away in **CENTRAL LOVELL** - about halfway between Bethel and Fryeburg - is **FARRINGTON'S INN ON LAKE KEZAR** (off Route 5). More a rustic resort than an inn, Farrington's offers a choice of fifty-one bottled beers plus lakeside dining. (open May to October only).

GARDINER's contribution is **151 WATER STREET** (151 Water Street), a lovely restaurant and bar with river view (the Kennebec) dining.

SQUIRE MORGAN'S (46 Market Street); **LITTLE WILLIE'S** (36 Market Street); and the **SEAMAN'S CLUB** (375 Fore Street). Beyond the Old Port area there's **RAOUL'S ROADSIDE ATTRACTION** (865 Forest Avenue, on Portland's "Miracle Mile"), where off-somebody's-wall decor, nightly entertainment (Wednesday-Sunday), and pitchers of Geary's (plus five others on tap; sixty in bottles) blend very well; and the **GREAT LOST BEAR** (540 Forest Avenue), with a respectable selection and a decor that includes a couple of very nice pieces of breweriana. Lastly, for its hominess - in spite of video games - and especially for its Maine Ale mirror (see page 41), I also like the bar at the **PIZZA VILLA** (940 Congress Avenue).

Spectacular is how I'd describe the view from the **OLD MILL PUB** (just off Water Street) in **SKOWHEGAN**. Constructed in 1906 as a carpet factory, the Old Mill is perched 150 feet or so above the swirling waters of the Kennebec. Grab a table on the open air back deck, choose from nineteen beers (two on tap; seventeen in bottles)...and prepare to be entranced. Just across Water Street is another Skowhegan spot worth visiting: **BLOOMFIELD'S CAFE & BAR** (40 Water Street) is a most inviting bar/restaurant set in a built-in-1908 former Rexall drug store.

"Oldest bar in the state" boasts 38-year old Mike Miller of his **BLUE GOOSE TAVERN** (69 Sabattus Street) in **LEWISTON**. "Prohibition was lifted in Maine in July of '33; we opened in October." Whatever, the Goose is a neat little bar with a fine draught (five taps, including Geary's) and bottle selection. A don't miss: the 1933 period photo, to the left of the bar, portraying a trio of Goose bartenders of long ago flanked by stacked-high Schlitz bottles.

Just up from the ferry slip on **PEAKS ISLAND** is **JONES' LANDING**, certainly one of Maine's more idyllic spots to enjoy a beer: there's Casco Bay in the foreground, the Portland skyline in the background, indoor/outdoor tables.

PORTLAND is, not surprisingly, a good beer-drinking town. The restored Old Port Exchange section, especially, fairly teems with meritorious places. Most meritorious, of course, is **THREE DOLLAR DEWEYS ALE HOUSE** (446 Fore Street), with ten taps foaming forth Geary's, Bass, Whitbread, Guinness, George Killian's Irish Red, Spaten Munich, Watney's, Harp, Grolsch, and Bulmer's Woodpecker Cider (there're over sixty others in bottles, too), plus a wonderfully archaic machine that cranks out the tastiest popcorn - and it's free - this side of Casco Bay. Then, right next door, there's **CADILLAC JACK'S** (442 Fore Street). Drive up in your BMW or SAAB (maybe even a Caddie?) and enjoy. Jack's includes a bar centered around a pair of gorgeous Richfield gas pumps, a circa 1950 Coke machine, a 1948 Wurlitzer, plenty of neon . . . plus, of course, a Cadillac - or the side of one, anyway, a '59 Caddie convertible - hanging prominently across from the bar. When you're done looking, check out the brew lineup: eight on draught, over fifty in bottles. Still on Fore Street (396 Fore Street) is - assuming it's opened: see page 61 - **GRITTY McDUFF'S**, Portland's original - and only - brewpub. Also in the Old Port is **HORSEFEATHERS** (193 Middle Street);

Their matchbook cover declares "Maine's Best Kept Secret." Well, no longer: the **HARBOR VIEW TAVERN** (1 Water Street, off Knox Street) in **THOMASTON** is a nifty little spot. Its beer selection is all bottles and not that extensive, but the lots of photos and other interesting stuff on the walls plus the choice of inside or outside (in season) seating makes a stop worthwhile.

Certainly **WALDOBORO**, settled by Maine's only sizable German influx ("The sea captain told 'em he was taking them to Pennsylvania: it was the original con job" chuckled Dean Ness of the Waldoborough Historical Society Museum as he explained the early days of the community), should have a beer emporium worthy of note, reasoned I...and I was right. The **PINE CONE PUBLIC HOUSE** (Friendship Street) has Geary's and Moosehead on tap, fifteen fine selections in bottles, and intimate dining overlooking the Medomak River. More important are 35-year old proprietor Henry Cabot's plans to be making his own beer and ale in the near future. With a wood-fired bake oven/brew kettle combination in place in the basement, Henry's just about - as of July, 1988 - ready to roll.

In **WATERVILLE** my choice would certainly be the **YOU KNOW WHOSE PUB** (on the Concourse, behind Main Street) with four draught picks (including Geary's), a handsome decor, and an almost-good-as-new Dawson's Calorie Controlled Beer/Ale clock still in full sway to the right of the bar.

Still ticking away at the You Know Whose Pub

Massachusetts

One of New England's more unusual places to enjoy a beer is the **ROTUNDA LOUNGE** (469 Main Street) in the heart of **ATHOL**. The Rotunda and its companion, Lucky Lanes Bowling, are both located in what was the city's movie palace ("one of the finest in New England," bartender Al Dargelis will tell you proudly), the York Theater. Part of the theater's lobby now houses the Rotunda; another part a snack bar. The lanes, a dozen candlepin alleys, are set up where once the audience sat. Chandeliers, wonderfully decorative detail, the old water fountain, etc., are all still in place. Have a beer and/or bowl a few: it's worth a stop.

For **BOSTON** - the big B; home to more bars, taverns, taprooms et al than whole states put together - I relied heavily on input from friends and associates and the written word as well as doing a moderate amount of researching myself.

Esquire magazine likes, among others, **DAISY BUCHANAN'S** (241 Newbury Street), **MIDNIGHT COURT** (164 Milk Street), and **29 NEWBURY STREET** (29 Newbury Street). Pierre Ryan, from away over in East Aurora, New York, touts **DOYLE'S CAFE** (3484 Washington Street) as "a great place, a great bar." George Keough, a breweriana buff from Hanson, Massachusetts, is high on the **PLOUGH AND STARS** (912 Massachusetts Avenue) for its patron mix, pub atmosphere, and the fact that "you can join in a conversation without knowing the participants." Nathan Cobb, also a breweriana buff and an employee of the Globe, sent along an article he wrote for the Calendar section back in 1985. Entitled "Beer Bar," the article included the **WURSTHAUS** (4 Boylston Street, **CAMBRIDGE**), and the **OLDE IRISH ALEHOUSE** (Route 109 at Route l, **DEDHAM**), as well as the aforementioned Midnight Court. Nathan's view was - and is - that beer bars should be chosen for their draught selection. "If you're after bottled beer, drink it at home," he suggests. Nathan's vote for the best Boston beer bar in 1985 was the **SEVENS ALE HOUSE** (77 Charles Street), and it would still be up there today as far as he's concerned with, in his words, "a pretty good draught selection including the new, locally-produced Harpoon Ale." (Note: in my one, admittedly short, visit to the Sevens I failed to grasp its appeal. It seemed little more than just another bar . . . although obviously an "in" bar: the place was packed and there were quite a few more people waiting on line outside the door). The Sevens also ranks high with Chris Little, an Avon, Connecticut associate who knows both his beer and Boston. Chris also likes the **BEACON HILL PUB** (149 Charles Street) and the **PURPLE SHAMROCK** (1 Union Street), which he characterizes as "very Irish, with good live entertainment." While on the topic of good Irish places, the **ORCHARD PARK BAR AND GRILL** (208 Waverly Avenue, **WATERTOWN**) comes highly recommended by Burlington-native-turned-Bostonian Mary Lou Peduzzi. "The bartenders are like right off the boat from Ireland" promises Mary Lou. Yet another Irish place (they're not terribly hard to find in the Hub!) is **McCARTHY'S TAVERN** (1592 Tremont Street) with a relatively old bar and Irish flags galore. The **CLOCK TAVERN** (342 West Broadway, South Boston) is aptly named: if you miss the huge E. Howard & Co. sidewalk clock out front you're in trouble.

Admire the clock, but then go on in . . . to a world where little has seemingly changed over the decades; where a Croft clock still gives the time; Pickwick Ale is still advertised via a large light-up sign; etc. The **SUNSET GRILL & TAP** (130 Brighton Avenue, Allston) came highly recommended as a place with an excellent beer selection. And the selection is good, but anyplace that lists Sierra Nevada as being brewed in Nevada (it's brewed in Chico, California), misspells "weiss" and serves its brews at a temperature that makes one wary of frostbite doesn't earn too many points on these pages. One of the more beautiful bars in America - for enjoying a beer or otherwise - is **LOCKE OBER** (4 Winter Place). Enter and marvel at its 1875 grace and opulence (but be properly dressed -which means a tie and jacket for the guys - or don't expect to enter at all: Locke Ober is as formal as it is beautiful).

Let's not forget, of course, the **COMMONWEALTH BREWING COMPANY** (138 Portland Street) and its marvelous ale/porter/stout selection. (For more on

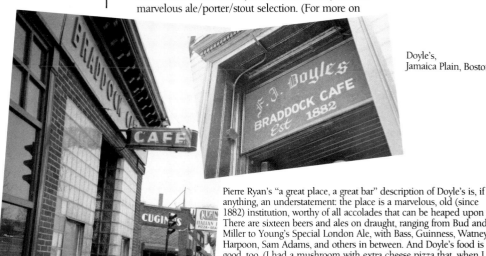

Doyle's,
Jamaica Plain, Boston

Pierre Ryan's "a great place, a great bar" description of Doyle's is, if anything, an understatement: the place is a marvelous, old (since 1882) institution, worthy of all accolades that can be heaped upon it. There are sixteen beers and ales on draught, ranging from Bud and Miller to Young's Special London Ale, with Bass, Guinness, Watney's, Harpoon, Sam Adams, and others in between. And Doyle's food is good, too. (I had a mushroom with extra cheese pizza that, when I think of it, still gets me to smacking my lips!). Large murals adorn the wall, the ceiling is all tin, the booths old and lovely, the crowd diverse, the atmosphere lively without being rowdy, etc., etc., etc. If ever there were a place where one could enjoy a pint or two and just sit and watch the world go by...this is it.

Commonwealth, please see page 61). Nor could one overlook that most venerable of Boston's drinking establishments. Founded in 1868, famous for its Latin motto ("Suum cuique" - "To each his own") and large portraits of Sox hall of famers Tris Speaker, Jimmie Foxx, Joe Cronin and others, **JACOB WIRTH** (31 Stuart Street) is just a great old place. To sit. To reflect. To drink beer.

"He was a bricklayer and there was no work: it was either build it or starve" was how Jim McNally responded when I asked him why his father, John, had decided to build the **OLD TIMER** (155 Church Street) in **CLINTON** in 1932, when both prohibition and the depression were in full sway. It was a good decision: over a half -century later the Old Timer is still going strong, serving lunch and dinner - and, in

Jim's words, "a lot of beer" - seven days a week in a delightful English Tudor setting.

In **FALL RIVER**, **LIZZIE'S** (123 Third Street) enjoys a lovely setting in a restored older building.

What's thirty feet long, is made of mahogany, features four gorgeous cut-glass cabinets, and has been moved twice in its seventy years of existence? The answer is the bar/back bar at **20 RAILROAD STREET** (20 Railroad Street) in **GREAT BARRINGTON**. Built in 1919 for New York's plush Hotel Commodore, the bar was moved to the Berkshires later that same year ("Things were more wide open up here with respect to prohibition," expounded the bartender), to a location a couple of doors from its present setting. But it's at 20 Railroad now (moved there in 1933), and is a must-see for bar aficionados.

GREENFIELD's contribution to beer drinking is the **VICTORIA DINER/BAR** (Chapman Street). Converted from a diner to a bar in 1933, the Victoria is tiny. And certainly not fancy. But the original tin walls and ceiling are still there, and, until relatively recently, so were the original marble tops on the tables. Sadly, though, they've all been smashed in the last five years ("Our clientele is changing," noted the bartender.). When your stay at the Victoria is done, cross the street for a looksee at an ancient painted-on-alley-wall sign for the Victoria Theatre and its long ago "Vaudeville/High Class Photoplays."

In **HOLYOKE** it's **THE BUD** (30 John Street, just over from City Hall), a familiar haunt for several generations of the city's businessfolk and politicos. With its 1913 cherry and mahogany bar, terrazzo floor, brass and copper fittings, and tall polished wood, almost private booths - plus Bass, Beck's, Lite, and, of course, Bud, on tap - The Bud is a place one could settle into without much difficulty at all.*

LAWRENCE checks in with two places, neither fancy, but both worth a visit. First is **HAYE'S TAVERN** (167 South Union Street), an old bar that's in the process of reclaiming its age. Proprietor Alex Buoanno had just removed about twenty layers of wallpaper to uncover a long hidden - and most pleasing - back bar. More refurbishing is planned. Plus, bartender Dennis John (and several patrons!) took great pains to point out, Haye's is the only bar in the country with a hot top (like asphalt) floor. On the other side of town is **DAIGLE'S** (168 Broadway), with a sign proclaiming it to be the "Friendliest Bar In Town." Daigle's - soon to become **EMERSON'S** (will it still be the "Friendliest Bar"?) - main attribute is its original bar and back bar, plus live country and western music Friday and Saturday nights.

On the men's room wall of the **OLD WORTHEN** (141 Worthen Street) in **LOWELL** is inscribed "Edgar Allan Poe was here." "Ha ha ha" thought I. Well, it turns out that he was here. And so have been quite a list of other notables, including Jack (ON THE ROAD) Kerouac, a Lowell native, and Judy Garland, who dated a Lowell native. But back to Poe:

*P.S. Being old and/or serving good beer doesn't necessarily guarantee success: The Bud closed shortly after I was there in spring, 1988. Let us hope it's open again soon.

legend has it that the storyteller/poet penned "The Raven" during one of his stays at the Old Worthen, a stagecoach stop years ago ("years and years ago," 23-year old barmaid Robin Morris wanted to assure me). "The Raven" was published in 1845 . . . which gives an idea of the O.W.'s age. Sadly, while still a great old gathering spot (appreciate especially the 2½-horsepower engine pulley-driven fans and the wonderful tin roof), the Old Worthen yet (as of late April, 1988) suffers from a May, 1987 fire. Restoration to its former grace is promised: let us hope so. A few blocks away, closer to downtown Lowell, is the **LAST SAFE AND DEPOSIT COMPANY** (160 Merrimack Street), located in an 1890's former bank headquarters and most notable for its small but richly paneled dining alcove.

LYNN was one of my biggest challenges. I figured there'd be - in a city of close to 80,000 with tons of neighborhoods and lots of old - a gold mine of un-mucked up bars. But I soon found out otherwise. "They've all been done over," I heard repeatedly. Finally a cop on the beat told me about **McDONOUGH'S PUB** (Summer Street, just off Commercial), said it was "the last of the Mohicans" as far as local neighborhood bars go. Maybe so, but I was disappointed. The sense of character just didn't seem to be there. But what was there - and that I really liked - was an outside horseshoe pit: pitching shoes and drinking beer go so well together. Further inquiries lead me crosstown to the **FOUR WINDS** (234 Broadway). Properly seedy, the Four Winds has four draught choices, darts and shuffle bowling, even a water view (it sits beside Sluice Pond). Plus, patron Chuck Snevis informed me, it's the last of the stand up (i.e., no bar stools) bars in Lynn. I found the Four Winds to be very comfy; got a special kick out of the placement of the sink in the men's room.

Hayes Tavern and patron Rick - Rockin' Rick - Diodati form a tableau vivant on South Union Street.

In quaint and charming **MARBLEHEAD**, I found **JAKE CASSIDY'S** (259 Washington Street), a trendy restaurant and bar with an old time advertising motif. Of particular interest (at least to me): the old beer labels laminated into the top of the bar. Also in Marblehead, in the Old Town section, is the **SAIL LOFT** (15 State Street). Known locally as Matty's, the Sail Loft has a nice nautical feel to it, serves a good pint of George Killian's. (Note: don't expect to park in front. You can't. Try to grab a spot on nearby Washington Street.).

In **METHUEN** your best bet is the **GAUNT SQUARE PUB** (5 Pleasant Street, part of the **RED TAVERN**), nestled in a former guest mansion and featuring a rather extensive list of U.S. micro bottled brews.(Note: Gaunt Square opens at noon on weekends but not until 5:00 P.M. on weekdays). There's also **MARGGRAF'S TALLY-HO** (74 Swan Street), a rustic and comfy wood-paneled bar and restaurant topped - roof-wise - by a small collection of signs, including a circa 1940 faded but still attractive "Schlitz On Draught."

Heading into lovely old **NEWBURYPORT** I gave a ride to a hitchhiker who told me that Jacob Barley was the place to go in town. Well, Jacob Barley turned out to be **JACOB MARLEY** (23 Pleasant Street), of Dickens' *A CHRISTMAS CAROL* fame. But not to mind, it's an alright place anyway: kind of cutesy on the inside but the outside is a gorgeous 1880 red brick mill (the bartender thought it had been a shoe factory, but he wasn't real sure) highlighted by a knockout of a smokestack. A short stroll away is the **GROG** (13 Middle Street) with a wonderfully warm atmosphere and, as with Jacob Marley, a good beer and ale selection. (If you feel like something softer head for **FOWLES NEWS AND SODA SHOP** (17 State Street), as neat an older soda fountain as you're likely to find.)

I had a hunch I'd find a goody or two in decidedly ungentrified <u>NORTH ADAMS</u>, and I was not disapointed. Almost side-by-side are **SCULLY'S CAFE** (Center Street) and the **MOHAWK TAVERN** (Marshall and Center Streets). Both are vintage, feature a lot of wood. The Mohawk possesses, also, a nice beamed high ceiling, interesting green formica-fronted bar, and a slate floor. Scully's, while perhaps not quite as attractive, would be my pick of the two: it has a handsome original bar/back bar and an atmosphere that I found calming - "We're the quietest bar in town," 27-year old bartender Steve Haskins assured me - and friendly.

In <u>NORTHAMPTON</u> one should head directly to the **NORTHAMPTON BREWERY/BREWSTER COURT BAR & GRILL** (11 Brewster Court). For more on central and western Massachusetts' only brew pub, please see page 65. Also in town and very definitely worth visiting is **SHEEHAN'S CAFE** (24 Pleasant Street), opened by Irishman John Dewey in 1901 as the workingman's answer to the gentleman's club. Dewey must have had rather elegant workingmen in mind: Sheehan's features a solid mahogany bar, beveled mirrors, curved walnut fretwork, all topped off by a row of stained glass windows. It's joy to behold. Then there's **YE OL WATERING HOLE** (287 Pleasant Street), known for its extensive beer can collection, its neighborhood feel . . . and its choice of over sixty-five brews.

<u>PITTSFIELD</u>, the community that garners my vote for the sizable city with the most plebian beer selection in New England (finding Genny on tap was a find!), offers **UNION STATION** (34 Depot Street), a cutesy restaurant/lounge in a former warehouse next to where the train station used to be (it's been torn down); **CHARLIE'S TYLER CAFE** (Tyler Street/Route 9 East), where you can cut the smoke with a knife, but which may be Pittsfield's oldest bar (and which serves the Genny); **THE HIGHLAND RESTAURANT** (100 Fenn Street), with large blow-up photos of from-the-area ballplayers Dale Long, Jeff Reardon, Mark Belanger, and others; and **PATRICK'S PUB** (26 Bank Row), which has probably the city's best beer - with its twenty or so choices in bottles - selection.

In <u>SALEM</u> the **LYCEUM** (43 Church Street) has a nice relaxing air, plus you can marvel that it was here, in 1877, that Alexander Graham Bell first demonstrated the use of the telephone for long distance conversing.

You'd expect a city the size and character of <u>SPRINGFIELD</u> to have a number of intriguing beer-drinking places. And it has. In the Indian Orchard section there's what I suspect is an undiscovered gem named **JOHNSON'S CAFE** (Main Street at Dr. Stusick Square, just south of Ludlow on Route 21). If a lovely back bar, original 1937 wooden booths, and a pace that's super unhurried sound good to you, Johnson's may be just what you're looking for. At the other extreme is the **BAR ASSOCIATION** (98 State Street, off Court Square), which borders on being tastelessly gaudy, but at least an attempt has been made to create an atmosphere that's interesting. "Interesting" is also how I'd describe the **STONE WALL TAVERN** (1700 block of Main Street, next to the Paramount), which really is built into a stone wall or, more accurately, the stone wall (of the Conrail, nee New York, New Haven & Hartford, bridge) is built into it. Step in and see what I mean: you'll almost feel a part of the bridge. (Just don't bring the whole gang . . . the Wall is small!). Also on Main Street is **TILLY'S** (1390 Main Street), a very modern, very pretty restaurant with a large, open bar and an abundance of exposed brick and light, bright wood. Just off Main is the charming **STUDENT PRINCE AND FORT** (9-14 Fort Street). Longtime friends Al and Nellie Winterfield of Wallingford, Connecticut had written me about the Student Prince, which they like for its food, its beer (seven draught choices, including DAB, Spaten Munich, and Spaten Munich Dark), and because, in their words, "the collection (of steins) on display is something to see." All that I can add is that I wholeheartedly concur: the place is great. Another spot well worth visiting is **THEODORE'S** (201 Worthington Street), which proprietor Ted Rauh has painstakingly restored and has decorated with all kinds of old stuff, and which features a

stately pre-prohibition cherrywood bar he got out of a VFW hall in Athol. Ted also owns **SMITH'S BILLIARDS** (next door, at 207 Worthington Street), with sixteen billiard tables and a smallish bar in a second-story walkup that's been a billiard room since 1910 or so. Sure it's upstairs, but go ahead: the original tin ceiling and ornate colonnades will make the climb almost a pleasure. Springfield's last pick is here strictly for its raffish exterior: to gaze longingly at the **TIC TOC LOUNGE** (355 Dwight Street, on what is known locally as "The Strip") is to risk being hypnotized by its flashing neon letters. Great 1930's gaud!

If you're in **STURBRIDGE** and in the mood for a bit of elegant, try the **WHISTLING SWAN** (502 Main Street, Route 20), a most pleasing restaurant with a very acceptable bottle beer list.

TAUNTON offers up a trio of places worthy of note. What is now **ARTIE'S PUB** (47 Weir Street) was built in the 1870s as part of the Hotel Belmore. Much of its former elegance is gone, but a coziness - and a fine-looking tin wall and ceiling - remain. Behind a rather garrish exterior is the intriguing interior of **BLINK'S** (445 Bay Street, in the Whittenton section). Ask proprietor Chester Martin to run the water through the old (very old!) rinsing trough; admire the solid brass footrail; look for the several mistakes in the pre-pro hand-laid tile floor; enjoy the great (which translates to a lot of good '50s stuff!) jukebox selection; inquire about the origin of the bar's name (hint: founder Henry Perreault, Sr., Chester's wife JoAnn's great-grandfather, had a glass eye to replace a real one he'd lost in the Spanish-American War and had the nickname of _____ .) The last Taunton goody is the **POLISH-AMERICAN CITIZENS CLUB** (314 Bay Street, Pulaski Square, also in the Whittenton section). What makes the P-ACC special - apart from the warmth of its patrons - is the magnificent Smith Brothers mural that hangs in a place of honor across from the s-shaped bar. Painted in full color, the 4' x 6' or so mural depicts two horsemen in a Polish village. Swans, thatched-roof houses, and the wording "Niech Żyje Polska" ("Let Polish live," 66-year old customer Matt Dykas proudly translated for me) round out what is truly a select piece of breweriana.

A cute place - on the inside - is **NAP'S RESTAURANT** (595 South Main Street) in **WEBSTER**, with dining room on the left, tap room in the center, and original diner on the right. I especially liked the half-century old large light fixtures that adorn the Nap's back bar.

Hidden away in the very center of **WESTFIELD** is the **CITY HOTEL** (43 Elm Street), an art deco masterpiece - in the rough - both inside and out.

WORCESTER is home to a number of worthy beer-drinking establishments. **GUERTIN'S CAFE** (Grand and Southgate Streets) doesn't look like much from outside, but inside it's a 1905 bar with original tin ceiling and some handsome fretwork. **MOYNIHAN'S PUB** (897 Main Street) has been a favorite with Clark University students since 1933. The **LEITRIM** ("No I.D., No Admit, No Excuses") **PUB** (265 Park Avenue) is another popular-with-college-kids hangout. The **CONEY ISLAND** (158 Southbridge Street) is basically a hot dog eatery, but it does have an adjoining bar and is well worth a visit just to admire the two-story high hot-dog-in-hand neon sign out front. Although it offers a surprisingly blah beer selection, the **FIREHOUSE CAFE** (1 Exchange Place) is fun: the bar is fashioned out of the back of a 1921 Mack fire truck. The **HOTEL VERNON** (Millbury Street at Kelley Square), also known locally as the Yacht Club, offers splendid pirate/seascape murals set amidst fading beauty. **MAXWELL SILVERMAN'S TOOL HOUSE** (Lincoln Square), a fairly posh restaurant in a 100-year old former factory, features what is

probably the city's most extensive beer list. If you're in the mood for zany, don't miss **RALPH'S CHADWICK SQUARE** (95 Prescott Street, off Grove Street), which comes with a Harley and go-karts hanging from the ceiling, fake palm trees, lots of neon, stuffed animals, live bands every night, etc., etc. Ralph's doesn't open until 6:00 and is difficult to find, but if you're looking for an off-the-wall place, this is it. My vote, among all the talent in town, for the best just-drinking-beer spot in Worcester goes to the semi-cavernous **WHITE EAGLE POLISH CLUB** (118 Green Street). Nothing fancy, just a relaxing, friendly atmosphere - complete with American and Polish flags flanking a portrait of JFK above the bar - plus a jukebox selection that I'll wager is as eclectic as any in the land.

The City Hotel, Westfield

New Hampshire

If the prospect of eating and drinking in a former jail cell intrigues you, then head for ***TIO JUAN'S MEXICAN RESTAURANT AND WATERING HOLE*** (Bicentennial Square) in **CONCORD**. I usually sidestep places with names that include the likes of "watering hole," but Tio Juan's - even though it has but your basic beer list - is worth not avoiding. Located in what was Concord's police station until the late 1970s, you really can eat in one of fifteen old cells ("very popular," manager Paul Letourneau informed me). Novelties aside, both Tio Juan's restaurant and bar are most attractive, with a lot of brick and a lot of warmth. If the brick doesn't get to you, drop over to ***JOHNNY BABE'S CAFE*** (one of several focal points in the Eagle Square Marketplace), where the stone will. Both the lounge - downstairs - and especially the restaurant - upstairs - feature rather magnificent exposed interior stone walls.

A most comfortable place to enjoy a brew and/or Tex/Mex/Cajun cuisine is the **WORK DAY CAFE** (487 Central Avenue) in **DOVER**. The beer selection's good, plus there's live entertainment all seven nights of the week. Dover, a splendid tribute to the beauty of well-preserved red brick factory neighborhoods, also features ***McWHO'S? TAVERN*** (4-6 New York Street), a place that's almost sure to be lively, what with darts, shuffle bowling, and a huge tv. The sign outside reads "Food & Ale," and two of the four taps are ale, plus there's a well-stocked cooler (Who'd believe Iron City on the banks of the Cochecho!?).

Several of the folks that I spoke with in Concord said "You gotta go to **HENNIKER**, to ***DANIEL'S***" (no street address necessary - you can't miss it). And so I did. What makes Daniel's so great is not its beer selection - although it's good - but its location, perched over the rushing waters of the Contoocook River. Very pleasant.

I found the pickings slim in **MANCHESTER**. The better part of a day and a lot of leads turned up but one place worthy of mention. This dearth may be because - with its rich ethnic fabric - the city's more interesting places are its private social clubs . . . of which there are many. (The Ukrainian American Citizen Club looked especially intriguing). But back to the one place. It's called **CHESTNUT'S** (464 Chestnut Street) and on the outside it's definitely ho hum, even ugly. Inside, although it's another of a growing list of "Let's decorate with old-timey advertising" establishments, it's an Old-Timey Advertising establishment that's very well done. There're some fine old signs (including a large Goebel - "If It's Goebel...It's Good" - tin beer sign from the days when Goebel was a biggie in and around Detroit), plus a wooden carousel horse, the front of an Edsel (with its lights on!), a hanging circa 1950 balloon tire bicycle, Andrews Sisters' era Wurlitzer, etc. That's upstairs. Downstairs is the ***SCORE CARD SPORTS BAR*** with a blend of new and old sports memorabilia (including a raft of black and white baseball glossies, long-ago catcher's

masks, and a very sizable 1959 Red Sox/Narragansett team photo). The Sports Bar, with almost nightly sports trivia and wide-screen tv coverage of the Sox, Celtics, and Bruins, stocks over thirty beers and ales.

I had to work hard to find anyplace of distinction in **NASHUA**. The city's years of tremendous growth have taken their toll. "There used to be all kinds of old places on the cross streets, but they're all gone now" summed up a shopkeeper. Finally a policeman told me sbout ***STAN'S PLACE*** (58 West Hollis), and while Stan's is no gem, it does have personality, tin roofing, and nice booths. How old is it: "You got me" is how waitress/bartender Brenda Guertin responded to that one, but she could tell me that it's been Stan's (named for proprietor Stan Slosek) for twenty-four years; before that it was Rommie & Mary's; and, way back in its youth, it was the Ritz.

Downstairs there's a pair of lovely Frank Jones Brewing Company lithographs; upstairs there's a veritable mini-museum of Portsmouth breweriana. Where? At the ***ISAAC DOW HOUSE*** (Old River Road), a 150-year old farmhouse-now-gracious-restaurant in **NEWINGTON**. Don't expect to be mesmerized by the malt beverage selection - all in bottles and quite humdrum - but come and enjoy anyway.

127

The bars of **PORTSMOUTH**, long a mecca of fun and frivolity, include the **MALT HOUSE** (Albany Street Extension), a contemporary bar and restaurant with seven beers on tap located in the former Frank Jones' malthouse; the **PRESS ROOM** (77 Daniel Street), a warm and cozy brick and pine-paneled pub complete with wood stove, darts, old typewriters and a nice beer and ale selection (the Press Room was voted Best Portsmouth Bar by *Portsmouth Magazine*. I would agree.); the **SPRING HILL TAVERN AT THE DOLPHIN STRIKER** (15 Bow Street), which also features a warm brick and pine-paneled atmosphere, plus a glassed-over well built into the bar. There's a good beer selection, too. Rounding things out is the **LIBRARY AT THE ROCKINGHAM HOUSE** (401 State Street), an elegant

drinking and dining spot once favored by - and owned by - Frank Jones. In fact, there's a large - and very nice - lithograph on tin portraying the brewery at its peak that yet hangs in a place of honor in the dining area immediately to the right of the entrance. It's definitely worth checking out.

"Gracious" is the word for **WOLFEBORO**, which prides itself on being "America's Oldest Summer Resort." And "gracious" is also the word for the **WOLFEBORO INN** (44 North Main Street). Built in 1812, the Wolfeboro, open all year, offers beautiful dining on Lake Winnipesaukee and a noteworthy ("We've got forty-two different ones," proclaimed the bartender) beer selection.

Rhode Island

Sentiment brought me back to SURKONT'S CAFE (530 Broadway) in **PAWTUCKET**. Once, many long moons ago, I'd visited and chatted with the then owner, former Brave/Pirate/Giant hurler Max Surkont. But times change. The place I'd visited was torn down in 1980 as part of a city redevelopment plan. And Max passsed away in 1986. While

the new place won't win any bar beautiful awards, Max's son, 33-year old Glenn Surkont, enjoys talking about his dad, the Cafe's softball team (4-1, and in first place in Pawtucket's Over-Thirty League at the time I was there), and the baseball memorabilia that lines the walls. It's a nice way to mix beer and our national pastime.

Glenn, on the right, with his softball team's star pitcher, Red "Tin Can" Murray on the left. What does a star pitcher in Pawtucket's Over-Thirty League (Red's 41, although he's not fond of admitting it) drink: for Red it was Old Milwaukee the day I was there, with a 16-ounce can going down real easy.

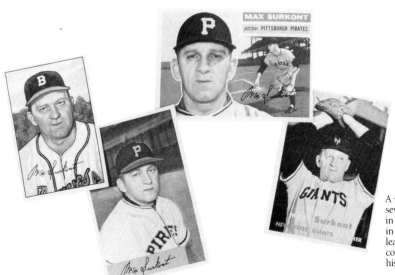

A veteran of the mound if ever there were one, Max Surkont spent seventeen years in organized ball, starting with Cambridge (Maryland) in the old Eastern Shore League in 1938 and ending with the Giants in their last year in New York in 1957. In 1953 he set a then major league record by fanning eight consecutive batters. Yet, Glenn confided in me, his dad loved his bar more than baseball: "This was his area; these were his friends."

The Dorrance: an old
favorite of old friend - and true bar
afficionado - Jim Starkman of Fairport, NY

In **PROVIDENCE**, there's the **CUSTOM HOUSE TAVERN** (36 Weybosset Street), which has Bass and Watney's on tap and features Hope in bottles; the **DORRANCE BAR** (70 Dorrance Street), a nothing-fancy Irish bar with a great old exterior sign; the **TALK OF THE TOWN** (147 Washington Street), also an Irish bar but one that's a mite fancier than the Dorrance; **PLAYERS' CORNER PUB** (194 Washington Street), an interesting, lively older bar with an abundance of area sports photos and pennants; and **SPAT'S** (230 Thayer Street), a bustling gathering place on the East Side near Brown that's locally touted as having "been there forever." In addition, there are several bars and restaurants in the Arcade (Westminster Street), a truly beautiful National Historic Landmark that's been a focal point of downtown Providence since 1828.

For delightful dining - and a favorite of mine, Yuengling's Lord Chesterfield Ale - overlooking the Warren River, try the **WHARF TAVERN** (Water Street) in **WARREN**.

The lovely seaside resort of **WATCH HILL** slumbers for most of the year, then comes alive for the summer season. A great place to enjoy it is on the outdoor deck at the **OCEAN HOUSE**, a rambling bright yellow wooden-frame Victorian hotel that rewards its guests with a magnificent view of the Atlantic. (If you're in the mood for a Moxie or a frappe - or just want to take a peek at the soda fountain and restaurant that almost appears to have stepped out of Natchez or Savannah circa 1947 — drop in at the **OLYMPIA RESTAURANT AND TEA ROOM** - "Since 1916" — on Bay Street.)

(401) 765-6923

MONUMENT SQUARE TAVERN
•
3 MONUMENT SQUARE
WOONSOCKET, RHODE ISLAND

Although Coors and Old Milwaukee do not make for an overly exciting draught choice, the **LOG CABIN TAVERN** (55½ Pleasant Street) in **WESTERLY** is a dandy little place. Described as "friendly" and "a neighborhood workingman's bar" by bartender Marie Thomas ("I've been here through three owners"), the circa 1948 Log Cabin's interior has deco overtones, a cozy feel.

Fellow breweriana collector Pat Connelly of Coventry likes the **PHOENIX HOTEL** in **WEST WARWICK**; says it reminds him "of the type of bar that a stagecoach used to pull up to: a real saloon."

It's refreshing to find something being modernized to look old. "Back to the future," as it were. That's exactly what owner Leslie Plante is doing with the **MONUMENT SQUARE TAVERN** (3 Monument Square) in **WOONSOCKET**. Tin roof, back bar, tile floor: all are new. You'd hardly know it though, they look so right at home on the ground floor of the century-old (1888) Linton Block Building.

P.S. One last spot in the Ocean State: old friend Don Bull, of Stamford, Connecticut, recommends - sort of - the **FOS'CLE** ("on the main drag into town") in **GALILEE**. Actually Don says "It's a dump," but one he loves. Seems as how all the tourists stay upstairs in the restaurant section, while the locals all head for downstairs, reached only via an unobtrusive passageway. Don recollects that he and wife Bonnie may be the only folks from away ever to make it down there to where the real atmosphere is.

Vermont

Let's start the Green Mountain State off with yet another deco-in-the-rough place of note (I like deco!): it's the **POLISH-AMERICAN CLUB** (37 Rockingham Street), **BELLOWS FALLS**. Built as the Chimes Club in 1937, it's now a private club . . . but if you look reasonably respectable the chances are they'll buzz you in.

Sometimes you save the best for last. Sometimes you include it real early...which is what I'm going to do with Vermont. The best beer selection in the state - and, for that matter, certainly one of the best in New England - is unquestionably at *THREE DOLLAR DEWEYS* (6 South Main Street) in **BRATTLEBORO**. There are nine beers and ales (John Courage, Harp, DAB Light, Toby Amber Ale, Watney's, Whitbread, Bass, Guinness Stout, and Calgary Lager) plus Woodpecker Cider on tap. Then there's sixty-two or so more choices in bottles. And 27-year old co-owner Ray McNeill is thinking all the time: he plans to add Double Diamond and Grolsch to the tap list, and to feature Catamount Amber as soon as it's ready to roll on draught. Located in a somewhat out of the way location on the outskirts of downtown, Deweys (not affliated with the Three Dollar Deweys in Portland) is open seven days a week from 4:00 (Ray: "We tried lunch but nobody came.") until closing. Opened in July of 1985, the place isn't much with respect to exterior, but inside it's a don't-miss-it beerlover's haven. Also in Brattleboro, a handsome red brick river town, is the *MOLES EYE CAFE* (foot of High Street, across from the tarnished but still magnificent Paramount Theatre). Featuring live entertainment most every night, the Moles Eye was the Oak Room of the former Hotel Brooks, built in 1871. Although modernization has taken a toll, the Eye is worth a visit. While there, check out the rather neat Chicago Cubs' pinball machine, with some fine shots of Wrigley (before lights!), just outside the entrance to the men's room.

For a rundown on **BURLINGTON** please turn back to pages 111-116.

Routes 7 and 7A from Bennington to Rutland have oodles of old and new inns and restaurants. One with a nice cozy bar - and restaurant, too - is the *QUALITY RESTAURANT* (735 Main Street) in **MANCHESTER CENTER**. Be sure to order Catamount.

As I was standing in the street taking this shot, a pair of sweet-looking young teenage girls walked by: commented one to the other, "What the bleep (starts with 'f,' ends with 'k') is he doing taking a picture of that?" So much for Bellows Falls' innocence. But if Bellows Falls is not a paragon of innocence it is a veritable small hub of food and drink pop culture. Up Rockingham Street about two hundred feet is the Real Scoop, a neat 1930ish ice cream stand, while the Miss Bellows Falls Diner stands majestically between it and the Polish-American, pictured here.

Go to Montpelier and you, too, can be the proud owner of a Charlie O's/World Famous bumper sticker: Stacy and the sticker.

Quechee Gin Mill
U.S. ROUTE 4 & GILSON AVE.
QUECHEE, VT. 05059
DRAUGHT BEER 18 IN ALL
Newton Mfg Co. Newton Iowa

Thanks to Robin Carlson of Boxborough, Mass. for telling me about the *QUECHEE GIN MILL* (U.S. Route 4 and West Gilson Avenue) in **QUECHEE**, which offers up "antique decor in a casual setting," Maxwell Parrish prints . . . and eighteen (18!) beers on tap, satisfying most any malt beverage desire you might have. See the gorge first . . . then see the Gin Mill.

I "did" the twin cities of **MONTPELIER** and **BARRE** with an old fraternity buddy, Chris Barbieri (now the president of the Vermont Chamber of Commerce, no less), and his wife Laurel (an English teacher at Craftsbury Academy), who live in nearby Worcester. Before teaming up with them I made a

quick stop at a place myself, *CHARLIE O'S* (70 Main Street, Montpelier). It's a good thing: Chris and Laurel wanted no part of it, describing it as a rough and be on the ready spot. (Laurel: "If you want a fight, that's where it'll happen."). I rather liked it, though. Thought it had character, a degree of age, and lots of photos and stuff hanging everywhere. Plus, who could resist checking out a place that brashly claims - on its outside sign - to be "world famous." (When I asked 21-year old bartender Stacy Shibley why the place was famous she admitted she didn't know, then offered me a Charlie O's/World Famous bumpersticker, commenting that if I and everyone else put one on our car then Charlie O's would be world famous!).

But back to Chris and Laurel. First stop was the **THRUSH TAVERN** (107 State Street, Montpelier), which Chris characterized as a spot that "hops after work, is dead thereafter." It was thereafter. The Thrush is attractive - located in the second oldest extant house in Montpelier, Chris informed me - but not much was happening. We moved on to what turned out to be my favorite, **JULIO'S**, located above a hardware store (44 Main Street, Montpelier; look for the Sherwin-Williams' sign). A Mexican restaurant with separate bar, Julio's features Catamount Amber on tap, much exposed brick, and the area's younger, liberal crowd. I'd noticed our next stop, **JACK'S BACKYARD** (9 Maple Street, Barre) coming into town and avoided it largely because of its vapid "An Adult Watering & Feeding Place" self-billing. Chris and Laurel, however, said it was a must. I wouldn't go that far, but the selection - headed by Bass on tap and Catamount in the bottle - is good and the popcorn - grab a pail and help yourself - is great. Last on the agenda was a Chinese restaurant, the **ORIENTAL RENDEVOUS II** (435 North Main Street, Barre) with little atmosphere and even less service, but the place in the area to head if you feel like some serious - there are several draught and a solid sixty bottled choices - taste testing.

The Northeast Kingdom's sole entry is a most appealing German restaurant tucked away in **NEWPORT CENTER**. The **FORSTHAUS** (Route 14, south of Route 100) offers fifteen bottled beers, including some select German ones ("We're a German restaurant; of course we have German beer": proprietor Gunter Hartmann), as well as a nice German menu.

I hadn't spent much time in **RUTLAND** in a good twenty years, and was saddened to find that the Bardwell House, a lovely old hotel and restaurant where I once spent a rather enjoyable New Year's Eve, has been converted to senior citizens' housing. "Converted about four years ago," Carol Roeckl-Smith, the bartender at **MURPHY'S** (31 Center Street) told me. She also told me about **ZEMO'S DUGOUT** (95 State Street); that is was probably the only old place left around. Murphy's, she informed me, had been an old, original bar until five years ago. Now, although not old, it is attractive. And five taps - Bass, Bud, Guinness, Heineken, and Bud Light - isn't hard to take in Rutland. I enjoyed a pint of Bass and headed off for Zemo's...only to find it closed. There I was, looking in at what could easily have been an Edward Hopper painting - sans people - and all I could do was that: look in. Seven booths, a wonderful little u-shaped bar, standup hatrack, tin roof, and a cash register that remembers World War II. I admired it for a long time. One last place of note in Vermont's second-largest city really isn't a bar at all (although beer and liquor are served). It's a Chinese restaurant named **KONG CHOW** (48 Center Street, across from Murphy's). Established in 1938, Kong Chow, I suspect, hasn't changed much in its fifty years. Its polished wood walls and inviting booths are definitely worth a looksee (but, as with Zemo's, better looksee early: they close at 9:00.).

STOWE is not my kind of town: too many cutesy shops, too many cutesy people. Still, there are two spots, almost side by side, that are definitely worth visiting. The older of the two, **THE PUB AT STOWE** (Mountain Road) characterizes itself as an authentic English pub, with authentic English cooking and,

more to the point, authentic English beer. With six English/Irish choices on draught plus another eleven by the bottle I'd say they've succeeded admirably (there are fifty or so other worldwide selections as well). Save some taste buds for neighboring **MR. PICKWICK'S PUB** (at Ye Olde Englande Inne, Mountain Road), though, where you can select from eleven tap and over eighty bottled choices. Both pubs, true to their heritage, serve a full menu of British fare, and Mr. Pickwick's has a large and lovely outside dining/drinking area during the summer season.

With my obvious enthusiasm for diners, I was delighted to discover the **CHELSEA ROYAL** (Marboro Road, Route 9 West) in **WEST BRATTLEBORO**. Built around a 1939 relocated-from-Brattleboro diner, the Chelsea Royal is a most attractive restaurant with a varied brew selection.

The 92-year old **CRAFTS INN** (West Main Street) in **WILMINGTON** offers outside dining and/or brew overlooking the Deerfield River from late April until early October.

Zemo's Dugout . . . and Pat and Jackie

I, of course, couldn't resist going back to Zemo's Dugout in the morning. And am I glad I did. The proprietors, Jackie and Pat Garofano, are delightful people. Pat explained that the "Zemo" name came with the place when he and Jackie purchased it in 1973. The original owner, a short and stocky guy, was nicknamed Zemo - "little monk" in Italian - and he and Jackie just stuck with the name. Jackie notes, proudly, that Zemo's is the only bar in Rutland with no video games, no jukebox, no swearing, and - although Pat was a little uneasy about including this one - that doesn't serve unescorted females. They open early (10:00) and generally close early (9:00). If you're ever around Rutland don't fail to drop by. And if you're ever around the first Saturday of December, especially don't fail: for their annual Christmas party Jackie puts on, Pat assured me, "an Italian buffet that's the best of anyplace."

Revere

AS IN PAUL AND HIS RIDE

Views from a 1905 printing of PAUL REVERE'S RIDE, published by the L.H. Nelson Company, located right in Longfellow's home town of Portland, Maine.

What does Paul Revere, forever enshrined in our hearts and memories for his April 18, 1775 ride to warn that the British were coming, have to do with beer?!

Was his home brew the talk of Boston's malt and hops mavens?

Probably not: although "The Messinger of the Revolution" tried his hand at many avocations and occupations - silversmith, coppersmith, political cartoonist, music publisher . . . even dentistry for a short while - he is not known to have been a home brew devotee.

Did he like beer?

The chances are that he did. Most of his contemporaries were known to have lifted a pint now and again so there's good reason to believe that Paul went along for the ride (sorry, I just couldn't resist that one) from time to time, too.

Did that stalwart New Englander, Henry

Wadsworth Longfellow, choose to make Paul's ride famous because "Revere" rhymes with "beer?"

It's possible, but not probable . . . although one William Dawes made essentially the same ride that same night - going to Lexington and Concord via Boston Neck, while Revere went by way of Charlestown - and certainly very few folks recall *his* name today.

Did he enjoy a brew or two ("one, if by land, and two if by sea") to top off that famous ride?

He may very well have. Revere and Dawes are known to have replenished themselves with food and drink in Lexington before pushing on to Concord, but we'll doubtless never know for sure whether that drink was the amber nectar: history, alas, doesn't always record it all.

Actually, these questions are just to throw you off. The real answer is that there was a brewer - not in New England; not even close to being in New England - so inspired by Paul Revere's stirring ride that he brewed a beer (actually an ale - and a very fine one at that) to commemorate it. That ale - still brewed and about to celebrate its 14th birthday - is generally available in New England's finer beer stores. Can you guess its identity?

answer ▶
(No peeking, though, until you've at least ventured a guess!)

"Liberty Ale . . . .

We brewed that in April of 1975. In fact we brewed it on April 18th. I'd been dying to brew an ale for a long time, and I decided that I wanted to do something for the Bicentennial because I like the old, old idea - British really, but also European generally - of brews made for the season, or brews made for an occasion. So I thought 'I want to do something for the Bicentennial . . . but I don't want to join the mob in 1976. It's going to be chaos: everybody's going to be joining the Bicentennial. There'll probably be Bicentennial beers and every other damn thing.' So I said 'Let's do an ale and let's make it a Bicentennial ale. What could we celebrate now? Well, Paul Revere's ride was on the 18th of April in 1775. So, on the 18th of April in 1975 we brewed Liberty Ale!"

1986 interview.

Maytag Washing Machine Company) explained in a March, (who, incidentally, is the great grandson of the founder of the Anchor's president and brewmaster, Fritz Maytag. As Fritz Beer fame) of San Francisco, Liberty Ale was the brainchild of Brewed by the Anchor Brewing Company (of Anchor Steam

Liberty Ale

. . . and the answer

Smith Brothers... More Than Just A Cough Drop

◆

NEW BEDFORD'S DYNAMIC DUO: SMITH BROTHERS . . . AND DAWSON'S, TOO

Think of Smith Brothers and you almost automatically think of cough drops. Ah, but old timers around New Bedford know better. They know that Smith Brothers used to stand for something far more exciting than stemming a cough! It used to stand for some mighty tasty ales.

The Large and Small of it

The large and small of Smith Brothers' breweriana: the earthernware jug ("Smiths' Ale Gives Strength") measures a full foot and a half in heighth, while the circa 1905 porcelain bottle stopper weighs in at but one inch.

1914 ad for Smith Brothers Cough Drops

No, Their Names Weren't "Trade" and "Mark"

Smith Brothers' Cough Drops have been around doing their thing about as long as anyone cares to remember. Originally concocted by the brothers Andrew and William W. Smith as an offshoot to their most successful Poughkeepsie, New York restaurant and confectionary, the drops are now manufactured in Chicago, far, far from their Hudson River birthplace...but Andrew and William W. are still right there on the label.

From the grocery business to wholesale liquors to brewing: such was the route of several New England brewers, Smith Brothers among them. There were four Smith Brothers, Michael, Bernard, Joseph, and James, with James the dominant influence. Born in Somerset, Massachusetts in 1858, he moved to New Bedford with his family as

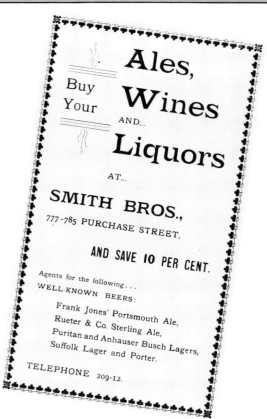

Anhauser Busch

Correct English was perhaps not a forte of Smith Brothers. In this 1900 ad they managed to both forget the hyphen in Anheuser-Busch and misspell it as "Anhauser."

and champion checker player as well as successful brewer - passed away in 1922. With younger brother Joseph at the helm, Smith Brothers opened up for beer business again in 1933. Edward Lahey, perhaps better remembered as longtime U.S. Brewers Foundation prexie, took over upon Joseph's death in 1937 and guided the firm for the rest of its years.

Up against ever-increasing brutal competition from the nationals, plus a relative giant, Dawson's, less than three blocks away, Smith Brothers called it quits in mid-1951. The brewery - equipment, trucks and all - was put on the market in October for $250,000. There were no takers. A four and one-half hour, two-alarm blaze destroyed much of the former brewery's facility in March, 1961. There months later the rest was razed. Most of what was once the site of Smith Brothers is now, most unglamourously, a parking lot.

an infant. After modest schooling and employ in a local shoe factory, he decided to seek his fortune in the grocery business. Next came wholesale liquors . . . a business that exposed James and his brothers to both substantial profits and the marketing of beer. Smith Brothers acted as agents for a host of brewers, including Frank Jones, F. & M. Schaefer, Suffolk, Rueter & Company, Stanley & Company, even Anheuser-Busch.

In 1903 the brothers decided to go all out -"the whole nine yards," as a Mainer friend of mine would put it - and build their own brewery. After but fifteen years of brewing, alas, Massachusetts went dry and they were forced to turn to the manufacture of ice. James - who was an avid baseball fan (he was co-owner and president of New Bedford's entry in the old New England League)

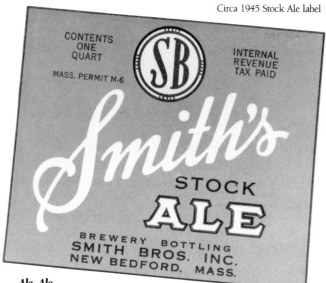

Circa 1945 Stock Ale label

Ale, Ale

Stock ale and a light dinner ale were Smith Brothers' mainstays in their eighteen years of brewing after repeal, although porter (from 1938 to 1946), stout (1933 to 1937), and bock (1938 to 1942) were all brewed at one time or another as well.

...And Dawson's, Too

The city that gave the world Moby Dick - "It's a Whale of a City" boast bumper stickers around town - also gave New England two breweries. And while Smith Brothers is the namesake of this chapter, it was New Bedford's "other" brewery - Dawson's - that was far and away the more important of the two.

Born in Lancashire, England in 1837, Benjamin Dawson came to America in 1858 at

On The Move

New Bedford - a city that has gone through three distinct periods: whaling, textile manufacturing, fishing - is proud of its past. But it's also proud of its present. And - for personal reasons - it's a city that will always have a very special warm spot in my heart.

the age of 21. At first home was Harrisville, Rhode Island, where he pursued the trade he'd learned in Lancashire, that of weaver in a textile mill. After six years in Harrisville, Dawson and his wife Helen, also a native of England, came to New Bedford. At the start, our future brewer continued as a weaver, finding employ in the Wamsutta Mills (makers of Percale sheets), but in 1869 he went out on his own, opening a retail

grocery store. From there, in 1885, it was on to wholesale liquors. Known as Dawson & Son (the son's name was Joseph), the business became the largest wholesale liquor operation in the New Bedford area. Successfully selling Frank Jones and other ales and lagers obviously inspired Dawson: in 1899 he went ahead and built New Bedford's first-ever brewery.

If all of this sounds familiar, it should: it's essentially the same road - millworker to grocer to wholesaler of liquors to brewer - travelled by James Smith. There were other parallels: both were active in politics (on directly opposing sides, however: it was not uncommon for voters in New Bedford to be stopped on the street and asked "What are you - Dawson or Smith Brothers?"); both took their companies into the ice business during prohibition; both passed away in the early 1920s.

Benjamin Dawson, a man for whom the American dream became a reality, died at his home in New Bedford on the morning of

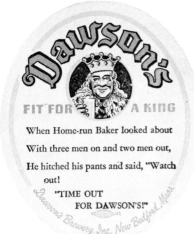

When Home-run Baker looked about
With three men on and two men out,
He hitched his pants and said, "Watch out!
"TIME OUT FOR DAWSON'S!"

"Watch Out!"

Although Frank "Home Run" Baker's career was pre-prohibition (or at least the great majority of it was; he held down the hot corner for the Philadelphia Athletics and Yankees for thirteen seasons, 1908-1922, leading the league in home runs four times), this coaster is definitely not. It was part of a series, each featuring a different poem on both sides, put out by the brewery in the latter part of the 1940s.

Photo courtesy of Haverhill Public Library

Published by Libby's Book Shop   Market Square, Amesbury, Mass.

Hand Colored

"Naturally Better"

They may have been delivering Harvard in this wonderful late 1930s photo, but the sign atop the Model Package Store on White Street in Haverhill indicates that Dawson's was their featured brand. And the sign's "Naturally Better" wording was true: Dawson's was proud of the fact that it used no substitutes or coloring matter, only natural ingredients in their purest state.

The Star Cafe

What I especially like about this circa 1940 photo-view postcard is that, while it states "hand colored," most of the card is actually just good old black and white. Included in the color category, though, is the Dawson's Ale-Beer sign - it's colored yellow - above the entrance to the Star Cafe. A recent midmorning stroll through Amesbury, a pleasant smallish city of magnificent Victorian homes, disclosed that the Dawson's sign is no more. I'd fully expected that, of course (although one can always hope!). But I was disappointed to find that the Star Cafe is history, too. ("been gone for at least twenty years," commented longtime Amesburyite Donald Mitchell, standing across the street from what is now Ben's Uniforms.)

Where have you gone, Star Cafe?

137

December 18th, 1920. The brewery that he'd crafted continued on, of course. Ice was the major product during prohibition, al-

and-then-some of the brewery's capacity... from 300,000 barrels a year to 700,000 barrels a year.

An Inside Look

Photos courtesy the Standard-Times

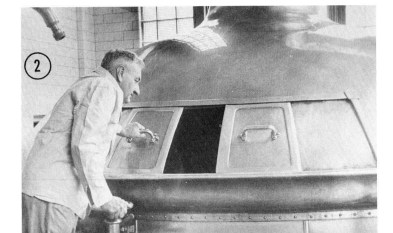

In its last full decade as Dawson's, the 1950s, the brewery was twice the subject of features in New Bedford's daily, The Standard-Times. Here, courtesy of the paper's photo morgue, is an inside look at Dawson's when it was humming. Clockwise from upper left: bottles coming off the line, ready to be put into cases (that's foreman Zygie Kwiatkowski, seated with cap, keeping watch over things); first kettleman Adolph Stuck checking the wort; brewmaster Theodore Schueler (a mighty important man at Dawson's for the better part of two decades, he was an eighth generation master brewer, four generations on his mother's side and three on his father's had been brewmasters before him.) amidst his laboratory's quality control apparatus; and cases stacked up and ready to be loaded.

though part of the facility was used as a dairy. More important was the fact that, regardless of the facility's other uses, the majority of the brewing apparatus was kept in good repair, so that when happy days returned in 1933 Dawson's was ready to roll. Over $200,000 spent in the months after repeal for improvements and the most modern equipment available just helped it roll with that much more vigor. An additional $500,000 was put into plant in 1937, and the end of World War II saw a doubling-

Dawson's Calorie Controlled Ale can (that bears a 1952 copyright date)

Calorie Controlled

No one seems to know with any degree of certainty what "Calorie Controlled," used by Dawson's on its packaging and in its advertising all during the 1950s, meant. Thirty-one year old Keith Whitmore, a breweriana collecting friend from Waltham, Massachusetts who specializes in Dawson's, theorizes that it was the first low calorie malt beverage. My own hunch, however, is that it was more than likely just a promotional ploy, a nicely alliterative play on words toward but one goal: increased Dawson sales.

Time Out For Dawson's

Just about the time that the war was, thankfully, nearing its end was the time Dawson's seems to have adopted the slogan that's still fondly recalled by many a beer buff around New England: "Time Out For Dawson's."

It was a slogan that would serve them in good stead: folks *were* taking time out for Dawson's. By the 1950s the brewery on Brook Street was one of the undisputed big guns in New England brewing. Its output of 154,917 barrels in 1950 made it, after Narragansett, Harvard, Haffenreffer, and Hampden, the fifth largest brewing company in New England (although it ranked but 63rd nationally). Scarcely more than a decade later, in 1962, sales had risen smartly to 216,312 barrels, jumping Dawson's to second place - behind only Narragansett - among New England's brewers (and 53rd nationally).

Those were the glory days. But you could kiss them goodbye, for the factors - overpowering competition from the nationals paramount among them - that did in every other independent New England brewer were already catching up with Dawson's. Within five years, in 1967, Dawson's was sold to Rheingold Breweries, Inc., a semi-national New York-headquartered corporation that routinely ranked among the top ten brewers in the nation. Asked why, in a November, 1987 telephone interview, the family decided to sell out, Benjamin's grandson, 88-year old Isaac Dawson, put it rather simply: "We got some money for it."

had run

Time ∧ Out For Dawson's

The Rheingold/Ruppert Era

By the time Rheingold purchased Dawson's, in 1967, it was not the powerhouse it had once been. To be sure, it was still a monster compared to Dawson's (sales were over three and a half million barrels in 1967!), and it owned the still strong-selling Ruppert/Knickerbocker labels, having bought out Jacob Ruppert, Inc. in 1965. But Rheingold pegged much of its hope for its newly acquired New Bedford plant not on Rheingold or Knickerbocker, but on a brand new low calorie product they christened Gablinger's (after the Swiss doctor who developed the formula). It turned out to be a weak peg: Gab sales (or non sales, as was the actual case) got mired in a mess of government bureaucracy and legalities, and never really did get far off the ground. Rheingold, itself, was acquired by PepsiCo, Inc. in February of 1973. PepsiCo, however, had seemingly little or no interest in the brewing operations: it was after the highly profitable string of soda bottling plants owned by the brewery. Within a year PepsiCo shut down Rheingold's major brew facility, in Brooklyn, New York. Chock Full O' Nuts, a New York coffee and luncheonette corporation, saved the day by buying Rheingold in March of 1974. In spite of Chock Full's best efforts, however, Rheingold could not be turned around. As big as it was, it was being gobbled up by yet-much-bigger brewers. In 1977, Rheingold, all its labels and all its facilities, was sold to C. Schmidt & Sons, of Philadelphia. One of the first things Schmidt management did was shut down the New Bedford operation. Over three-quarters of a century of brewing on Brook Street came to a close.

June, 1974 newspaper advertisement

A great tasting beer-A light beer with less calories than skim milk

99 CALORIES

GABLINGER'S BEER

12 Fl. Oz.

YOUR GROCER HAS IT

"...With Less Calories Than Skim Milk"

The comparision with skim milk was an apt one for many who tried Gab . . . they thought it had about as much flavor. Whether it was the taste, the brown can (ugly!), the mug shot of the good doctor on the label, or just an idea that was mishandled...whatever, Gablinger's was, very simply, not a success.

139

"Among the Finest and Most Modern"

"More than a half million dollars has recently been spent in enlarging the plant's facilities and capacity, and the new plant has been pronounced by many brewery experts to be among the finest and most modern in the country."

Modern Brewery, June, 1937

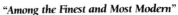

Times Change

Today what was Dawson's is utilized by a hodge-podge: auto salvage, auto repair, used tires, liquor storage. Sad, but true. But at least it is utilized.

And standing.

Memories

I chatted with several folks who were in and about the old brewery the day I was taking photos (November 4, 1987). Their memories were good.

Al Andersen (who looks remarkably like Art Carney), 62-year old carpenter, son of former Dawson's chief engineer, and buddy of Andre Fornier, right, the 47-year old present-day owner of what was Dawson's.

Yeah, we get guys coming by and asking about the brewery and taking pictures. Maybe an average of ten-twelve a year. That I see. I don't care. Doesn't bother me.

Andre Fornier

I own all of this, the whole brewery. Since 1979. Two years after they closed. It's not bad, not bad at all. I changed it over to industrial. I got a class three license now, junk yard license. And I got a body shop that I rent out, too, And a tire shop on the other side. I rent them out. Basically, I didn't do nothing (to convert the brewery to industrial). I made the ramp, to come in up here. And overhead doors and stuff like that. But there ain't a hell of a lot you had to do; it was so unique already. It's like you say, it's built like a bomb shelter. That's what it was; it was a fallout shelter.

Andre Fornier

There used to be an old standing joke here in the city of New Bedford. It was one of my father's favorite jokes. About two blocks that way was Smith's Brewery. Smith produced a stock ale, which was quite dark and quite heavy in body. And Dawson's made a light dinner ale. It was almost a lager. One year they decided to see who could sell the most in the month of June. And so they kept very careful records. And in the thirty days of June they totaled up all the ale that they had sold . . . and it was a dead heat. Absolutely tied. So to settle things once and for all, they sent samples of the two ales up to M.I.T. to have it analyzed, to see which was the best. And about three weeks later the same report came back to both breweries, and said: "Neither horse is fit for work."

Al Andersen
(Note: Al fairly roared over that one: I managed a smile.)

Joseph Hayes, 72-year old retired carpenter who lives across Brook Street from the former brewery.

I've been here, maybe, twenty years. And in the old days of the brewery the aunt had the house. And in those days sometimes the hop smell would be in the air and if she had laundry out it would hit the laundry: you could smell it real strong. I liked the smell, but my aunt didn't, though.

Joseph Hayes

Dawson's was good stuff. Especially what was drunk here, because it was fresh. Down below in the bottling room there was a porcelain sink that was attached to the wall and that had three spigots. One was ale, one was beer, and the third one was water. That was just for rinsing out what used to be called a seidel, a glass mug with a handle on it.

Al Andersen

I remember when Ruppert took over. They speeded up the machinery, expecting that they would produce more: get this thing really hopping. You could hear the machinery running faster. And their trucks'd be racing back and forth.

Joseph Hayes

They were pretty liberal with their help. There was kind of an unspoken local rule that if you worked here they didn't mind if you drank on the job. As long as you didn't get in trouble with it. And as long as you tried to keep it to a case a day. Of course, that's kind of hard to do in an eight-hour day. But some guys went over, over the case. The guys that worked here for years and years, especially the guys in the fire room. Years ago, before they put oil in here when they fired those things by hand with coal, those guys could consume some beer. They'd sweat off ten pounds a day if they didn't drink a case of beer.

Al Andersen

We were going to use it (the brewery) for a Halloween party one time. There's a lot of vats and there's a lot of fermenting tanks that are still here. That are like big swimming pools. We were going to have them (the kids) go through and have different things come out and scare them. But we didn't do it. We would've run into too many problems about being unsafe. So we didn't bother.

Andre Fornier

My father was the chief engineer here when it was Dawson's, when they were still making Dawson's Ale and Dawson's Lager Beer. It was a big deal (being chief engineer). It requires a first class engineer's license. It was impressive for an immigrant kid: he came to this country when he was 18. His name was Einar. It's an old Norwegian name. Einar was a famous Viking, Einar the Red.

Al Andersen

142

Time Out For Dawson's

In factory, dock and foundry,
In every major industry,
New England's workers all agree
Time out...For Dawson's!

Executives work with all their might
to speed production left and right.
But when they hurry home at night -
Time out...for Dawson's!

All work, no play . . . you know the rest.
Take time out for good cheer.
If you wish to do your best,
Call for Dawson's Ale or Beer!

1945 radio jingle

Avenue Package Store, 1120 Acushnet Avenue, New Bedford

There were two copper kettles in there, for cooling the mash, and they had to knock out most of that wall to get 'em out of here. It was an engineering feat. And those copper kettles were taken down to the North Terminal here and loaded on a big barge and towed down to New York and put on a freighter and sold to the brewery in Japan. This was 1968, early in the year.

Al Andersen

Where they knocked the wall out.

"The Friendly Beer"

My own favorite memory - discovery, actually - of Dawson's occured not ten blocks from the brewery. I'd decided to walk around some, looking for a lunch spot. Suddenly there it was: a good 25-foot long Dawson's "The Friendly Beer" painted sign still hanging in there on the side of the Avenue Package Store. One word came to mind to describe it . . . beautiful. Just beautiful.

143

There's Always...

◆

. . . SOMETHING ELSE YOU WANT TO INCLUDE

No matter how hard you work at it there's always more "stuff" — facts, photos, lore, breweriana — than space. Here, in what is in reality a miscellaneous section, are two six-packs and then some of that "stuff."

"Made in the Berkshires"

For a solid half-century, from 1867 until prohibition, Pittsfield had its own ale, even its own malt tonic. "Made in the Berkshires," as the ads of the brewery made clear. Begun by one Michael Benson as a truly ramshackle affair (accounts of the day describe it as a "common woodshed," twenty by twenty-five feet in size), the concern was bought by Bavarian native Jacob Gimlich and his partner John White a year later, in 1868. As Gimlich & White, the firm prospered. In 1891 the brewery, still run by Mssrs. G & W, became the Berkshire Brewing Association. To celebrate the turn of the century, the veteran brewers introduced Mannheimer Export Lager. And they were not at all bashful about it. A 1900 ad extolled Mannheimer thusly: "After thirty years of successful business we have reached the height of our ambition. We have placed upon the market for family trade a Lager Beer far superior to any. Our MANNHEIMER EXPORT LAGER BEER has reached the acme of fame. Bright and sparkling, healthful, refreshing and purity are but a few thoughts synonymous with Mannheimer." Whew!

Gimlich died in 1912; the brewery in 1918. Nothing of it remains today. On its former site, at the confluence of Columbus Avenue and Ononta and South John Streets, now stands the Second Congregational Church and its parking lot.

Left to right: circa 1940 Clyde Cream Ale bottle; circa 1895 Enterprise porcelain tray; circa 1905 Enterprise serving tray, courtesy the Hug collection

An Enterprising Name

Two entirely different brewing facilities have carried the "Enterprise" name in Fall River, Massachusetts' long and illustrious industrial history. Number one was located at 50 Glasgow Street. Founded in 1894, it was constructed of wood and burned to the ground in 1898. Rebuilt of more traditional - and far sturdier - brick, it operated independently until 1910 when it became part of the Old Colony Breweries Company, a three-brewery Fall River combine. It was closed in 1916.

After prohibition the former Old Colony Brewery, 866 Davol Street, bounced back as the Spindle City's only brew operation. Founded in 1896 by Rudolf F. Haffenreffer (son of the founder of Boston's Haffenreffer & Co.) it, of course, had also been part of the Old Colony Breweries Company before prohibition. Renamed the Enterprise Brewing Company, it operated - still controlled by the Haffenreffer family - until 1963, brewing a variety of ales and lagers under a variety of names, including Old Tap, Boh, Clyde, White Seal, and King Philip.

Today nothing remains of either former brewery - or, for that matter, of any of Fall River's other three 20th century breweries. "Progress" - and interstates - have taken their unfortunate toll.

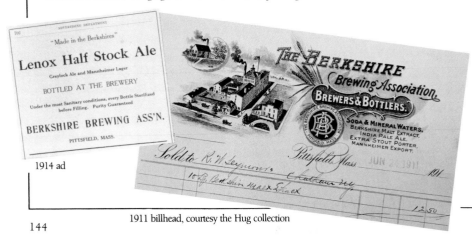

1914 ad

1911 billhead, courtesy the Hug collection

John Bradley, Maine Brewer

For a state that has the "Maine Stein Song" - made famous by Rudy Vallee in the 1930s - as its state university's theme song, Maine has had precious few breweries in its almost 170 years of existence. (The fact that it spent so many of its first 135 years legally dry — see pages 86-87 — is, of course, a good reason why!). Consequently, I was thrilled when I unearthed this 1860 receipt in a Portland used book store a while ago . . . especially because Cape Elizabeth, then as now a gracious Portland suburb, seemed a most unlikely location for a brewery.

Reliable information, alas, proved elusive. William B. Jordan, Jr., in his A HISTORY OF CAPE ELIZABETH, MAINE, gives the brewery's address as Brewery Road, now Highland Avenue, and Ocean House Road. City directories of the day indicate that John Bradley operated the concern as the Forest City - Portland's nickname - Brewery from 1850 or so until the early 1870s, using his residence at 17 York Street in Portland as his depot. At some point James and/or Patrick McGlinchy, also early Portland brewers, may or may not have been involved in the

Cape Elizabeth operation. (Jordan says yes; city directories indicate no.) The facility appears to have been used as a brewery through 1881, when it became a canning factory. It was completely destroyed by fire in September, 1883.

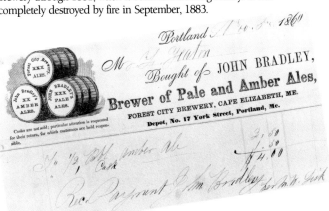

Half-Eckart Bros.

This circa 1890 ceramic bottle stopper should've read "Eckart Half-Bros.": the brewery was founded in 1865 by George F. Eckart and Frederick F. Ehrsam, half-brothers who immigrated to America from their native Saxony, Germany. Also known as the Eagle Brewery, Eckart Bros. brewed lager, ale, and porter until 1920, when operations ceased with the advent of prohibition.

Do Cows Really Like Beer?

d 'em only the best and they'll taste the best, reasons sentday Stamford, Connecticut beef baron Fred Grant; so 2,000 steers get to luxuriate on a 100% pure organic diet includes spinach, yams, dandelion roots . . . and beer. of beer. "Beer is a very important part of the digestive cess," explains Grant. Ah, but do they like it? "Beer is cally not a steer's favorite drink," Grant will admit, adding t I'd say the cows are comfortable."

The Massachusetts' Brewery That Really Wasn't

The bottles were embossed "State Line, Mass.," but Losty's brewery (1856-1903) was actually 200 feet or so over the line in Canaan, New York. State Line's former post office was within sight of the brewery, however, and the resultant better service may have prompted the Bay State address. Whatever, all that remains of State Line today is a cluster of houses, and a small cluster at that . . . but it's more than remains of the brewery, which has been reduced to small bits of foundation on the side of a hill.

Give Me A Mule Head

Several of brewland's more distinctive after-prohibition brand names were claimed by West Haven, Connecticut's Wehle (pronounced "Way-lee") Brewing Company. There was Ox Head and Cab and Old Eli and, most distinctive of all, Mule Head. (Other names used were less charismatic: Burton, Buckingham, and just plain Wehle.) Opened in 1933 in what had been the Weidemann Brewing Company prior to prohibition, Wehle was headed up by Raymond J. Wehle, president, and Harold J. Wehle, secretary/treasurer. After eight years of moderate success they sold out, in late 1941, to William W. Swayne of New York City who, in turn, sold controlling interest to Edward B. Hittelman, president of Brooklyn's Edelbrew Brewery, in August, 1942. Following an initial pledge to put affairs on a sound footing, however, Hittelman - amidst shareholder allegations that he had transferred Wehle's wartime grain and bottle cap quotas to Edelbrew and "did not attempt in good faith to operate the Wehle plant" - closed the brewery. It was never reopened. Nothing of the facility, which had been located at 1093 Campbell Avenue, remains.

A nice graphic little collection of Wehle breweriana: from left, a circa 1936 Wehle Beer can; a circa 1935 Cab coaster; a circa 1938 Mule Head serving tray; a 1934 billboard; a circa 1938 Ox Head Beer In Cans sign; and a circa 1935 Cab Cream Ale tap knob.

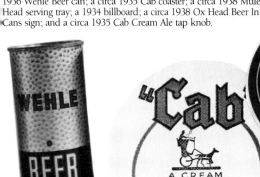

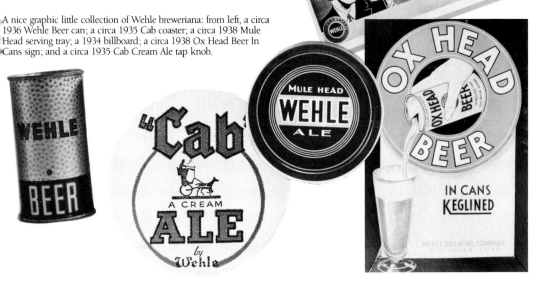

145

Hartford and Her After Repeal Breweries

Before the big P (prohibition), Connecticut's capital city had four - count 'em and see page 80 - rather substantial breweries. But was there life - brew-wise - after prohibition? The answer is a semi-resounding "yep." Two of the four - Aetna and New England Brewing - came back on the scene.

Aetna was the successor to Hartford's first brewery, founded in 1865 by Charles Herold. Name changes (to the Herold Capitol Brewing Company in 1879; Columbia Brewing Company in 1896) followed before the Aetna name was adopted in 1900. Lager, ale and porter were brewed. Early-on during prohibition the company tried the manufacture of cereal beverages, but with no more success than most of its contemporaries and the plant lay idle for most of the dry spell.

Refurbished in 1933, the Aetna Brewing Company opened up and operated - brewing Aetna Ale - until 1939. In that year the brewery's last chapter was begun, but as the Dover Brewing Company. Dover continued until 1947. Brands were Dover Ale and Dover Beer. In 1947 the company went into receivership after having been attached by several suppliers for monies owed. A year later, in December of 1948, a Superior Court judge authorized the brewery's sale - for a meager $25,000 - to one William Moiger of Glastonbury, who announced plans to move a nutmeg mill operation into the facility.

Nothing of Charles Herold/Herold Capitol/Columbia/Aetna/Dover remains extant today.

A 1900 ad and an enamel-over-metal serving tray from about the same year. Aetna appeared to specialize in ornate - and attractive - type faces in addition to fine ales and lager.

New England Brewing Company's story isn't too awfully different than Aetna's, except that there's a bit of Ronald Reagan in its history.

Founded in 1897, New England Brewing was built for output: its capacity was a most considerable 200,000 barrels and it had its own complete bottling facilities. Both ale and lager were brewed.

After prohibition, the brewery was slow to get back into things, but in 1936 it reopened, the largest brewery in Connecticut, with J. Harold Murray at the helm. While not exactly a household word these days, Murray was a well-known stage, screen, and radio star at the time, having starred in movies with the likes of John Gilbert and Myrna Loy. Weary of show biz, he decided to try the beer biz. As he said shortly after taking over as brewery president: "Whatever artistic leanings I may have I use in planning advertisements that make my product click." The only problem was that his product -Nebco Beer and Ale - didn't click. In spite of a seventeen-person sales force (including Josephine Moore, one of but two brewery saleswomen in the country), New England Brewing did not live up to expectations. Floods in 1936 and 1938 hurt, both times forcing a halt in production. The brewery went into receivership in 1937; J. Harold returned to show biz in 1939; the brewery was reorganized in 1940; and became a branch of Waterbury's Largay Brewing Company in 1944. Operations ceased in 1947. Nothing of the former brewery, which was located at 503-529 Windsor Street, remains.

A four-decade span of New England Brewing Company memorabilia; the serving tray (enamel-over-metal, a la Aetna) is from circa 1900; the ad is from 1911; the portrait of J. Harold Murray is from 1937.

The Big Nine

Think of large brewery horses and you think of Anheuser-Busch and their Clydesdales. And that's ok. But other brewers, too, have been known for their horses at one time or another. Genesee, Carling, and especially Hanley come to mind. No Clydesdales for Hanley, though. Their pride and joy was a nine horse team of Roan Belgiums. Known as "The Big Nine" (their total weight exceeded 20,000 pounds!), they were used for exhibition purposes only, displayed at most of the leading fairs and horse shows throughout the country. (P.S. Hanley's horse team was most appropriate: James Hanley, the brewery's founder, loved horses and owned some of the finest thoroughbred stock in the country. His Prince Albert, in fact, was touted as "the fastest harness horse in the world" in the very early years of this century.)

No Thanks, I'd Rather Pour It Over My Head

There's beer for drinking . . . and there's beer for hair setting. And at no time was this truer than back in the mid and late 1940s when the "beer do" was all the rage. This period cartoon pokes fun at the plight of the guy or girl who didn't know the benefits of pouring the bottle over one's head rather than into one's glass.

"Stop! You're drinking up my wave set."

Painchaud's Liquors,
257 Winter Street, Haverhill,
Massachusetts, circa 1910.
Courtesy Haverhill Public Library

Wouldn't It Be Great . . .

Wouldn't it be great to be able to step back in time and walk into such as Painchaud's and stock up on the wherewithall to do some rather serious taste testing and do that rather serious taste testing; to find out if New England's brews of yesteryear really were as fine as legend - and many an oldtimer! - has it that they are? Wouldn't it be great . . .

When $12,000 Bought a Brewery

If you'd been in the vicinity of Lynn, Massachusetts in 1911 you could've picked yourself up a nice little brewery for $12,000 and change. The Waterhill Brewery, located at 44 Woodman Street, went under the auctioneer's gavel, but the five-year old operation didn't bring much: some lucky buyer became the new owner for $7,450 plus assumption of a $5,000 mortgage. (The lucky buyer, however, didn't re-activate the facility as a brewery. Today it's long gone; on the site is public housing.)

"Two Be-er Not Two Beer"

A circa 1895 Seymour, Connecticut business card with a wonderful - from a beerlover's point of view - takeoff on Shakespeare's "To be or not to be."

1948 photo

A Shave and a Haircut Beer

It was, surprisingly, not the Board of Health that put a stop to what had become a custom in at least one Stamford, Connecticut tavern in the late 1940s: the furnishing of an electric shaver for the convenience of patrons. Though the shaves were strictly self-service, local barbers filed a complaint, the state beverage control commission agreed with the barbers, and that was that. Bye bye shave and a beer.

1915 Prohibition rally card

But They Had To Live With It Anyway

Forty-six of our then forty-eight states eventually ratified the so-called "Noble Experiment," prohibition. The only two that weren't naive enough to believe that it would work were right her in - where else?! - New England: Connecticut and Rhode Island.

Under The Tadcaster Tree

◆

Worcester: What wonders awaited me at the end of the exit ramp?

Worcester is a city that's long intrigued me. I must have passed through it a good forty or fifty times on I-290, but I've never, ever spent any considerable time in it. Once, many moons ago, I set out to track down what remained of the old Bowler/Brockert/Worcester brewery, but my car was in bad shape, it started snowing like crazy, and by the time I finally arrived in "The Heart of the Commonwealth" Old Trusty was sputtering and wheezing so badly that I figured I'd better just turn around and head back home. Which I did.

It's an intrigue - this intrigue of mine with Worcester - that has transcended the city's brewing history, substantial though it's been. I guess I've wanted to find out at least a little of what Worcester is all about. Friends advised me not to expect "a big Portland" or "a small Boston"; that there's not much happening. Another knowledge-able soul, who grew up in a community adjoining Worcester, cautioned me not to go on an overcast day. "It's a gray-enough

city as it is," she counseled. A recent *Yankee* magazine cartoon poked fun by showing two kids, one saying to the other: "We used to live in Pawtucket but my dad wanted to wake up in a city that doesn't sleep. So we moved to Worcester." And my son, Carl, who's been to many a concert at the Centrum, gave it a ho hum "It's alright."

On the other hand, another recent issue of *Yankee* devoted seven full pages to an article entitled "Renaissance in Worcester." And *Worcester Evening Gazette* reporter Bob Blezard, talking with me about New England's micro movement, opined that, while Bostonians like to think of Worcester as Metro West, folks in Worcester are ever-increasingly coming to consider Boston to be Metro East.

I liked that.

Three Breweries Not So Long Ago

First, of course, let's take a gander at Worcester's brewing past. In the early years of the century - this century - Worcesterites had not one or two, but three, local breweries to satisfy their every malt beverage desire. With one of them (see page 149) you had to belly up and order quickly or forever lose your chance, but the other two were significant operations.

The city's creme de la breweries was Bowler Brothers, founded in 1883 by brothers John and Alexander Bowler. From an output of barely more than 5,000 barrels their first year, Bowler Brothers grew by large leaps: within twenty years they were providing Massachusetts and surrounding states with over 160,000 barrels of brew a year. The brothers' success was, in fact, the culmination of three generations of brewing. Both their father and his father before him had been brewers in England. Both brothers were born in Ipswich, England, coming to America as infants in 1859 because their father had accepted a position as brewmaster for a Troy, New York brewery. Neither brother wasted any time

From a circa 1902 Bowler Brothers' advertising booklet

A nicely embossed bottle from - obviously - either 1902 or 1903. It didn't get much use!

They Must've Been Doing Something Wrong

"Shortlived" is not really the right term for Gindele and Reuther. "Here today, gone today" is more like it. Messrs. Gindele and Reuther constructed their brewery, located at the corner of Canterbury and Hammond Streets, in the spring of 1902, but they had precious little time to enjoy it. By late 1903 they were out of business. Nothing remains of the brewery today.

in carrying on the Bowler brewing tradition: before their teenage years were through they were both experienced brewers. John honed his skills at a brewery in Brooklyn; Alexander in one at Elmira, New York. Then they joined together in Worcester.

Only One Ale

Only one ale in all the world for me!
So sings the connoisseur, and all the rest agree.
Only one ale, the Bowler Brothers' brew,
"Tadcaster" is the brand - What
Ails
You?

Only one ale, of all the ales the best
I'll take Tadcaster - the De'il can take the rest.
Only one ale as fine as ale can be -
"Tadcaster" is the brand - What
Ails
Me?

Only one ale, the difference you will see
When you take a friendly mug or two with me
Of old Tadcaster, none equal to be had,
'Tis brewed by Bowler Brothers - What
Ails
Tad?

Only one ale, note well its amber hue,
Pure as a dew-drop, take a sip of dew,
Blended with sunshine and zephyrs - just you try
A mug of old Tadcaster Ale - When
You're
Dry.

Although the brothers brewed lager as well as ale and porter, their English heritage dictated that their pride and joy be ale. And it was: Tadcaster Ale, named after the town of Tadcaster, England. Nor were they the least bit modest in their claims for it. Phrases such as "Best Ales and Porters on Earth," "The Acme of Perfection," Has No Equal," and "The King of all Ales" appear routinely in Bowler advertising copy. "It has the unmistakable old English tone and fragrance, and a color that rivals translucent amber. No man, however critical, need blush to offer a mug of Tadcaster to his most hypercritical friend. Tadcaster is an ale that wears and both makes friends

and keeps them" puffed an article in the January, 1900 Worcester Sunday Spy.

For three and a half decades Bowler Brothers thrived, becoming one of the more important breweries in New England, until done in, of course, by prohibition. With the arrival of legal dryness, the brothers turned to other interests. Alexander passed away in April of 1930; older brother John the following February.

Brewery Number Two

Before we return to the continuing tale of Bowler/Brockert/Worcester, let's pause and look at what little is known of the city's other major brewery. Founded in 1896 as the Worcester Brewing Company, with George Bierberbach as president, the venture failed and fell into the hands of receivers within a few years. In May of 1899, however, a new group headed by Michael J. Finnigan took over. The name of the operation was altered to the Worcester Brewing Corporation. Ale, lager and porter were brewed.

Though of consequence, the Worcester Brewing Corporation's brews never reached the status or enjoyed the "sizzle" of Bowler Brothers' much-heralded Tadcaster Ale. Operations continued until prohibition, when Worcester Brewing finally did achieve equal status with its intra-city rival: they both went out of business.

Bowler Comes Back

"Bowler's Ale Is Back On Market" headlined an article in the May 3, 1934 issue of Brewers News. And indeed it was, brewed with plant and equipment described as "completely modernized." The new proprietor was John J. Tiernan, owner of a substantial chunk of the Savin Rock Amusement Park, West Haven, Connecticut. Tiernan installed himself as treasurer, while J. Alexander Donoghue, who'd been with the brewery for sixteen years prior to prohibition, was named president and general manager. Their reign, as the Bowler Brewing Company, was shortlived, however: the venture flopped almost immediately, with the plant and equipment sold for $52,000 in the latter half of 1935.

The new purchasers were a varied lot. They included Anthony J. Pinkevich, chairman of the Cremo Brewing Com-

pany, of New Britain, Connecticut, who became president; M. Joseph Stacey, present-day Worcester city auditor, who was the treasurer; and Oscar Brockert, who took on the role of brewmaster (in addition to serving in the same capacity at Cremo: see page 93). The "Bowler" name was dropped forever: the new venture became the Brockert Brewing Company, in honor of Oscar, a man who knew his way around the world of brewing. Cont'd. on page 153

Circa 1900 matchsafe and bottle opener

Fiftieth Anniversary

Do You Use Ale?

Are you a Judge of Good Ale?

Do You Like the Best?

IF YOU HAVE NOT TRIED

BOWLER BROS.'
❋ TADCASTER ALES

GIVE YOURSELF THE BENEFIT OF THE DOUBT, THEN YOU WILL KNOW THAT TADCASTER IS PURE AND WHOLESOME, UNMATCHED IN FLAVOR, PERFECT IN TONE AND BOUQUET.

Connoisseurs Prefer it to All Others!

YOUR FRIENDS will like it!
YOU WILL SAVE money and get the Best!
THE BEST, in MATERIALS used.
THE BEST, in the ART of BREWING!
THE BEST, because we KNOW HOW!
To MAKE THE BEST ALE Made
In THIS or any OTHER country.

❧ ❧

Brewed by BOWLER BROS., LTD.,
Worcester, Mass.

❧ ❧

Bottled by Thos. Glynn & Son,
Newburyport, Mass.

87

Bowler Brothers envelope, 1916

Pre-Prohibition Tadcaster Breweriana

I love this ad. Humble the Brothers were not! But they could afford to be boastful: at the turn of the century and for several years thereafter, Bowler Brothers was tops in sales in Massachusetts and second in sales in all of New England. An especially noteworthy moment occured in the summer of 1903 when Sir Thomas Lipton, the well-known Scottish sportsman and tea magnate, ordered a supply of Tadcaster Ale for use aboard his steam yacht. The Brothers "are felicitating themselves on the order" was how the press of the day stated it.

Advertisement in the Official Program of the City of Newburyport, Massachusett's 50th Anniversary of Incorporation as a City, 1901

. . . And After-Prohibition Tad Breweriana, Too

Late 1940's Tadcaster labels

For many of its post-prohibition years, the brewery was concerned not only about the success of its ale, porter, and lager, but its Massachusetts Semi-Pro Basketball League team as well. Here's the Tad five - plus five - as they appeared in February, 1947, when the team was leading the loop with an almost unblemished 11-1 record. That's then-brewery president Joseph Stacey (see page 152), looking properly pleased, standing in the second row, far right.

Reflections on a Quarter of a Century Plus . . .

M. Joseph "Matt" Stacey was a key man at Brockert/Worcester Brewing Company for twenty-seven years, first as treasurer (1935-42) and then as president (1942-62). Now 76, Matt clearly enjoys talking about his adventures in brewland, is proud of the fact the WBC went out of business "clean": that the brewery's investors got their money (and more) back, and that his employees were given time to find other means of livelihood. Here are some of Matt's reflections, as shared with me in a most enjoyable two-hour interview in his office - he's auditor for the City of Worcester -at City Hall.

The brewery was completely dismantled during prohibition. It was used as a bonded government warehouse run by a couple of their (Bowler Brothers') former employees. At one time there was more Star Cars and Moons (both former makes of automobile) stored in that building.

After prohibition a man named Tiernan started up, equipped it (the brewery), all on conditional bills of sale and a big mortgage by Worcester County Institution for Savings. All they produced was draught beer. But Uncle Sam got 'em for bootlegging and grabbed 'em for income tax, and so he (Tiernan) walked away from the whole thing. They got him for his previous (to repeal) activities.

My predecessor, Tony Pinkovich, was the one who brought me up to Worcester. I was teaching school at the time in Meriden, Connecticut, the same town he was from. He went up there (Worcester) to buy some equipment in 1935, and when he saw the big mortgage and conditional bills of sale, he made a deal to take over the balances. That's how the brewery got started.

It was named the Brockert Brewing Company. Oscar Brockert brewed at Connecticut Valley for Waxey Gorden. We started off as a draught brewery only. That was sometime in 1935. I think we took possession sometime in October. We came out with beer - draught beer only - St. Patrick's Day of 1936. We came out with bottled beer sometime in the fall of 1936.

In 1946 I bought the name "Tadcaster," which was controlled by the H.E. Shaw Tobacco Company. They turned out certain products and were tobacco wholesalers here in the city. When the copyrights (to the Tadcaster name) had expired, they picked them up. I think it was sometime in the twenties. They never used the name for beer. They used it for fountain syrups, concentrated fountain syrups. Same logo, with the hop leaf in it. And they also used it on razor blades and a few other products. They sold me the rights to use the name on anything with alcohol in it. We used the name "Tad," too, which is a shortage of Tadcaster.

When we brought the name (Tadcaster) back it didn't get the reaction we thought we were going to get. But the Brockert name was a little tarnished. We'd had trouble with our product. It was off-taste. It gave people the runs. Then we had a bunch of the Irish people that worked for the brewery before (prohibition) that tried to get their sons in (into jobs at the brewery) and couldn't, so they started the propaganda that Brockert's gave 'em the runs.

There was a brewery in Bridgeport, Connecticut that didn't last too long after prohibition by the name of Dugan's. (note: Matt is referring to the Bridgeport Brewing Company, which brewed Dugan's Ale from 1934 to 1941.) A wholesaler out of Bridgeport talked me into putting out the beer for him under the Dugan name. So I made an investment in labels and cases and crowns and everything else. Then he backed out. But I went ahead anyway. That was in the fifties, and it was the revitalization of the Worcester Brewing Company. I came out with six quarts (of Dugan's) for $2.00. I called it the "Big Six." It was a big seller. Then Narragansett came out with twelve king-size bottles - which was a new type of bottle, sixteen ounces - and they were going house afire. So I came out with the Dugan's in a twelve-pack for $1.95 retail. The thing there was we came out with these twelve king-size in a twelve-pack for $1.95, plus deposit, and we boomed. We boomed. So Dugan's took over, practically, 70% of our sales. Tadcaster just slipped back in the background. Dugan's was just beer, no ale. It was my lifesaver in the fifties. I went back and increased our barrelage by about 20%. My barrelage ran anywhere from 40,000 to 50,000 barrels a year.

I used the name "Black Label": Brockert's Black Label. And I made a foolish mistake. I shipped some beer (Brockert's Black Label) into West Virginia during the war (WWII), maybe a couple of carloads, and they (Carling's) picked me up on it, crossing state lines. They had a patent on it. I could use it (the "Black Label" name) within the state. They couldn't stop me from using it in Massachusetts. But then they were going to sue me, so I gave up my rights to Black Label. If I ever knew Carling's was going to put up a plant in Massachusetts I'd have never given up the rights, no matter what, because I could've made them pay me a bloody fortune. I cursed it when they came into Massachusetts. I said "I threw away a million bucks."

We used to have stock ales that would run 12-14% (alcohol) by volume. You'd have two, three glasses of stock ale you'd have a pretty good bun: you'd have a feeling that you're a little intoxicated. You've heard of a boilermaker: a glass of beer and a shot of whiskey. Well, I've seen 'em here in my day - people coming from the wire mills - when there was Leahy's barroom on Millbury Street. I think it's out (of business) now. As the wire mill emptied at 3:00 they'd have the bar set up with about sixty to seventy glasses of beer and whiskey ready for the customers. Already filled. And some of the boilermakers, they'd pour the whiskey right into the beer. The first time I ever saw it was in that place (Leahy's).

We sponsored some of the best basketball teams in the country. In order not to spend money on advertising - we couldn't afford it - I'd gone to public things. And basketball was big here. We had some tremendous basketball teams. Heinsohn played for me. I had Joe Hughes. I had all the guys wanting to play for me because I can afford to give 'em beer and pick up their tab. I had more college players come into Worcester, playing against local boys here. This was during the summer. They wanted to keep in condition. We had the high school boys, too. And they knew Stacey would bring in - the brewery would bring in - the best players, and they could play against the best. Then, at the end of the season, there was an all-star team picked from all the teams, and they'd play the Celtics. We'd bring in the Celtics here and we'd pack in 5,000-6,000 into Crompton Park, that park near the brewery. Outdoor basketball under lights. That used to be a helluva thing: it kept the kids out of trouble. The girlfriends would come. We had four nights a week for basketball. It was our best form of advertising: the Tadcaster five. And then in the end, when Dugan's started going over, we changed it to Dugan's.

You want a story? You know Richie Gedman (Red Sox catcher)? His father was running my labeler when he married the mother, and later when Richie was born. The father's name was Richie, too. He was a handsome looking guy, over six foot. The boy doesn't look anything like him. The boy takes after the mother: the boy was stubby. He (Richie, Sr.) worked for the brewery for about five years, 'til we closed down. He died just about a year ago, but the mother still lives within two blocks of the brewery.

Now you've seen the expressway (I-290) go through: that was supposed to go through my buildings, where the garage was and everything else. And I wasn't using that last building. I wasn't using it at all. All we had was the cooper shop and junk up there. I figured that was gonna be worth a half a million, but it didn't happen.

My son, Robert, took it more emotionally than I did (when we closed). He was going to the University of Pennsylvania at the time. He took it seriously. He figured the brewery was his. You see I controlled, I'd say, 68% of it. He's a lawyer now, and top computer man. Systems man.

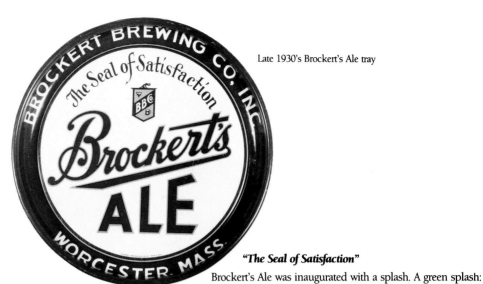

Late 1930's Brockert's Ale tray

"The Seal of Satisfaction"

Brockert's Ale was inaugurated with a splash. A green splash: it made its debut in Worcester taverns on St. Patrick's Day, 1936. Not bad for an ale named in honor of a man born in Lithuania, the son of a Lutheran minister.

Oscar, The Brewmaster

One of seventeen children, Oscar Brockert began his studies of the art of brewing in his native Lithuania. In 1905, at the age of twenty, he came to America to "make his fortune," as he later put it. He studied at the National Brewers Academy, then worked for a number of Eastern breweries. During prohibition he taught at the Academy, giving instructions on how to best make near beer. Having a brewery - and its brands - named after him had to be one of life's sweetest accomplishments for Oscar Brockert.

It was a sweetness that didn't last long, however. Oscar left after a year. His son, Bill, took over as brewmaster until he, too, left, in 1940. But while the Brockerts' years were short, they were good. Those, plus the war years, were the days when New Englanders still preferred hearty ales: exactly what Brockert's specialized in. And when New Englanders did most of their beer-drinking in the local taproom: again, exactly what Brockert's specialized in. Eighty percent of the brewery's business was in the form of draught beer, with virtually all distribution within a less than

Circa 1938 Brockert's Ale inside-of-matchbook copy

one hundred miles radius, from Pittsfield to the west, to the Hartford area to the south.

Immediately after the war, the company's name was changed one last time, to the Worcester Brewing Company. The president for what would be the brewery's last run was Joseph Stacey, who'd replaced Anthony Pinkevich following the latter's death in October, 1942. The once highly-revered Tadcaster name was revived. Packaged beer was given more emphasis, with both a twelve-pack of sixteen ounce bottles and a six-pack of quarts added to the product mix.

But the same problems - the power of national advertising campaigns, desire for weaker, blander brews, etc., etc. - that beset New England's other brewers beset Worcester Brewing, too. "Competitive conditions in the brewing industry have changed so radically in recent times thay continuation as a brewer locally proved impossible," Stacey is quoted as saying in a closing-the-brewery-down article (in which, adding insult to injury, Stacey's name was misspelled as "Stacy" five times) in the June 2, 1962 Worcester Telegram. Worcester Brewing at least got out while the getting was okay. Stacey's proud that the company was still solvent. In fact, he'll tell you that "The investors got twice their money back when we liquidated. We were one of the few New England breweries that didn't wind up bankrupt."

Several views, inside and out, of the former brewery, located at 60 Ellsworth Street/81-87 Lafayette Street, plus one of George Sigel. While George has little interest in beer, he does like old things: his pride and joy (he carries pictures and all) is a fully-restored 1948 Packard Deluxe.

Bowler Brothers/Brockert's/Worcester Brewing Today

I'd like to think of the brewery today as faded elegance, but from all information at hand it appears as if what was Bowler Brothers/Brockert's/WBC was never that much to look at, even in its prime. Let's, then, call it faded basic. Most of it is owned by Boston Beef Company, Inc., and its sister operation, Ellsworth Cold Storage, Inc. Part is also utilized by George Green Electrical Corp., distributors of electrical equipment.

Ironies abound: whereas "BB" once stood for Bowler Brothers, today it means Boston Beef; whereas 1883 one reflected the brewery's founding year, today it's part of the logo for Schonland's ("Schonlands: Since 1883"), one of the many brands carried by Boston Beef; and the brewery that Brockert's/WBC was closest to, the Cremo Brewing Company, is also now utilized as a meat packing and processing plant.

Circa 1963 Dugan's bottle

Dugan's Premium Beer

Dugan's was Worcester Brewing Company's primary brand from 1952 until the company's closing of its own brewery in 1962. It, as well as Tadcaster, was then brewed by Boston's Haffenreffer & Company under contract to Worcester Brewing until 1964. At that point, the Worcester Brewing Company dropped from the scene completely. Narragansett, who'd bought out Haffenreffer in 1964, continued use of the Dugan - but not the once proud Tadcaster - name for an additional two years, until 1966.

George Sigel, one of Boston Beef's owners, calls the building "fascinating," and was most gracious in giving me an hour or so tour. Boston Beef, a meat packer and processor, actually makes use of only a small percentage of what was once New England's second-largest brewery. The greater portion is used for nothing: it just sits there and rots and collects dust. As we walked through one empty - and ghostlike - section after another, George asked me if I could still smell the malt. I had to - sadly - say no.

The Miss Worcester, 300 Southbridge Street

"If you visit only one diner, choose this one" scribed Ann Sullivan in a 1979 *Worcester Magazine* article entitled "Diners Serve Up Memories As Well As Food." It's probably still true today. With its marble counter and tiled floor, the Miss Woos (rhymes with "booze") is as fine an example of diner beauty as you're likely to find.

Intrigue Satisfied

And now . . . what you've been waiting for. The inside scoop. What New England's second-largest city is really like! Four days, obviously, does not make one any sort of real expert. Actually, I thought I knew all I cared to after the first day. It was a gray day, and Worcester was a gray city. Period. Just as my friend had said.

But, still, I said to myself, the home of Polar Beverages and Table Talk Pies (I grew up on Table Talk apple) and Connie Mack (actually from neighboring East Brookfield) and the first bicycle built in America and great ethnic diversity and a lot of other good things (the city's restored Mechanic's Hall has to be, quite simply, the most beautiful concert hall in the country!) can't be that bad.

And it isn't. On the second (and third and fourth) day the

sun came out. People seemed friendlier. I felt friendlier. And I made a discovery: Worcester is filled with lots and lots of great pop culture. Neat things like diners and old signs. And neon. Lots of working neon. I'm not saying that Worcester is Neon City or The Great White Way, but . . .

Back to diners, though. In 1891, the city's own Charles Palmer applied for America's first diner patent for his Night Owl Lunchwagon. (Some oldtimers still use the term "night owl" for what the rest of us call "diner.") The Worcester Lunch Car Company, born in 1906, manufactured many of the country's more elaborate diners in its fifty-six years of operation. And four Clark students, in a student guide to Worcester that they published in 1974, came right out and stated: "Worcester doesn't have the nightlife or the culture which you might expect in cities of its size, but it does have diners."

Well, the nightlife and the culture have come a long way since 1974. But the diners have hung in there, too.

Nightlife, culture, neon, diners, ethnic diversity, history: what more - other than its own brewery, of course - could a city want? Worcester, you're ok.

But just try telling that to the uninitiated . . . back home in Portland, I was suiting up for my weekly go at tennis when the guy using the locker next to me, making small talk, asked "Will, have you been anyplace lately?" I responded, "Yep, I've been in Worcester all week." "No," he said, "have you been anyplace?"

I just let it ride.

All views, February, 1988

Upper row, left to right: Boulevard Diner (155 Shrewsbury Street); The Miss Woos' "Booth Service" sign.
Second row, left to right: Worcester Heritage Preservation Society's "Information Diner" (Worcester Common); Edgemore Diner (just over the Shrewsbury line on Route 20).
Third row, left to right: The Coney Island (158 Southbridge Street); The Coney Island.
Bottom, left to right: Ralph's Chadwick Square Diner (95 Prescott Street); Uncle Will's Diner (866 Hartford Turnpike, Route 20, Shrewsbury). In spite of its *great* name, Uncle Will's closed during the summer of 1987.

155

Very Way Down East

◆

ON DRINKING BEER IN EASTPORT/LUBEC, MAINE

What's it like drinking beer in the easternmost place to drink beer in the United States?

I wondered.

I thought perhaps - just perhaps - Bass or Watney's or Whitbread might be popular, what with the easternmost place to drink beer that much closer - geographically, at least - to jolly old England than the rest of the colonies.

Or would Moosehead and Labatt's and Molson's and O'Keefe dominate, Canada being right next door?

A third thought was that made-in-Maine Geary's Pale Ale (lobster on the label and all) might have cornered a chunk of the market: Maine is Maine, and Maine products are Maine products. (Portland Lager more or less fits into this Maine product category, too).

The last possibility - the one that I knew was certainly the most distinct - was that very way Down East would be the same as most every other place in the country, with the all-too-usual lineup of Bud, Miller Lite, Heineken et al.

I wondered. And so, doing my best to put any preconceived notions asunder (a friend in Portland had commented "It's a good thing you're going up there to drink beer. . . because there's not much else to do." Talk about preconceived notions!), I decided to drive Down East to find out.

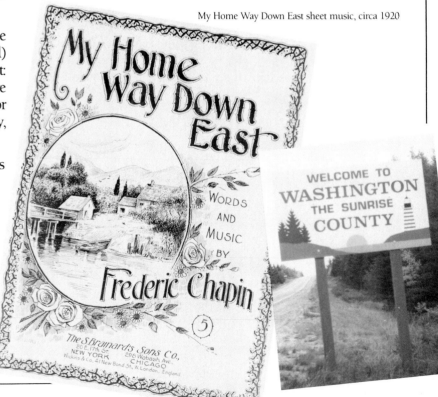

My Home Way Down East sheet music, circa 1920

The Sunrise County

If east of Ellsworth is considered "way Down East" (which it is), then Washington County - which includes both Lubec and Eastport - must be considered "very way Down East." The county's own nickname for itself is "The Sunrise County," for the perfectly good reason that, as the easternmost county in America, it enjoys each day's sunrise sooner than does any other county.

Washington County is also huge (larger than Delaware and Rhode Island combined) and wild, with 1.47 million acres of woods and 133,000 acres of lakes and ponds. FODOR'S NEW ENGLAND calls it "as close as you can get to a frontier feeling and still be on the East Coast."

First Stop, Lubec

To reach Lubec (pronounced Lou-beck), you have to turn off U.S. Route 1 at Whiting, and take Maine Route 189 the last ten miles into town. When you get there you may be sorry you did: Lubec, once the sardine packing capital of the world, has fallen upon high unemployment and hard times. The result is a downtown that's largely boarded up. As ghost-townish as Water Street, Lubec's main drag appears, however, it's the "best it's looked in years," Mary Coggins, proprietor of one of the few operating shops on Water Street, the Homestead Sales grocery store, informed me. She also informed me that Lubec is basically dry. Beer (and other alcoholic beverages) may be purchased for take out only. There is no place in town where alcohol can be served on premises.

A couple of oldtimers in Mary's store filled me in. It seems that the town's no on-premise consumption statute dates back to the early 1940s: after years of open rowdiness when there were eight or so bars on Water Street catering to the everpresent thirsts of workers from the Quoddy Dam Project — an attempt to harness the area's extremely high tides for electricity — the town fathers reacted . . . and shut down all the bars, and other drinking establishments, too.

It's been that way ever since. But things may change: "Every year it comes up for a vote . . . and every year it gets closer." This is how the owner of the Home Port Inn, a lovely inn and restaurant (in which no alcoholic beverages can be served) up the hill from Water Street, put it. She's obviously hoping.

The Easternmost Community in America

Lubec (named after Lubeck, Germany) is proud of being the easternmost community in America. Once a thriving sardine canning town, it has seen much of its prosperity fade away. Two sardine factories remain in operation, however, as does the only smoked herring plant in the country. There's also a row of truly beautiful 19th century homes lining Main Street as it winds its way up from Water Street.

The Easternmost Place To Buy Beer in America

By my reckoning, Wasson's Market, about a third of a mile inland from Water Street, is the easternmost place in Lubec - and America - to buy beer. "We sell a lot of it," proclaimed 20-year-old Denise Tinker, with Bud and Coors being the favorites. Other brands in Wasson's one cooler include Busch, Bud Light, Miller High Life and Genuine Draft, Colt 45, Lowenbrau, Coors Light, Schmidt's, Pabst, Milwaukee's Best (both regular and Light), O'Keefe and Schooner. Not too exciting.

I did find a six-pack and a half of Portland Lager buried in the bottom shelf. ("It's just beginning to catch on," volunteered Denise.) I purchased the six-pack, but at $6.04 including tax and deposit, I couldn't help but wonder just how much Portland Lager was really going to "catch on" in what is, in reality, an economically depressed community.

Last Stop, Eastport

"The first thing you notice about Eastport, Maine is the herring gulls, hundreds of them, crying and wheeling above rotting wharves, whitening the blue morning sky. In the seconds it takes you to drive through the business district, you begin to wonder if the gulls are causing the only stir in town. Every third or fourth shop has a FOR SALE or CLOSED sign in a dusty window; some buildings look too flimsy to last the winter. Eastport, in the midst of a workday morning in late August, seems inert, empty."

from "Portrait of a Declining Town," *Saturday Review,* October 5, 1968

Eastport is your basic flannel shirt, baseball cap, pick up truck kind of place. Located just three miles from Lubec as the crow flies, it's a good thirty-five miles as the car drives.

As I headed into downtown Eastport on an October Wednesday afternoon, I had the feeling that not much has changed in the twenty years since David Butwin wrote the above words for the *Saturday Review.* After an afternoon, evening and morning, driving and walking around, I still feel that way.

Eastport's main street, also called Water Street, is not unlike Lubec's, with a lot of closed stores. It doesn't have nearly as much of a boarded-up look, though ... and it's definitely not dry. I'd given a ride to 23-year old construction worker Chris Brown, on his way into Eastport for an evening of camaraderie and Budweiser, who told me of several good spots. A spot he overlooked, however, turned out to be THE spot...the easternmost place to drink

a beer in the entire U.S. of A., the WA-CO Diner.

Yes, a diner.

But a diner that serves beer (including the only draft I could find in town), is filled with beer signs and, very often, beer drinkers. I chatted with Betty Ferguson, owner - for the last year and a half - of the WA-CO. She told me how the WA-CO (from the names of the two men who started it all, Watts and Cole) began life as a lunch wagon in 1924; that the first permanent structure was built in 1934; that the present-day building ("The New WA-CO") was constructed by her dad in 1971 because "he wanted a more modern place." Beer has been on the menu since 1934, and Betty sells a fair amount of it, with Miller Lite, plus Michelob Light and Coors Light, being the big sellers. Busch on draft, at the oddball price of $3.68 a pitcher ($3.50 plus tax) sells well, too. "The Canadians drink a lot of it," comments Betty.

But still . . . a diner?

It's 6:00, and Jack Hicks and Keith Folls, both 27 and both from Eastport, are splitting a Narragansett: "Well, we can drink here for a buck and a nickel, or we can go across the street for a dollar and a quarter" explains Jack. From two stools away, Earl Morse, 66-years old and a man who obviously knows his way around Eastport, chimes in that on payday nights, Friday and Saturday nights, he's seen the WA-CO full, people

The Easternmost City in America
While Lubec is the nation's easternmost town, Eastport is its easternmost city (and, living up to the name its had since its incorporation in 1798, its easternmost seaport, too). Now, ironically, Eastport is the smaller of the two, with a population that's dipped under 2,000. Such was not the case in 1893 when the state of Maine decided which locale got a city charter and which did not: Eastport, then a bustling canning and transportation hub, had the 5,000 citizens necessary to qualify as a full-fledged city.

Candidate Number Two

There is one other candidate for the title of *Easternmost Place To Drink Beer in America*, Stinson's The Cannery. As with the WA-CO, it's on the water side of Water Street ("We're about on the same plane, really" is how Betty Ferguson summed up my dilemma). But the WA-CO was open when I came to town on October 7th and 8th (1987), while The Cannery was not. It's an "Open for the Season" place. . . and the season had ended the weekend before.

I tracked down Bernie Cecire, co-owner of The Cannery, as he was closing things up for the winter. Bernie sells a lot of beer, bottled only ("The economics of installing a draft system are not attractive enough."), including a fair amount of Geary's. He laughed heartily when I asked whether he thought Eastport is a good beer-drinking town: "Oh, yes! Washington County, I think, in general, and probably Eastport in particular, probably drinks more beer per capita than most other areas in the state or the Union. That'd be my guess, anyway."

Lastly, Bernie is bullish on Eastport, thinks it's "being discovered" and that in five or ten years it'll be a far different place than it is now. His only concern: whether its being far different will be good or bad.

Adorable

I would use the word "adorable" to best describe the WA-CO's exterior. Inside, it's more or less your regular diner, with a counter flanked by sixteen stools, and six booths spread along the side.

Signs give the day's specials (Crabmeat roll with French fries, $4.00; Liver and onions, $3.25; Baked beans with coleslaw and hot dogs, $3.50) and the homemade pie roster (Banana cream, coconut cream and chocolate cream at $1.50 each; squash at $1.35: "Cream pies cost more to make," Betty tells me.) There's a large poster giving the various schedules for the local Shead - the Shead Tigers! - High School athletic teams.

But there's also a large sign devoted to the WA-CO's beer selection. It's a fairly lengthy list although, alas, it's a fairly basic one, too: Budweiser, Michelob, Michelob Light, Miller High Life, Miller Lite, Coors, Coors Light, Narragansett, Busch (draft), and Kingsbury. The Kingsbury, which is non-alcoholic, is 75¢; all other brands are $1.05, except for Michelob and Michelob Light which will set you back a nickel more.

drinking beer. "Enjoyed many a 'Nasty-Gansett' here myself," he adds.

It is Wednesday, however, and the WA-CO (they pronounce it WHACK-O in Eastport) is more empty than full. I order a Narragansett. And a fish and chips. "Do you want those fish with bread crumbs or batter?" I'm asked. I go with the batter. Soon, I'm digging into what looks like fish fritters, five of 'em, big and greasy, but good, and more French fries than I could ever put away.

When I've eaten all I can, I order an after dinner drink. Another Narragansett. This one I especially enjoy, basking in a glow that only a lover of both beer and the East Coast could understand.

Who Wants The Handsome Waiter?

◆

THE BREWERIES OF SPRINGFIELD AND CHICOPEE

Perhaps it's a throwback to Salem and her witches; perhaps it's the region's dry sense of humor . . . whatever it is, the brewers of New England — more than any other section of the country — have made use of less than Calvin Klein types: ugly (or distinctive, if you prefer) gentlemen. Just whose gentleman was the most distinctive is up for discussion, but there can be no denying the handsome waiter's place on the ugly honor roll.

Although brought into prominence by the Hampden Brewing Company, the waiter was conceived by Hampden's predecessor, the Springfield Breweries Company, which, in turn, had been the successor to Hampden. Sounds confusing, I know, but it was actually the stuff that beer baron dreams were made of.

Once upon a time there were five breweries in the Springfield/Chicopee area: the Springfield, Highland, and Liberty brewing companies (all in Springfield); the Consumers' Brewing Company (in Chicopee); and the Hampden Brewing Company (in the Willimansett section of Chicopee). Then along came the consolidation movement that swept through Boston, Pittsburgh, St. Louis and many another American brewing center: four of the five Springfield/Chicopee breweries joined together to form the Springfield Breweries Company in April of 1899. Only Liberty remained independent, but it, too, eventually joined the fold in 1910.

Once it got rolling, the Springfield Breweries Company was not bashful: its advertisements proclaimed it to be "New England's greatest brewing institution." Indeed, it was right up there. From an output of 200,000 barrels a year in 1899, the combine grew to the point where it was churning out some 350,000 barrels a year prior to prohibition, up among the very top

Cont'd. on page 162

Circa 1940 Hampden Mild Ale bottle

Circa 1950 coaster from the Lido, Winsted, Connecticut

A Lot of Folks Wanted Him

Born in Springfield, nurtured in Willimansett, the handsome waiter tickled many a beer drinker's fancy . . . and helped sell a heap of Hampden Ale and Beer throughout New England and neighboring New York.

Circa 1905 tray, Providence Brewing Company, Providence

Circa 1915 tray, Enterprise Brewing Company, Fall River

Circa 1910 sign, James Hanley Brewing Company, Providence

Circa 1940 tray, Hampden Brewing Company, Willimansett

You Be The Judge

Here, for your viewing - and voting - pleasure, are the four leading contenders for the Least Likely to Succeed in a Singles Bar Award. Left to right we have, representing the Providence Brewing Company, Mr. My Choice; James Hanley's The Connoisseur; Enterprise's Half Stock Ale man; and the Pride of the Pioneer Valley, our Handsome Waiter. You be the judge.

Check It Out!!!

Springfield/Chicopee breweriana collector Dave Graci holding an original Springfield Breweries Company handsome waiter tray outside his Dave's Y Package Store on Chicopee Street in Chicopee. Included in his store is quite the display of old time Pioneer Valley breweriana. If you're in the area why not stop by and, as Dave suggests in his ads, "Check It Out!!!"

Culver Pictures

Guess Who . . . and Why

Before your mind relaxes from the hard task of judging, can you guess who this man is (hint: he's probably the most successful children's book author of all time) and what he has to do with the Springfield/Chicopee brewing scene?

For the answer, please turn the page.

Culver Pictures

Answer: He's Theodor Geisel - far better known as Dr. Seuss - and Springfield's his hometown. He was born in the "The City of Firsts" in 1904. Of greater interest is the fact that his father and grandfather before him - both also named Theodor - were big wheels in Springfield's brewing world.

The eldest Theodor, a native German, joined forces with Christian Kalmbach to purchase the small, 1,000-barrel capacity brewery of the estate of Oscar Rocke in 1876. Within a decade, the brewery, known as Kalmbach & Geisel (and nicknamed the Mammoth Brewery), had grown over forty-fold. By the early 1890s capacity - and sales - had topped 75,000 barrels. *The Springfield Graphic* reported in October of 1892 that K & G had received an offer of free land if they'd move their plant to Milwaukee. They declined.

In 1894, Geisel bought Kalmbach out, incorporated the business, and changed its name to the Highland Brewing Company. When Highland joined forces with Springfield Breweries, Geisel the eldest became a vice-president. In 1902 he went out on his own again, organizing the Liberty Brewing Company, which he also sold, in 1910, to Springfield Breweries.

Son Theodor H. Geisel, born in 1879, joined his dad at the Highland Brewery as a teenager. He was most active at Liberty, both before and after its inclusion in Springfield Breweries, remaining as General Manager after it became an SBC branch.

Incidentally, Theodor the youngest came about his distinctive nom de plume in an intriguing way: while an undergrad at Dartmouth, he was Editor-in-Chief - as Theodor Geisel - of *Jack-o-Lantern*, the college's monthly comic magazine. Involved in an infraction of school rules and afraid he'd lose his editorial post, he began using his middle name (which was also his mother Henrietta's maiden name) . . . Seuss. The "Dr." came later, after he'd dropped out of Oxford University. Hesitant to disappoint his father by coming home sans doctorate, he simply appended "Dr." before his middle name. Thus, save for a few variations, it's been ever since . . . and for the more than forty children's classics (over 100,000,000 copies sold!) he's written and illustrated, including THE CAT IN THE HAT, AND TO THINK THAT I SAW IT ON MULBERRY STREET, THE 500 HATS OF BARTHOLOMEW CUBBINS, and HOW THE GRINCH STOLE CHRISTMAS.

with respect to New England brewing organizations.

The end of legal beer, of course, put one big damper on things. Soft drinks - Springfield Beverages, Hampden Beverages, and Liberty Beverages - were produced, but unsuccessfully. In the fall of 1924 all remaining operations were discontinued, and the corporation liquidated. The former Highland plant was razed to make way for Massachusetts Mutual's giant-sized headquarters. The Springfield Brewing Company's facility was sold to a realty company, eventually burning down. The Liberty plant survived, but appears not to have been used for much of anything. Only Hampden fared well. Bought at auction by successful New York businessman Karl. H Bissell in 1923, it was kept operational during the entirety of prohibition producing malt extract and near beer (and, locals will tell you, perhaps a little of the real stuff, too!) .

Cont'd. on page 169

View of the Highland Hotel from the front cover of the Court Square Theatre's April, 1916 program. The hotel's copyrighted slogan: "Every Meal a Pleasant Memory."

Strictly a Figment

Legend has it that the handsome waiter was, in real life, a waiter at Springfield's storied Highland Hotel. He was actually, however, strictly a figment of some clever promotion person's imagination: there never was, alas, a living, breathing handsome waiter at the Highland or any other place. (Sorry, ladies!)

The Highland
HILLMAN STREET
SPRINGFIELD'S LEADING RESTAURANT
THE IDEAL PLACE FOR AFTER THEATRE PARTIES
BEST NOONDAY LUNCHEON IN THE CITY
11-30 TO 2-15   50 CENTS
D.H. SIEVERS & CO.   TEL. 7800

The Springfield Breweries Company

Formed through the combination of four area breweries in 1899 - with a fifth coming aboard in 1910 - the Springfield Breweries Company was a giant among New England breweries. Successively headed up by Franklin Pierce (grandson of THE Franklin Pierce, our 14th president), Michael H. Curley, Thomas J. Flanagan, John W. Glynn, and Theodor R. Geisel, SBC grew until it was among the very largest brewing organizations in New England.

Springfield Brewing Company

Organized in the 1860s, the Springfield Brewing Company didn't really start to hum until it was purchased by brewing magnate Selig Manilla in 1890. His expertise - and money - spearheaded rather phenomenal growth: from 4,000 barrels sold in 1890 to 100,000 at the time of its merger into SBC. The brewery's greatest moment had to be in 1896, when its Tivoli Beer crossed the Atlantic and won a Gold Medal and First Prize Diploma at the International Exposition at Baden Baden, Germany against one-hundred twenty-six German and American beers. A German newspaper of the day warned Germany's brewers to bestir themselves if they wished to retain their prestige!

Circa 1895
foam scraper

"Touches the Right Spot"

¶Too much cannot be said in praise of our Hampden Ale. ¶Ale drinkers are invariably delighted with Hampden and unfailingly enthusiastic in its praise. It touches the right spot every time. ¶The dealers who draw Hampden are not less pleased, for they are assured of a constant and increasing ale patronage.

Springfield Breweries Co.
Springfield, Mass.

Hampden Brewing Company

Ale - pale, stock and porter - was the pride and joy of Willimansett's Hampden Brewing Company. And that's as it should have been, for the brewery's roots, stretching back to 1868, were almost exclusively English and Irish. (See Old Breweries Never Die, pages 91-92.)

Hampden Pale Ale ad from 1910, the year Liberty was acquired . . . and the Springfield Breweries combine was complete

Circa 1905 postcard view of the Liberty Brewing Company, 183 Liberty Street, Springfield

Liberty Brewing Company

Liberty, the last holdout (it was not acquired by SBC until January of 1910) was a small brewery. Output for 1909, its last year as an independent, was but 30,000 barrels. Opened in 1903, Liberty was proud of being the first brewery in America to be constructed and equipped throughout by union labor. A metal plate over the brewery's office door carried the words "Union Built."

And extremely rare and downright nifty piece of breweriana: an 1890's three-tiered metal Highland Brewing Company lunchpail

Circa 1898 Consumers' Brewing Company embossed bottle (courtesy of Dave Graci)

Highland Brewing Company

Famed for its Bavarian Beer (a "thick mash food beer," with a very low percentage of alcohol and very high percentage of nutriment), its Pilsener and its Export, Highland liked to boast that its brews were made on the highest point in Springfield . . . and were of the same grade. Highland also brewed a Cream Ale and a malt extract, which in combination with iron, was a staple among many of the area's large hospitals.

Consumers' Brewing Company

Being absorbed into Springfield Breweries spelled the death knell for the Consumers' Brewing Company. Founded as the Chicopee Brewery in 1879, it passed through a number of changes in ownership (John Greim and William Ritter) and name (Crystal Spring and Consumers') before being closed in 1899 as a consequence of the SBC takeover.
(P.S.: You've undoubtedly often wondered where a wild and somewhat crazy name like "Chicopee" comes from. Well, wonder no longer: it's Indian for "birch bark place.")

163

Roll Me Over

In its heyday, the Springfield Breweries Company was one class act. I mean, how many breweries publish a monthly magazine. And one that you had to pay for, at that (5¢ the copy; 50¢ the year). Called *Clover*, it contained a fairly dazzling assortment of jokes, toasts, adages, and current events, plus advertisements for its own and other products. Here, culled from the pages of three 1908-1910 issues, are a few *Clover* goodies. Put yourself in a pre-Vietnam, pre-World War II, pre-Depression, pre-World War I mode . . . and enjoy.

Jokes

"Just throw me a half-dozen of your biggest trout," said the man with the angler's outfit.
"Throw them!" exclaimed the astonished fish dealer.
"That's what I said," replied the party of the first part.
"Then I'll go home and tell my wife I caught them. I may be a poor fisherman, but I'm no liar."

The Customers - "Is your Limburger cheese good?"
The Delicatessen Dealer - "Madam, it is unapproachable."

Little Willie - "Sweet Lillie, will you let me kiss you?"
Little Lillie - "Have you ever kissed another girl?"
Little Willie - "No, never! I vow I haven't."
Little Lillie - "Then go away and don't come back till you have learned something about it. I am not going to have you practicing on me."

A Bangor clergyman, pastor of a popular church there, received a caller at his parsonage the other day, a young matron carrying in her arms a chubby-faced youngster.
"I want the baby christened," the mother said.
After the ceremony the clergyman started to write out the baptismal certificate required by the Board of Health. Forgetting for a moment the date of the month, he remarked to the mother.
"The is the ninth, isn't it?"
"No, indeed, sir," replied the young matron indignantly, "it's only the second."

First Straphanger (in a whisper) - "Why did you give that woman your seat? She isn't bundle-laden, tired, or pretty, or even polite."
Second Straphanger - "Well - er - you see - she is my wife."

A certain little boy in a Woonsocket school had fallen into the habit of saying, "I have wrote" and "I have went."
The teacher tried in several ways to break him of the habit, but all in vain. So one day she had him remain after school and write the two phrases one hundred time each, thinking that in this way he would surely remember to say "I have written" and "I have gone."
A few minutes before he finished his task the teacher was called out of the room. She told him to wait until she returned. When she returned she found on the desk the phrases correctly written one hundred times, and beside them a note saying:
"Dear teacher - I have wrote "I have written" one hundred times and I have went home."

In The Clover

Adages

To err is human; not to tell of others' errors is divine.

How easy it is, the night before, to get up early in the morning.

You needn't pack up any worries; you can get them as you go along.

To find out what you can do, try. To find out what you can't do, try.

The memory of quality lasts long after the price is forgotten.

Some defeats are only instruments of victory.

Toasts

May you have more and more friends and need them less and less.

Here's a toast to all of you here
No matter where you are from;
May the best day you have ever seen
Be worse than your worst to come.

May you never kick without cause and never have cause to kick.

Wherever we're whirled in this whirligig world
Let us be for ourselves our own judges,
And for troubles and cares and the hammer-verein
Give pooh-pooh! and a couple of fudges.

The Commonwealth Brewing Corporation

As operational as Hampden was when repeal arrived, Liberty was not. Purchased by Leo Kaufman, and operated (along with a former wholesale grocery facility on Chestnut Street) as the Commonwealth Brewing Corporation, Springfield's only post-prohibition brewery lived a year-to-year, even week-to-week, existence for most of its dozen or so years (1933 to 1945; after which it was operated as the Springfield Brewing Corporation until its final shutdown in 1948).

One contact in Springfield/Chicopee (all started, I might add, by Officer Raymond Bousquet of the Chicopee police . . . but more on that later) lead to another, and before too long I was fortunate enough to be conversing with Milton Allen.

In the beer business one way or another for most of his adult life, Milton was a salesman ("but I did a whole lot of other things, too") for Commonwealth from 1937 until 1945, with time out for military service. Now 72, he lives with his wife Pauline in the Forest Park section of Springfield, where I spent several hours chatting with him. In his words are the highs and the lows - and the humor, too -of life at what one competitor termed a "wildcat" (translation: under-capitalized and under-staffed) brewery.

The Salesman: Milton Allen in a recent photo.

"He Made a Dollar Go Farther"

"My boss was a real smart man. He was the best boss I ever had and one of the smartest men I ever knew. Leo Kaufman. He lost an eye when he was a kid. From measles. But he could see more with the eye that he had than most people (with two).

Probably two or three times a month I would drive him to Boston. You know, in those days breweries, especially small breweries, were hand to mouth operations. You had to have money every week. So I would drive him to Boston and we'd visit three or four wholesalers and pick up checks. So we could start the next week's brewing. It was a small plant. And, as I say, like all small companies in those days it was hard. I can remember going out and working and calling up at 1:00 and saying 'I've got $500.00 in collections, and the boss might say 'We're all set today. Don't bring it in. Stay on the road.' On the other hand, he might sat 'We're short, can you bring it in?' So I would drive back from wherever I was and turn in my collections, and I'd go back out on the road again. He made a dollar go farther than most people I've ever seen. I mean he really worked at it."

1934 photo

The Brewmaster. Born in Germany in 1869, (Louis) Albert Kuhn's career in brewing spanned the better part of seven decades. He died in Springfield, September 1, 1950.

A Little Late

To illustrate his boss' penchant for work, Milton told me a little story. I can still hear him chuckling as he told it to me. "That man could go to work at 5:00 in the morning and work until 2:00 the next morning. Many a time I would go back to the office to write my orders up and he'd still be there working. He didn't have a car. I'd give him a ride home. Then go home myself. That could be 10:00, 11:00, 12:00 at night.

A customer in Holyoke got married. He ran a package store and his clerks were selling tickets for a dance for him. A party and a dance: bring a girl and come to this party; it's going to be at the hotel in Holyoke. Ok, so I went home and got dressed and so on, and I said I'll bring my orders down to the office and then I'll pick up the date and we'll go to Holyoke. So I got there and I started to write my orders out and he (Leo) asked me to do this and asked me to do that. And I could see I was running late. Well, I called up and said I'm gonna be a little late. By the time I brought him home - and I'm trying to hurry him - it's now a quarter of eleven. I went to the girl's house and she came to the door in her nightgown and her mother right behind her, and I got holy blue hell."

"Mr. Kuhn Made a Nice Bock"

Bock, a favorite of the Springfield Breweries Company, was a tradition carried on by Commonwealth.

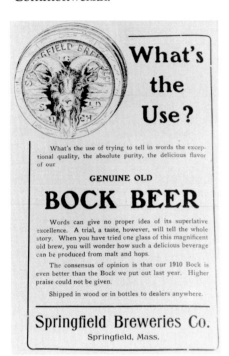

Pre-prohibition SBC bock ads. The small announcement with the wonderfully refreshing prices (65¢ a dozen!) is from 1916.

Milton Allen recalls Gold Medal Bock:

"We had a genuine bock. We used to sell a hell of a lot of it. In throwaway bottles. Used to put 'em up in dozen packs. Twelve packs. They were very popular around Springfield, yes sir. That was Gold Medal Bock. You know, real dark beer is made with roasted barley malt. The difference between real dark beer and fake beer is that they (the makers of fake dark beer) put the coloring in: you see the little black dots in the foam if it's coloring. If it's real bock the foam is pure white. The beer can be dark but the foam is pure white. Our bock would stand up to any bock that was made. Mr. Kuhn made a nice bock beer."

Circa 1940 Gold Medal Bock bottle (a non-throwaway, with a State of Maine excise tax stamp affixed to the neck . . . still there almost a half-century later)

BARNEY THE BARTENDER

The special, only here for a short while, nature of bock is captured so very nicely in this 1939 cartoon by Don Barry.

Just What Is Bock, Anyway?

Just what is bock, the legends surrounding its name, and the why of its association with a goat are questions that generally stump even the most devoted of beerophiles.

Borrowing liberally from the section on bock (Bock Beer: It Used To Be A Big Deal) in an earlier work, FROM BEER TO ETERNITY, here are some answers.

First, what bock beer is not: it is not the dregs cleaned out of brewing vats in the spring. How the dregs rumor got started is anybody's guess, but it's a rumor with absolutely no basis in fact.

The distinctive flavor and dark brown hue of the special brew is the result of the roasted or caramelized malt that is used in brewing it. It is also often aged longer than lighter beers. It has traditionally made its appearance in the spring.

Historians believe bock had its origins in the fourth or fifth centuries among the tribes of northern Europe. As part of the annual harvesting of crops, the very best grains were selected, steeped in water chosen by the tribe's priests, brewed into beer, and then placed in underground caves to age all through the winter. With the arrival of spring, the beer was brought forth, consumed with great relish and ceremony, and blessings were offered both as thanks for the previous fall's harvest and in the hope of a bounteous crop in the year ahead.

Although the significance of bock changed down through the centuries, its symbol as a sign of spring did not. Until relatively recently - bock has been pretty much relegated to oblivion in the last several decades - a placard with a goat on it displayed in a tavern window was as sure a sign of spring as a robin or the crack of the bat.

Why a Goat?

Why a goat instead of an elephant or an anteater? And, while we're at it, whence cometh the word "bock?"

Historians are basically uncertain with respect to both of these questions but they've had fun trying to figure them out. One theory holds that two rival German brewers happened to meet in a tavern way back when. Each was outspoken on the merits of his own brew . . . and the demerits of his rival's. After much jawing, they decided to settle things once and for all. Each brewer was to wolf down as much of his rival's beer as he could. The winner would be the one who could stand on his feet and keep drinking the longer . . . as that would prove his beer were the stronger. After many hours, as both contestants were fading fast, one of the two ventured to the door for some air. Just then a goat sauntered in, banged into the quite tipsy brewer, and knocked him off his feet. "I win!" declared the still-standing brewer. "It was the goat," snarled the loser. What he actually snarled, of course, was "It was the bock," because bock is the German word for goat. Word of

the contest spread, and bock came to be the accepted name for stronger, heartier brew.

A second, entirely different story revolves around the city of Einbeck, Germany. During the Middle Ages, Einbeck was famed through Europe for its superior quality beer, especially its dark beer. The city's name was sometimes spelled "Einbock" and often pronounced that way as well. It's thus theorized that people requesting Einbeck beer would call out "Ein Bock" and that eventually this came to be shortened to just plain "bock."

Then there are those who feel that the word "bock" most likely comes from astrology. After all, goes the theory, the special brew was made from grains brewed under the sign of Capricorn, the goat. Goat is bock in German. etc., etc.

Three different theories. Each somewhat plausible; each somewhat implausible. Take your pick. More important, the next time spring rolls around why not try to track down some bock and give it a try. You might be very pleasantly surprised.

167

When Boston Was Cut Off From Springfield

But Leo Kaufman had a heart, too. Milton recalled the time of the Hurricane of 1938. "Springfield was cut off from Boston. Or we'll say Boston was cut off from Springfield. Nobody could get through. For about a week the roads were blocked because the trees and telephone wires and telephone poles and everything else had been knocked down. After about a week, I got to the office one morning and the boss said that a truck was leaving for Boston that day. Now how's he gonna get there? Well, he's going through Fitchburg and so on and so forth. It'll be much longer, but they'll have a truckload of beer in Boston.

So I left and went out on my territory. One of my first stops was a customer in West Springfield, and he seemed to be very upset about something. I asked him what the matter was and he said that that day, that very day, his son was supposed to report to Harvard Graduate School of Business Administration. He had to be there. The trains and buses weren't running; the roads weren't open; there was no way for his son to get there. I said 'Does your son care how he gets there?' He said 'No, he's gotta get there!' So I called the boss and told him the situation: that the young man had to get to Boston. He said 'You get him and bring him over to the office by a quarter past ten. That's when the truck is leaving.'

So I told Jack (the customer) to get his son and get him ready. I'd pick him up at his house and bring him over to the office. He grabbed the phone, called his son, told him to get dressed, pack his bag - he's going to Boston. The son said 'How?'. He said 'Never mind how. You're going!'

And he did. By Commonwealth beer truck.

Circa 1940 Dartmouth Cream Ale bottle

The Product: Actually, Dartmouth Cream Ale was but one of quite a number of brands put out by Commonwealth. Others included Worcester Star Ale, Finnegan's Ale, Oxford Club Ale, Victory Ale, New England Ale, Bay State Ale and Beer, and, of course, Gold Medal Tivoli Beer.

Corned Beef Sandwiches and Good Brew

Bosses and beer trucks are great. But what's a brewery without a brewmaster?

Commonwealth's brewmaster was a rather legendary figure. Legendary in Massachusetts, anyway. His name was Albert Kuhn, and he'd been around, starting as a brewmaster at the Conrad Decker Brewery in East Boston in 1883. It was his brew that had won the Gold Medal (and First Prize Diploma!) at Baden Baden away back in 1896 (see page 163). By the time he retired during World War II, Albert Kuhn had logged a most impressive sixty-eight years in the brewing industry.

"Our brewmaster was Mr. Kuhn when I went to work there. He had worked as a brewmaster for Springfield Breweries. It was his beer that won the award.

In his young age, he must have been 6'1" or 2". When I knew him he was already bent over. And he walked with a hump. He didn't say much. He sat at his desk out there. His son also worked there, in the plant. Allie, Jr. Allie was an umpire and quite an athlete and a coach, Allie, Jr. He was short and stocky. He coached some local high school teams and semi-pro teams. And he worked at the brewery, too, as the assistant brewmaster.

Our trouble was this: it was a small plant and in the summertime, when the demand for beer was high, the beer was not allowed to age long enough. It would be on the shelf a couple weeks and it would break down. In the wintertime, when business was slow, we had the best bottle of beer or glass of beer that you could imagine. On Saturday afternoon - I'd go out and make calls Saturday morning in those days - I'd be up at the office and the bookkeepers, Mr. Gallagher and his son, Ed Gallagher, and Tim Boller, would be in the office. I'd go down and get some corned beef sandwiches. And Mr. Kuhn knew when he had a good brew. The old man would come upstairs with this copper two-gallon kettle and he'd say 'Try this beer.' And, honestly, that beer was terrific. In the wintertime we had a wonderful glass of beer."

The Wrong Beer

"I met a customer on State Street, in front of a cafe. The cafe wasn't my account, but the customer was my account. He says 'You know, you oughta buy me a beer.' And I said 'Anytime. Here's a cafe right here.' So we went in. We sat down and Bill said 'You're paying for it so I'll have your brand.' And on tap they did have one of our brands, Worcester Star Ale. He was served first. He took a sip and made a face. 'What's the matter, Bill?' He said 'Taste it.' Well, I tasted it and it was TERRIBLE. I said to the bartender, 'What have you got there?' He said 'Worcester Star Ale.' I said 'That doesn't taste like our ale. I sell it and that doesn't taste like our product.' He got a little flustered, went down to the cellar, came back up, took the knob off, and put on another knob. 'You're right,' he said, 'it wasn't your beer."

Forty-five years later - for Milton Allen at least - there is still the memory of THEIR beer . . . and OUR beer!

Circa 1940 Gold Medal Tivoli tip tray

The Award: Gold Medal Tivoli was the sole brand name carried on by Commonwealth from the old Springfield Breweries' days. In light of Milton's comments, perhaps the wording on this tray should have, more correctly, read "Fully Aged . . . Wintertime Only."

Hampden's After Prohibition Rise and Fall

The first twenty or so years after prohibition were good times for Hampden. Lead by Karl Bissell as prexy and Edward J. Glynn (son of John W. Glynn, former head of Springfield Breweries) as treasurer and general manager, they - and their handsome waiter - flew quite high.

Within the first five years after repeal, the plant was twice considerably enlarged, with capacity increased to 245,000 barrels . . . three times greater than prior to prohibition. A three-story bottling plant was constructed in 1937 to keep abreast of the public's ever-increasing preference for packaged over draught brews. After a wartime lull, Hampden management continued to expand, pouring in over $2,000,000 in a five-year building program, 1946-1951, that increased capacity to 350,000 barrels. But then the seemingly inevitable - for small and regional brewers -

Circa 1948 Hampden Mild Ale - "Brewed by the Masters of Mildness" - six-pack container

Taken for granted today, the six-pack was developed in the later 1930s in response to changing purchasing habits: studies showed that the lady of the household was increasingly, as a routine part of the family shopping, doing the buying of beer . . . and that a unit of six was the best weight for her to handle.

Because of beer's close association with Germany in the minds of many, America's brewers worked especially hard to prove their patriotism during World War I, and again during World War II. If this coaster is any indication, Hampden worked as hard as any - and then some - to make it clear which side it was on.

ONE
25¢
WAR STAMP
BUYS TWELVE BULLETS
HAMPDEN BREWING CO.
WILLIMANSETT, MASS.

Circa 1942 Hampden Brewing Company coaster

hard times set in. A ten-week strike in 1952 didn't help. And the beer market's continuing shift from ale, Hampden's speciality, to lager hurt, too. A takeover of Lowell's Harvard Brewing Company in 1957 lead to a corporate name change, Hampden-Harvard Breweries, Inc. Four years later, in 1961, Hampden-Harvard was involved in another takeover. This time, though, it was the takee rather than the taker: western Massachusett's last remaining brewery was bought by Drewrys, Ltd., a large midwestern operation with breweries in Chicago and South Bend, their headquarters. Hampden and Harvard

Circa 1948 Hampden Mild Ale quart spout can

Hampden was a leader in developing mild ale. " 'S Mild - but Sturdy" was their slogan, and they sold it on draught, in bottles, and, starting in the late 1930s, in that new invention, the beer can."

In its last decade and a half, Hampden-Harvard acquired the rights to a number of once famous brewing names. Among them:

Name	Original Brewery Location	Year Acquired
Dobler	Albany	1959
Fitzgerald (Fitz)	Troy	1962
Hedrick	Albany	1967
Dawson's	New Bedford	1967

I asked Daniel Buckley, 76, a man who spent thirty-eight years with Hampden/Hampden-Harvard/Drewrys/Piel's in various sales and public relations capacities, if all these beers and ales were separate brews. "Supposed to be," he answered. And then, with a twinkle, added "I didn't get in the brewery far enough to find out if it wasn't." (Incidentally, I also asked Dan what in all of his thirty-eight years, was his happiest, most crowning moment. He only hesitated a second, then replied "Payday.")

Officer Raymond Bousquet: This Piel's Is For You

Officer Bousquet and an original portrait of Gottfried Piel that we found hanging in Encon's offices. It was Gottfried, along with his two brothers (who were not named Bert and Harry, but Michael and Wilhelm) who founded Piel Brothers in the East New York section of Brooklyn in 1883. Today, 105 years later, Piel's is still being enjoyed, a product of the Stroh Brewery Company.

"I've Been Looking For You"

When you hang around old breweries and backwater sections of town you never quite know what you'll find. But you can almost always count on No Trespassing signs and/or guard dogs as a more than occasional part of the mix. Thus it was no big deal to see a barbed-wire-topped fence adorned with "Warning: Attack Dog" signs surrounding part of the still extant (please see pages 91-92) Hampden/Piel's brewery. No big deal at all: just roll that empty oil drum over to the fence, climb up, and there's your unobstructed photo view of the brewhouse.

Suddenly, however, as the dogs are going wild and I'm jumping down from the oil drum, a Chicopee Police cruiser car comes charging out of nowhere . . . with the officer's finger pointing directly at me.

Oh no, I thought, now it is a big deal. And that feeling was certainly intensified when the officer jumped out of the cruiser with an ominous "I've been looking for you."

And he had been looking for me; even gone off his beat to find me. Noticing me taking shots of the Y Cafe (where I'd talked with Roger Racine), he'd gone in, found I was researching the brewery, and set out to find me . . . but to tell me of Dave Graci and his package store breweriana display. What a great guy! In addition to telling me about Dave, he also set me up with Daniel Buckley (from whom I learned of Milton Allen), and accompanied me around Encon (present-day owners of most of the former brewery) to make sure I was treated right. Officer Raymond Bousquet, you're ok!

---

continued to be brewed, but Drewrys was shipped to Willimansett by rail for distribution, too.

Then things get really complicated. Drewrys was absorbed into a Detroit-based conglomerate of breweries named the Associated Brewing Company within a year or two. Associated also owned Piel Brothers, a time-honored brewery located in Brooklyn. Hampden-Harvard was made a division of Piel's. And such it remained, even though Piel's became free of Associated in 1973, until the brewery was shut down in 1975.

Circa 1974 Piel's coaster

"Everybody Cried"

"Everybody cried because it was such a great place to work at" is how longtime brewery employee Roger Racine, interviewed at the Y Cafe ("You Are A Stranger Here But Once") in Willimansett, summed up the plant's closing in 1975. "They had predicted it (the closing) for about ten years. But when it did come - seeing that they had said 'This is gonna be our last summer; this is gonna be our last summer; this is gonna be our last summer': they kept saying it over and over - it really was a surprise."

Xxxxx vs. XXXXXXXXX

◆

"THE BATTLE OF LAWRENCE"

I can recall reading somewhere that X's were used to rate the quality of brews in centuries-ago England. If his or her majesty were to take a trip through the countryside, the equivalent of beer scouts would be sent out ahead of time to taste - and rate - each inn's brew. The rating would then be posted on the inn's door, something to the effect of:

X - not bad
XX - pretty good
XXX - real good

Peter Blum, Stroh/Schaefer/Schlitz (and all-around beer and brewery) Historian, advances a somewhat different theory. Peter believes that the use of X's originated in the distilling industry, with three X's signifying extra special . . . and four or five or more being merely a case of good old oneupmanship.

With this as background, I motored on down to Lawrence, Massachusetts — the former home of both Hacker's XXXXX Ale (brewed by the Cold Spring Brewing Company) and Holihan's XXXXXXXXX Stock Ale (brewed by cross-town Diamond Spring Brewing Company) — to try to determine the story behind what, for all the world, had seemed like "The Battle of the X's."

As so often happens, the real truth is somewhat different yet. As relayed to me by Jim Holihan, Diamond Spring president at

". . . a good business"

Facing off: a matchcover promoting Hacker's XXXXX Ale, and a label bearing Holihan's host of stock ale X's (in use from around 1950 to 1960). As explained by Jim: "Stock ale is a heavier ale. It's got more alcohol, it's got more body. And it's got a heartier - perhaps toward the bitter - taste. Stock ale was basically an ale that was aged. We did a good business with stock ale: people liked that kind of hearty, strong ale. It didn't run over 6% (alcohol by volume), but it ran practically 6%."

the time:

"Well, actually the X's meant, supposedly, strength. In other words, you tell the customer or tell the bar owner or tell whoever you wanted to tell that each X on the label represented 1% of alcohol. That was the whole game. Now Hacker's had five X's, and I guess we thought we'd outsmart them and put more than five. We'd point out that we're 9% alcohol. And we'd tell the public - not in advertising, but word of mouth - that the X's were alcohol. At one stage in the malt beverage business alcohol was important, very important. We really didn't have 9%. It was probably just about as strong as Hacker's.

They (Cold Spring) kidded us about it, of course. They'd say, 'Well, what do you think you're doing, using X's on your label to start with? We had the X's on there before you did.' And they did, too. And then the crack would be made once in awhile: 'How come you put nine X's on there: why didn't you put six X's, seven X's, or four X's?' And we'd say, 'Well, because it has 9% alcohol, that's why.' And they'd look at you like that, knowing that you couldn't have an ale up to 9%. They were very friendly competitors."

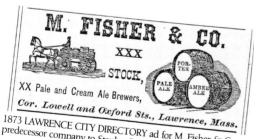

1873 LAWRENCE CITY DIRECTORY ad for M. Fisher & Co., predecessor company to Stanley & Co.

1881 LAWRENCE CITY DIRECTORY ad

A Stanley & Co. almost-barbaric-man-and-his-beer lithograph from the early 1880s. Courtesy of the Hug Collection

A Giant For The Time

Lawrence, prior to the coming of Cold Spring and, later, Diamond Spring, was not brewery-less. From 1874 to 1895 "The City of Workers" was home to Stanley & Co., a giant for the time: its 1879 sales of 28,184 barrels of ale and lager made it the largest brewery in Massachusetts outside of Boston (and larger than any brewery in Connecticut or Rhode Island, too). Stanley was absorbed into the British-owned New England Breweries Company, Ltd. in 1890. Production ceased in Lawrence in 1895 (although the Stanley name continued on as part of New England Breweries' operations in Boston).

Dreams

This truly magnificent 1912 Cold Spring lithograph is courtesy of breweriana collecting friend Tom Hug. And it's a favorite of his. Commenteth Tom: "I've had dreams about this girl! She's great."

1897 LAWRENCE CITY DIRECTORY ad

174

The Cold Spring Brewing Company

The older of the two participants in Lawrence's "Battle of the X's," the Cold Spring Brewing Company, was organized in 1895, and was incorporated in the same year. From the beginning, ale, porter and lager were brewed in a plant that company hierarchy liked to tout as "The Model Brewery of Essex County."

In a city that prided itself on the immensity of its textile mills - Lawrence was the wool worsted manufacturing capital of the world in the early 1900s - it would've been easy for a 75,000 barrels a year capacity brewery such as Cold Spring to get lost. Yet the brewery merited a full-page write-up in historian Maurice B. Dorgan's classic profile of the city, LAWRENCE YESTERDAY AND TODAY, published in 1918. Dorgan described Cold Spring as embracing "every improvement and facility known to the industry, is strictly sanitary and is scientifically operated."

During prohibition, or at least during the first several years of it, Cold Spring turned to the manufacture of soft drinks. With repeal it was, naturally enough, back to beer. Hacker's -named in honor of the company's brewmaster, William H. Hacker - became the company's major brand name. Cold Spring closed in 1952, a victim of the usual "smaller brewery lost in a sea of much larger competitors."

"Time For Hacker's"

The time when you could order a Hacker's Ale or Beer is long since gone . . . but colorful (and is this circa 1940 clock ever colorful when it's lighted up!) artifacts from Cold Spring's fifty-seven years of existence do fortunately remain.

There are almost two full pages of various and diverse German societies, twenty-four in all, in the LAWRENCE CITY DIRECTORY for 1898. Here's a sampling.

GERMAN SOCIETIES.

TURN-VEREIN.
Meets every Monday evening, at Turn Hall, 44 Park street. Pres., F. Martin. Sec., Hugo E. Dick, 131 Newbury street. Treas., August Frank.

TURNERS' SISTERS SOCIETY.
Meets in Turn Hall every Tuesday night. Pres., Mrs. Mary Hoppe. Sec., Mrs. Lena Weigel. Treas., Mrs. Anna Burger.

BAVARIAN READING SOCIETY.
Meets every Thursday evening, in Bavarian Reading Society Hall, 5 Knox street. Pres., George Seuss, 3 Howe's court. Vice-Pres., Henry Gebelein. Sec., George Richter.

HARMONIE LODGE, No. 5, D. O. H.
Meets every second and fourth Friday, in Turn Hall, 44 Park street. Pres., William Mohr. Vice-Pres., Emil Fiedler. Sec., Arthur Voigt. Treas., Herman Wiesner.

SCHILLER LODGE, No. 97, D. O. H.
Meets every Monday evening in Schiller Hall, 280 Prospect street. Pres., John Kannheiser. Sec., Charles Petzold. Treas., Herman Keil.

FREIHEIT LODGE, D. O. H.
Meets every Wednesday in Schiller Hall. Pres., Robert Kinstler. Vice-Pres., F. Pfefferkorn. Sec., George Bayreuther. Treas., Hermann Dick.

SISTERS SOCIETY OF FREIHEIT LODGE.
Meets first and third Wednesdays at Schiller Hall. Pres., Mary Wurzbacher. Sec., Miss Wilhemina Berthel, 58 Marston street. Treas., Mrs. Katie Wirth.

Lawrence . . . City of Immigrants

Lawrence, as with Lowell, Manchester, Holyoke et al., was created to be a manufacturing city. Named for the Lawrences, a wealthy Boston family whose financial clout made Lawrence possible, it became - to use the words of Steve Dunwell in his THE RUN OF THE MILL (Boston: David R. Godine, Publisher, 1978) - "the queen of immigrant cities." At one point over fifty nationalities and forty-five languages were accounted for in Lawrence, with German most definitely among the most accounted: Lawrence was home to one of the largest concentrations of German-Americans in New England, and boasted the leading German newspaper, *Anzeiger Und Post*, in the six states, too. Was it any wonder that Lawrence was - and is - a good beer-drinking town?

The Diamond Spring Brewing Company

Long before there was the Diamond Spring Brewing Company (aka Holihan's), there was Holihan Brothers. Founded in 1856 by Peter and Patrick Holihan, the firm specialized in the sale of fancy groceries. Wholesale liquors were soon added and . . . but wait . . . why not hear about all this directly from THE man who knows: James P. (Jim) Holihan. Jim - and his brother Bill - graduated from Yale on June 20, 1933. The very next day, June 21st, they started work at the family brewery ("for very few dollars a week," notes Jim, "because our Uncle Joe wasn't inclined to pay anybody for anything."). That brewery, of course, was Diamond Spring. In 1937 Jim became Diamond Spring's president, a post he would hold for

the next thirty-five years. As was most often a fact of life in a small brewery, though, Jim was a lot more than just president: during the brewery's peak years from 1945 to 1950 he was also the firm's secretary and treasurer, general manager, purchasing agent, sales manager, and advertising manager.

I was introduced to Jim by way of his niece, Heidi Holihan. An interview was set for a Thursday afternoon, October 28th (1987) at the Exeter (New Hampshire) Healthcare Center, where Jim, 78, was convalescing from arthritis in his legs.

As I drove down to Exeter I found myself getting increasingly excited at the chance to meet and talk with the man who, having headed Diamond Spring for three and a half decades, was certainly dean of New England's brewery prexies.

I was not disappointed: I found Jim to be warm, personable, candid - and extremely informative. The words on the next three and a half pages are his (often in response to Diamond Spring breweriana - which he loved - that I brought to share with him). I hope you enjoy them.

1881

1898

On The Holihan Brothers as Wholesale Liquor Dealers

"They bought a lot of Iroquois. And also they were agents, a little later on, for the Cold Spring Brewery, which was the other brewery in town. They sold about half the output of the Cold Spring Brewery in Greater Lawrence. This would've been in the early 1900s.

They did an excellent liquor business. In the Valley. And they did a shipping business, too. They did a great business in Maine. They (Maine) were dry. And the Holihan's, being a semi-mail order house, used to get orders from Maine, and they'd ship 'em up. It was illegal to sell it in Maine, but it wasn't illegal to ship it into Maine."

Circa 1915 label. Diamond Spring was always famous for the purity of its water: before the brewery, the spring's water was sold to the people of Lawrence as Knowles Diamond Spring Water.

On The Decision to Build a Brewery in 1912, when the Seeds of Prohibition Were Already in the Air

"Well, first of all - on prohibition, I guess they believed that it could never happen . . . like a lot of brewers thought. Never happen. And secondly, they were selling enough beer and ale to warrant putting the money into the building of a brewery, which was finished in 1912."

Circa 1915 bottle stopper. Jim: "I've never seen anything like this, except for whiskey. This had to be between 1912 and 1918."

On Drinking Beer - During Prohibition - at Yale

"I can tell you a lot of stories about beer down in New Haven (when in college during prohibition). I remember I was treasurer of the fraternity house, Beta Theta Pi, for two years. We used to buy beer - illegally, of course - from a fellow in West Haven. We never knew who made the beer, and we really didn't care. I think we charged the brothers 35¢ or 50¢ a bottle: you could have whatever you wanted at dinner or lunch. And I found out in 1933, before I graduated, that the man who made the beer was our former brewmaster, believe it or not. His name was Frank Klein."

Maloney's - "The Finest, Most Beautiful Beer Garden in the United States"

"Oh, God. One of our best customers in the 1930s and 1940s. To be honest with you, though, I can't remember that they had any beer garden. I can remember Maloney's Bar. First of all, they did a hell of a business. Secondly, they had a good location. It was an action spot. It was one block away from the main street, so there was a lot of foot traffic in there. It was a busy area. And there was a nice atmosphere there."

The Place to Drink!

THE FINEST, MOST BEAUTIFUL BEER GARDEN IN THE UNITED STATES

MALONEY'S

410 COMMON ST., Lawrence, Mass. (Near Hampshire St.)

1935 ad

On One of Haverhill's More Enduring Hotspots . . . Comeau's Cafe

"That was a good spot! They used to buy ten to fifteen halves a week. Now, ten to fifteen halves in those days was a pretty good account. Today if you can get a draft account with three halves a week you're doing a hell of a business. It was more a cafe, with dancing. And a band. Billy Comeau, who owned it, was a great friend of ours. We used to see a lot of him. But he was one of the worst chiselers in the business. He used to come up to the brewery and demand these big discounts. And we'd give him some free beer on occasion. To pacify him.

We had an account - imagine this - in Lawrence and we had one in Lowell that sold twelve ounces of beer for 5¢. Now that was back, but it's after 1933. And the guy in Lowell, the fellow was from Brooklyn, New York, and I'd have to go up there every Friday to collect. And I'd have to give so much of a discount. I mean they demanded that. We made money on it, though. In fact, he sold over one hundred half barrels a week. The place in Lawrence was the same way. A hundred halves a week is unheard of!"

While Maloney's is long gone, Comeau's - on Lafayette Square in Haverhill - is still going strong. This photo, emphasizing its great old side-of-building sign, was taken in October of 1987.

On Diamond Spring's Peak Year

"We sold 100,000 barrels in our peak sales year, 1947. That was our peak, '47-'48. We had good years and made some money. But we had lean years, too, and didn't make as much money. 100,000 was really cooking. We could have sold a little more, but we couldn't make it: we didn't have the capacity."

On Boston's Brewers

"They all stayed in there pretty well in the thirties. And through the war. The war gave 'em a hell of a lift because you could sell all the beer you were allowed to make. But the demise of the Boston breweries, overall, started almost immediately after the war. They were run by stodgy people who wouldn't accept new ideas. And the toll, once it started to come, came fast."

On The Impact of a "Big, Blond, Busty" Salesperson

"One of the reasons for Knickerbocker's popularity (note: Knickerbocker was the largest selling beer in Massachusetts for many years in the late 1940s and 1950s) was Dagmar. Do you remember Dagmar? She was on tv at night. Every man in the area looked at Dagmar. Big, blond, busty. She advertised Ruppert for about three or four years. Ruppert brought you her show."

On Volume vs. Profit

"Look at that! 'Brewed Better With Pure Spring Water': that was a good phrase. We were proud of our spring. Even before the brewery was built there it was reknowned for the water. And in the summer - if you can imagine this - we reduced the '3 for $1.10' to 3 for $1.00. And we had our pints at 6 for $1.00. We did it for volume. During the summer we'd sell more anyway... but at 3 for $1.00 it just flew. I'll say honestly, I don't think we made any money on it. As the fellow says, it's nice to see the volume. But it's also nice to make money."

On the Best (and the Worst) New England-brewed Beer

"Excluding our brand, of course . . . I think the Hampden Beer was as good as any. That would cover the ale, too. They made both, beer and ale. I thought both of their products were good. They had intelligent men running it: it was a quality brewery. They used good materials. The head of the brewery was a former brewmaster who was a hell of a chemist, et cetera, and everything that came out of there was a good-tasting product.

I think the worst beer, probably, was made in Worcester, by the Worcester Brewing Company. Brockert's, or Tadcaster. They had Tadcaster for awhile. It wasn't uniform. Up and down. And the brewery was sort of nondescript. An old building made over."

On Problems After The War

"I don't know if you know it, but the local brewers suffered terribly for three or four reasons after the war (World War II). They all did well during the war, but the decline came after the war when thousands, many thousands, of American soldiers came home and were used to only beer, as opposed to ale. They'd forgotten ale. Ale was not shipped overseas at all, to speak of. Brewers who were able to get Army or Navy or service business shipped beer.

That was one thing. Then the decline of draught beer that the local brewery depended upon started to give way, in the on-premise places, to bottled beer. In other words, a guy that sold ten halves a week would decide, through some smart salesman from Budweiser or Schlitz, to put in bottled beer for 15¢ or 20¢, and quite a lot of the people switched over to bottled beer. It was the pressure of the big breweries.

Then, in that era - let's say '44 to '48 - the grocery stores in our area came into certain licenses that enabled them to sell beer. Before that there were only fourteen (off-premise sales) outlets for beer and ale in Lawrence. We were very, very close personally to the fourteen stores. Fourteen stores is a low number of outlets, and we spent money on the owners. We spent money on the clerks. And we had their good will, to the extent that if you came in and asked for a beer or an ale, they would give you Holihan's. And about 25 or 35% of the public came in and didn't ask for a particular brand. But when the grocery stores became licensed, they went from the clerk who waited over the counter to the pick-up sixpack, in a cooler, by the wall. So the public had to get their beer by picking it up themselves, and the nationally advertised brands would do better."

Late 1950's point-of-purchase sign and Light Ale can. Jim: "Oh, boy, I haven't seen one of these for awhile!"

1944 ad for Imported Black Horse Ale: It would later be imported from Lawrence.

1965-1968 gallon beer cans

On The Importance of Black Horse Ale

"They (Dawes Black Horse Brewery, Montreal) let the rights go. They didn't protect it or were ignorant in knowledge, one of the two. And we were advised by a friend in Buffalo that the label could be picked up. Just picked up. Period. With no financial entanglements. Back in '59 we started working on it, and finally got it covered by the Federal government. Carling was tear-ass about it. Carling tried to stop it, and they didn't succeed. They wanted the label themselves.

I can tell you about the experience we had when we introduced Black Horse Ale. It was very high in alcohol. And, of course, we got it into most of the bars and package stores right away. We thought 7½% alcohol would be fantastic, the first thing people would go for. Our salesmen loved it. It got distribution and quite a few people tried it. But I remember we had two or three women call us at the brewery and complain that their husbands were coming back crocked, intoxicated, at night. They said they drank three bottles of Black Horse Ale instead of three bottles of Holihan's or something else. They gave us hell. We finally found out - it got through - that it was too strong. And we reduced it, then, to about 6¼ or 6%.

Black Horse was very successful for us. We sold more Holihan's, but Black Horse was coming along. We sold in about sixteen-eighteen states. We did a hell of a business in Miami, greater Miami, and shipped as far as Colorado. Just Black Horse, the distributor wouldn't touch Holihan's. Black Horse sort of sold on its own. First of all, it was an ale, and it was a good name. The ale business is not particularly competitive, because there aren't many ales made, mostly beer."

On The Short-lived Gallon Can

"It was an experience (the gallon can). My memories are that the package was a hell of a package. I mean the gallon idea. But nobody ever produced a tap that went in (the can) without spoiling one-half the beer. Plus the fact the taps cost the consumer $4.50-$5.00. They had to buy it. In other words, they pay for the gallon can and then they pay extra for the tap. I think they would have gone along with the idea if the damned taps worked, but they had more trouble when they used it."

On a Full Quart of 50th Anniversary Pilsner

"That was pretty good, that 50th Anniversary deal. It wasn't a special beer. We liked the word "Pilsener" very much: people thought it was sort of a foreign beer, a better beer. It made a good sales impression. We were very proud when we hit our 50th anniversary. Gee, that brings back memories."

"It Was Criminal"

"We were proud of the brewery. In 1912 they used the best bricks to build it that money could buy. There were special bricks made up in Epping, I believe. Epping, New Hampshire. It was criminal when they knocked that brewery down (in 1973) in favor of the apartments that are there now."

The brewery as it looked in 1933

On the Decision to Liquidate Diamond Spring in 1972

"Well, we had two or three things happen. First of all, we had family problems. We had internal friction. Plus the fact that we had two big wholesalers that handled Holihan's, one in New Haven and one in Pawtucket, Rhode Island, that got into financial trouble and had to quit us. That was the loss of about 200,000 cases. That was a deathly blow. So, between the pressure of the shipping brewers - nationally known - and their growth, the family, and the loss of two major distributors, we decided to quit."

(Note: New Haven's Hull Brewing Company kept the Holihan name alive for two more years, producing Holihan's Beer under license from 1972 to 1974.)

Back to me again . . .

It's impossible, of course, to do any kind of real justice to thirty-five years in three or four pages . . . but I hope we've captured at least some of Jim's spirit, and the joys and tribulations of heading a small brewery for the better part of one's life. Thank you, Jim.

Jim in a circa 1935 portrait, and in an August, 1988 shot

On His Favorite Moment in the Thirty-five Years

"I think my favorite moment was when I was elected a director of the U.S. Brewers Association (note: it was a position he'd hold for twenty-two years) in 1947. My other memorable occasion was when we celebrated our 50th Anniversary. We were really proud of being in business 50 years. And happy that our group was enjoying prosperity and good business.

A family company touches also those family members who are not directly involved in the business. Heidi Holihan, Jim's niece and the daughter of longtime co-manager Bill Holihan, was only seventeen when Diamond Spring closed. Yet she, too, remembers:

"It (the brewery) was a landmark in Lawrence, certainly. I remember going there when I was a little girl. On Saturday mornings was the time when there weren't a lot of people coming in and out of his (her father's) office. So it was a time when we could be together and he could catch up on his paperwork and I used to play with all the things in his office. Then I would sneak across the street, when no one was looking, over to the brewery itself and the bottling plant. I used to watch the farmers from all around: we used to give them all of the spent hops and grains to feed their animals. There was a tremendous amount of good will going on. They were all very happy, the farmers. They used to come and visit my father. We used to give out spring water to people, too. I remember my father was very happy that we could bring something into the brewery and use it, and it could still be used after for something else that was put to good use, like feeding the animals.

Heidi Holihan in 1977, five years after the brewery's closing

There was a room called the tap room, where local businesses used to come and be welcomed to have their office meetings and conferences and get-togethers. Everywhere I go, when people hear my name, they remember having been there on some occasion and how they were giving away all the beer.

It (the brewery) was a big brick building with these big, tall, thin windows with arches on the top. And a big spire on the top. That was the height of the brewery, and then there was a staircase that went down stories and stories below the ground to where the pumps and the spring was. They took a lot of care - they always had the water tested - to make sure nothing was in it. The two of them (Heidi's father and uncle), they always felt that the water was the most important ingredient in beer. There was always a lot of attention to making sure that the water was top shelf.

I felt that I always wanted to work there. What I remember was the day that they had stopped production and they were allowing people to come in and take what they wanted. And we had these huge old vats, you know, the wooden vats still there. It was old equipment; it had been replaced when the modern stuff came in, the stainless steel ones. There was a lot of cypress and special wood in there. I remember them pulling apart the vats to take the wood out. It was very sad to me. I wish I had had the opportunity to work with my father. I wish I had been a little older so that I could have worked there."

But back to the present . . . and the "brewing" scene in Lawrence today. Where once stood Diamond Spring is now a large apartment complex called British Colonial (which looks, I might add, about as British colonial as your average Chinese restaurant). Cold Spring has fared better: most of it still stands, utilized by U-Stor-Here, and also North East Machinery, Inc.

May, 1988

You Must Remember This

◆

HOW NEW YORK BEER MONEY TOOK THE BABE FROM BOSTON

From the beginning, beer and baseball have been a natural. After all, what can compare with the joy of a cold one after charging back in the bottom of the ninth to defeat arch-rival Mudville, 6-5?

It almost seems as if radio were invented so a brewery could send along the game to you.

Television, too.

The St. Louis Cardinals, Toronto Blue Jays, New York Yankees, Baltimore Orioles, and the old St. Louis Browns ("First in booze, first in shoes . . . and last in the American League") have all been owned by a brewer at one time or another.

We have Busch Stadium.

We have the Milwaukee Brewers.

But, alas, beer and baseball worked against

The Colonel: he wanted to do more than just bring the Yankees a pennant. He wanted to change the team's name, too. His choice was "Knickerbockers," after his brewery's best selling brand. Chided at the possible name change by the New York press, the Colonel stuck with "Yankees."

that greatest of all New England institutions, the Red Sox.

Let's go back to when the American League was a youngster. There was an almost-perennial first division team, and there was an almost-perennial second division team. Beer money - and Broadway plays - would change all that.

The first division team was the Red Sox. In their first eighteen years of existence, the Sox (variously also known as the Pilgrims and the Somersets) finished in the top half of the league fourteen times, won six pennants and five World Championships. In the seven year span from 1912 to 1918 they were especially hot, taking four flags and the Series all four times, too.

The Yankees were the second division

Cont'd. on page 182

Jake wanted these guys   *... not these guys*

Jacob Ruppert's original love of baseball did not come from his being a Yankee fan. He was a Giant fan, enamored of Mugsie McGraw and his team of true giants: Christy Mathewson, Laughing Larry Doyle, Rube Marquard, Chief Meyers et al. He considered the Yankees little more than a weak team in a weak league. Nevertheless, thwarted in his attempts to buy "the Jints," he bought the Yankees instead . . . and became as rabid a Yankee fan as there's ever been. One of his best remembered quotes: "My idea of a good ballgame is one where the Yankees have a thirteen-run lead in the top of the ninth with two out and two strikes on the hitter."

Early 1900's Sweet Caporal and Sovereign cigarette cards. It was tobacco - not bubble gum - that spawned the collectible card. The whole thing started in 1886 when Allen and Gintner, a Richmond, Virginia cigarette company, inaugurated a series of sports cards in lieu of their usual pretty lady cards.

Beer and Baseball and Ken Coleman

Broadcast booth memories aren't all of games won, games lost, home runs, and double plays. There're generally some beer memories in there, too. Such is certainly the case with "The Voice of the Red Sox," Ken Coleman. Now in his 33rd year of doing big league play by play, the 62-year old North Quincy, Massachusetts native has worked with Carling's during his ten years doing the Cleveland Indians, Hudepohl in his four-year stint with the Cincinnati Reds, and both Narragansett and Anheuser-Busch during his nineteen seasons at Fenway Park. Here are a few of his favorite beer stories.

"I remember when I came here (Boston); when I did my first game, opening day of 1966 at Fenway Park. I, of course, had been doing major league baseball: I had done the Cleveland Indians for ten years and had also been with the (Cleveland) Browns during that same span, so it wasn't like I was some kid that came into a job. But, nevertheless, like anybody that was in a new job, I was apprehensive about it and hoping that I would do well. And after the first game I was sitting in the press room and frozen - that was a very cold April day - and a fellow from the advertising agency for Narragansett came over to me and said 'Great game. Terrific game.' And I said 'Well, gee, that's real nice. Thank you very much.' And he said 'Yeah, those were two of the most professional pours I've ever seen.' And I realized, of course, that his idea of a great game was how you poured the beer and how big a head you got on it. The thing in those days (on television) was to get a very big head on the beer, because it looked more appetizing. In fact, that was one of the tricks they used to use: they would very often be sure that the beer was warm, so you'd get a very big head on it as you poured. And then, of course, if you did it without spilling over, you know, that was really terrific."

" . . . how you poured the beer and how big a head you got on it."

"When I was doing the Cleveland Browns' games the Carling Brewing Company sponsored the games. At that time they had their main brewery in Cleveland. It was up in a very tough section of the town. I went to the brewery once. When I first got there (Cleveland), I went to a Bock Beer Party that they had for the media. I went in and made an horrendous mistake - as I discovered as a newcomer on the scene and a New Englander - I ordered a bock beer. Everybody else was drinking Manhattans and martinis and scotch up in the executive suite, and somebody had to go down to the basement of the brewery and get me a beer. It was like "What is this guy doing: ruining the party?"

"The reason, or one of the reasons, Curt Gowdy came to Boston

At home at the mike: Ken behind the microphone in the den of his Cohasset home.

March, 1988

Red Sox schedule, 1975

Since 1925, when Fred Hoey first began broadcasting Red Sox games over the Colonial Network, the team has had three radio/television brewery sponsors: Dawson's, Narragansett, and present-day Anheuser-Busch, with 'Gansett the longest running and the best remembered.

was because back in the forties, fifties, and actually into the sixties, really, there was a period there when there was an identification factor with the announcers and sponsors more (than there is today).

Today people buy spots more than anything because they can't afford to buy three innings as they used to.

When Curt came to Boston - which would've been, I believe, in '51 - one of the reasons was that Jim Britt, who had been broadcasting in Boston for both the Red Sox and the Braves doing all home games - they didn't do any road games; he was doing all the home games - the Braves took on Ballantine as a sponsor, so Jim had to make a choice: to go with one sponsor or the other. And he opted to go for the Braves. So Curt came in and started working the games on the Red Sox, which had Narragansett."

"I recall going down there (to Narragansett) one night with Gary Waslewski, who was a pitcher of ours from Connecticut. I think it was after the '67 season. And I remember having the beer before it was pasteurized. It was absolutely delightful. It was most enjoyable."

"Once we had a State of Maine Day. And the day before a fellow from Narragansett, a fellow named Jim Nolan, said to me, 'You know, tomorrow is State of Maine Day and we're going to have a commercial, talking up that beer and lobster go well together, in which you'll have a live lobster in the booth. And at the end of the third inning you go over to the lobster, and the way you deal with a live lobster is you rub his tummy and he'll just lay out flat on his back.' And I said 'Yeah sure, Jim,' really thinking that he was putting me on.

So the next day I go in and, sure enough, they've got this live lobster in the booth, and, sure enough, we go through this rehearsal without doing the actual lobster part of it, but they explained this is what you do: I'm doing this at the end of the third. And I know damn well that the only thing I could think about through the first three innings was how I was going to deal with that lobster! I wasn't thinking very much about the baseball game."

(P.S. The lobster came through and did as it was supposed to do: all of Ken's appendages are still with him!)

181

"Babe Ruth! Babe Ruth! (We Know What He Can Do)" sheet music, 1928

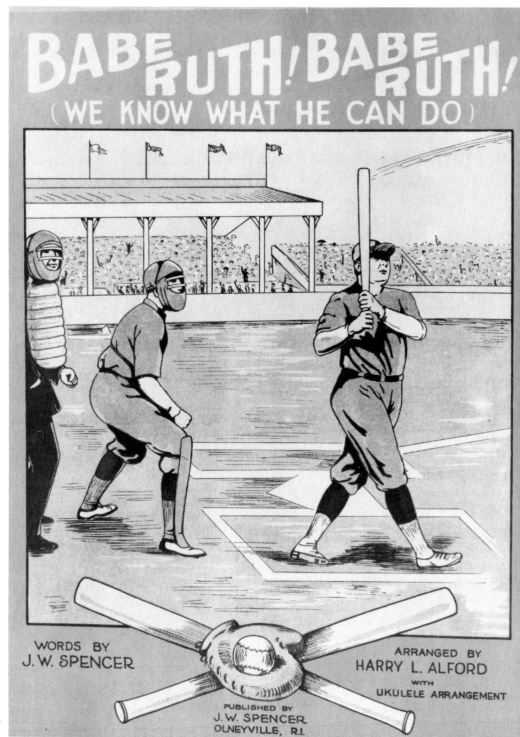

team. Known as the Highlanders from 1903, when they moved from Baltimore, until 1913, they finished in the first division but eight times, won no pennants, no World Championships in their first eighteen years of existence. In the seven-year span from 1912 to 1918 they were especially cold, finishing seventh or eighth (there were only eight teams in the league in those days) three times and no higher than fourth overall.

Then along came Harry Frazee. A Peoria, Illinois native and former bellhop and billposter who'd made good - more or less - in the New York theatre, Frazee and his partner Hugh J. Ward purchased the Red Sox in late 1916. Frazee, proclaiming that "Nothing is too good for the wonderful fans of the Boston team," put money into the team at first, and the club finished second in 1917 and on top in 1918. "Hairbreadth Harry," however, was a gambler at heart, seeemingly always involved in some theatrical deal or another. He particularly liked to back Broadway plays. And his specialty seemed to be bad Broadway plays.

Best known for his awesome ability with the bat, George Herman Ruth was no slouch on the mound either. He started his career as a lefty hurler, and most of his years with the Red Sox, 1914-1919, were spent as a pitcher. It's worthy of note - sad note - that in spite of a number of seven-game specials (1946, 1967, 1975, and 1986), the last World Series the Sox have won was way back in 1918 . . . with the Babe hurling two of the team's four victories over the Cubs.

The Yankees, meanwhile, had been purchased by New York beer baron Colonel Jacob Ruppert and partner Cap Huston in January of 1915. Born into the brewing business in 1867, Ruppert was a New York political, social, and business kingpin. He was a major real estate owner, a colonel in the National Guard, a three-term congressman, a principal backer of Admiral Richard E. Byrd's second Antartic expedition, and a noted sportsman. He also ran his Second Avenue brewery, Jacob Ruppert, Inc., with an iron, and very successful, hand.

Frazee, after a string of flops, needed money. Ruppert had it. What has become known as "Harry Frazee's Crime" and "The Rape of the Red Sox" started innocently enough: after the 1918 season pitchers Ernie Shore and Dutch Leonard and outfielder Duffy Lewis were sent to the Yankees in exchange for $50,000 and a trio of players that would be of little help to Boston. Before it was through, though, the Frazee to Ruppert pipeline would strip the Sox basically clean. Players the likes of Carl Mays (whose 27-9 record lead the Yankees to their first-ever pennant in 1921), Waite Hoyt (who went on to win 227 games for the New Yorkers and a handful of other teams, and to be voted into the Hall of Fame), Herb Pennock (who became a mainstay on the New York mound for ten seasons and who's also in the Hall of Fame), catcher Wally Schang, third-sacker Jumping Joe Dugan, shortstop Everett Scott, and pitchers Bullet Joe Bush and Sad Sam Jones all exited Boston for the Colonel's payroll.

Ruppert's most monumental purchase, of course, was the Babe: George Herman "Babe" Ruth, whose sale to the Yankees after the 1919 season — for $100,000 plus a $350,000 personal loan Ruppert made to Frazee — left Boston fans confused and disgusted.

The rest, as they say, is history.

The Babe went on to become "The Sultan of Swat," "The Wizard of Whack," "The Prince of Pounders." The Bambino. To rewrite how the game is played.

The Yankees went on to become the Team Dominant in baseball. From 1921 until the Colonel's death in 1939, they won ten pennants, seven World Championships.

And the Red Sox? Well, they went on to become the laughing stock of the league for all of the twenties and into the thirties. In the dozen years between 1922 and 1933, when Tom Yawkey took over, the Sox finished dead last an unbelievable nine times, never finished higher than sixth. They even made the Browns look good!

It would, in fact, be 1946 before another flag hung over Fenway Park.

You could look it up. And you could blame it on the strange combination of "Hairbreath Harry" Frazee, bad Broadway plays, and Jacob Ruppert and his beer money.

Eddie "The Brat" Stanky, with a career high of .320, was one of five Brave regulars to hit over .300 in their glory year, 1948. The others were Tommy Holmes (.325), Alvin Dark (.322), Jeff Heath (.319), and Mike McCormick (.303).

What A Year It Would've Been

The year 1948 was the year of the almost All-Boston Fall Classic.

The Braves - they were the Boston Braves then - hadn't won a flag since 1914. They were due. The Red Sox hadn't won since 1946. They weren't quite as due.

Destiny seemed as if it were going to bring the two teams together. The Braves held up their end very nicely, finishing six and a half games ahead of the second-place Cards. The Red Sox had to work a lot harder, however: their sweep of a two-game set with the Yankees, coupled with a Cleveland loss to the Tigers, forced the first playoff game in American League history, the Indians vs. the Sox in a single game winner-take-all duel. One more win and all of the City of Boston would've been rocking and rolling . . . but Gene Bearden's pitching and Lou Boudreau's hitting iced it for the Indians (who went on to beat the Braves, four games to two, to become World Champs).

So the world was deprived of Spahn and Sain vs. Ted and Vern and Dom . . . an All-Boston Series.

More germane to BEER, NEW ENGLAND . . . the world was deprived of an All-Narragansett Series: both teams were brought to you by the pride of the Ocean State.

Zeltner's, Of Course!

◆

A LITTLE BIT OF THE BRONX IN NEW ENGLAND

Circa 1900 Zeltner's
Old Fashion Brew bottle

Every A to Z book needs, of course, a "Z." And they're not always so easy to come by. We've done it, though, courtesy of former Bronx, New York brewer Henry Zeltner and his Zeltner's Old Fashion Brew. No, the Bronx is not part of New England, but Danbury, Connecticut is . . . and that's where Zeltner had one of his agents, Foley Brothers.

Old Fashion Brew

Zeltner, located at 170th Street and 3rd Avenue in the Morrisiana section of the Bronx, was not a large brewer. Inching into New England was undoubtedly a big step for him; Danbury probably about as far as he got.

Agents (which would bring us back to "A" if we wanted it to) were utilized by most brewers of any consequence to enable them to expand beyond just their local marketing area. Some agents were substantial, handling many brands, or the output of one of the national giants, Anheuser-Busch, Jos. Schlitz, Pabst, or Lemp. Some were tiny, distributing but a secondary brand or two. Many doubled as bottlers and/or wholesale liquor dealers and/or saloonkeepers. All were important in allowing brewers to increase sales, enlarge their marketing horizons . . . be that brewer Eberhard **A**nheuser or Henry **Z**eltner.

1897 DANBURY CITY
DIRECTORY AD

A Varied Lot

The Foley brothers, William, John, and Edward, were a varied lot. William and John were tobacconists and cigar manufacturers prior to William's entree into the wholesale liquor business in the early 1890s. John joined the business in 1896, about the time that Zeltner's became their primary account. Ballantine, just ale at first but later lager as well, was added in 1901, and by 1910 was the brothers' major line. So it remained until prohibition, except that by 1915 John had stepped out of the picture and younger brother (?) Edward had stepped in. With prohibition, the brothers dissolved their agency. Edward became a partner in a manufacturer of hatter's machinery; William just seemed to disappear.

The End

Index

Please Note: in the interest of space — and because of the alphabetical-by-town arrangement within the chapter — neither the bars/taverns/cafes of Quintessential They're Not nor the towns/cities they represent have been included here.